T0301302

The Innovation Policy of the European Union

To Finn,
with all my love

The Innovation Policy of the European Union

From Government to Governance

Susana Borrás

Associate Professor of European Politics, Department of
Social Sciences, Roskilde University, Denmark

Edward Elgar

Cheltenham, UK • Northampton MA, USA

Published by
Edward Elgar Publishing Limited
Glensanda House
Montpellier Parade
Cheltenham
Glos GL50 1UA
UK

Edward Elgar Publishing, Inc.
136 West Street
Suite 202
Northampton
Massachusetts 01060
USA

A catalogue record for this book
is available from the British Library

Library of Congress Cataloguing in Publication Data

Borrás, Susana.
    The innovation policy of the European Union: from government
to governance/Susana Borrás.
        p.   cm.
    1. European Union. I. Title.
    JN30B67   2003
    341.242'2—dc21

                                                            2003044896

ISBN 1 84064 993 3

Printed and bound in Great Britain by MPG Books Ltd, Bodmin, Cornwall

Contents

Figures

Tables

Preface and acknowledgements

The idea for this book started to take form in the mid-1990s, when I was completing my PhD dissertation and I realized the need for a more encompassing work about the EU's innovation policy. Yet, this book has taken a long time to come to fruition. The reason being that different projects have requested my most immediate attention, the most important of them being the birth of my two children – two lovely reasons. Writing this book has truly been a learning process. I have enjoyed exploring new areas that were relatively unknown for me, like for example the world of standards, and I have become fascinated by the political and social implications of the 'risk society' and the intellectual property rights regime. This learning and fascination is, I hope, reflected in the wording of the different chapters.

Most of the chapters of this book have been presented at international workshops. Chapter 2, 'Research and knowledge production' was presented at the workshop organized by Klaus Nielsen, 'Knowledge, Learning and Institutions', at Sofienberg Slot, Denmark, May 2001. Chapter 3, 'The changing regime of intellectual property rights', was presented at the 4th EUNIP Conference, Tilburg University, The Netherlands, November 2000. Chapter 6, 'Risk and the social sustainability of innovation', was presented in a second workshop organized by Klaus Nielsen 'Cognitive Processes, Values and Institutional Change', Rungsted, Denmark, January 2002. The concluding chapter was presented at the 5th EUNIP Conference in Vienna, December 2001. Furthermore, I presented Chapter 3, about intellectual property rights, at Linköping University, Sweden, where I was invited by Charles Edquist. Last but not least, I have discussed Chapters 3, 4 and 6 with colleagues of the innovation research group at Roskilde University in our periodical internal meetings, which have been a source of inspiration and encouragement.

Therefore, I am truly grateful to all the colleagues and friends in Denmark and elsewhere that have invested their time and energy providing rich comments, criticisms and remarks for the work in this book. I am particularly thankful to Sjoerd Beugelsdijk, Peter Biegelbauer, Jerome Davis, Charles Edquist, Marie-Louise Eriksson, Christian Friis, Lars Fuglsang, Birgitte Gregersen, Jaume Guia, Bjørn Johnson, Bengt-Åke Lundvall, Klaus Nielsen, Paul Nightingale, Bart Nooteboom, Ramon Ricard, Jacob Rendtorff, Margaret Sharp, Marianne van der Steen, and Jon Sundbo.

Other important people have contributed to make this book better. Andrew Crabtree has been a great help in improving my written English, and has helped to formulate my ideas more clearly. Erik Kristensen and Kenny Larsen have been precious research assistants, collecting information and classifying the large amount of material. Last, but, of course, not least, a special thanks to Dymphna Evans for her enthusiasm and encouragement as commissioning editor of this book.

A final word to my family. For particularly tragic reasons, my family has collectively known that science, culture and politics are unavoidably linked to each other. My great grandfather, Antonio García Banús was professor of organic chemistry at the University of Barcelona in the 1910s, 1920s and 1930s, until he was forced into exile by the dictatorship that ruled Spain for too many decades. Difficulties were also known by Miguel Batllori, my uncle, who has dedicated his life to Catalonia's cultural history in the context of Spain and Europe. They have stimulated my belief and hope that science and culture are the active building blocks of a united and peaceful Europe, based on the values of pluralism, freedom and democracy.

However, the ones I am mostly indebted to are my parents, Miguel and Nuria, my father-in-law, Jason (who recently passed away), and my husband Finn. Their invaluable support has been a constant stimulus in my work. My most sincere gratitude and love are for them.

The following remarks are important before reading this book. First, note that the data was last updated in December 2002. Second, since the numbering of EU Treaty articles changed after the enforcement of the Amsterdam Treaty, this book consistently uses the latest numbering system, but indicates in brackets the old article number. Third, for the sake of clarity, this book only refers to the European Union, and not to the 'European Communities' or 'European Community', as it was termed historically. And last, but not least, when the sources of the tables and figures are not indicated, they are my own creation.

The usual disclaimer applies. Any possible mistakes in this book are my sole responsibility.

List of abbreviations

3GPP	the 3rd Generation Partnership Project (of GSM mobile telephony standard)
AIA	Advance Informed Agreement, under the Cartagena Protocol on Biosafety
ANFOR	Association Française de Normalisation
ANSI	American National Standards Institute
BSE	Bovine Spongiform Encephalopathy (also known as 'mad cow disease')
CBD	Convention on Biological Diversity
CCP	common commercial policy
CEECs	Central and Eastern European Countries
CEN	Comité Européen de Normalisation.
CENELEC	Comité Européen de Normalisation Electrotechnique
CERN	Conseil Européen pour la Recherche Nucléaire
COST	European Cooperation in the Field of Scientific and Technical Research
CSF	Community Framework Support
DVD	digital versatile disc
DVB	digital video broadcasting standard
DVB-MHP	digital video broadcasting-multimedia home platform
ECJ	European Court of Justice
EEA	European Economic Area
EFTA	European Free Trade Association
EMBL	European Molecular Biology Laboratory
EMBO	European Molecular Biology Organization
EOTC	European Organization for Testing and Certification
EP	European Parliament
EPO	European Patent Office
ERA	European Research Area
ESA	European Space Agency
ESF	European Science Foundation
ESI	European System of Innovation
ESO	European Southern Observatory
ETSI	European Telecommunications Standards Institute
EU	European Union

EUREKA	European Research Coordinating Agency
FAO	Food and Agriculture Organization
FP	Framework programme
GATT	General Agreement on Tariffs and Trade
GDP	gross domestic product
GMO	genetically modified organisms
GSM	Groupe Spécial Mobile
HDTV	high definition television
HTML	hypertext markup language
i2i	innovation 2000 initiative
ICTs	information and communication technologies
IEC	International Electrotechnical Commission
IGC	intergovernmental conference
ILO	International Labour Organization
IMO	International Maritime Organization
IPRs	Intellectual Property Rights
IS	information society
ISO	International Standards Organization
ITU	International Telecommunications Union
JET	Joint European Torus
JRC	Joint Research Centre
MAC	multiplexed analogue components (a European HDTV standard)
MRA	mutual recognition agreement
NSI	national system of innovation
OECD	Organization for Economic Cooperation and Development
OHIM	Office for the Harmonization of the Internal Market
OJ	Official Journal (of the EU)
PCT	Patent Cooperation Treaty
RIS	regional innovation strategy
RTD	research and technological development
RTT	regional technology transfer
SEA	Single European Act
SEM	Single European Market
SGML	Standard Generalized Markup Language
SMEs	small and medium-sized enterprises
SPS	sanitary and phytosanitary measures (under WTO)
SST	social shaping of technology
TBT agreement	Technical Barriers to Trade (under WTO)
TEU	Treaty on European Union.
UMTS	universal mobile telecommunications system

UNCED	United Nations Conference on Environment and Development
UN	United Nations
W3C	World Wide Web Consortium
WHO	World Health Organization
WIPO	World Intellectual Property Organization
WSSN	World Standards Services Network
WTO	World Trade Organization
XML	extensible markup language

Introduction

Bohr: You know why Allied scientists worked on the bomb.
Heisenberg: Of course. Fear.
Bohr: The same fear that was consuming you. Because they were afraid that *you*
   were working on it.
                    Michael Frayn (1998), *Copenhagen*. London, Methuen Drama.

SCIENCE, TECHNOLOGY AND EUROPEAN INTEGRATION

Science and technology have always been at the heart of the European
political construction. In the 1950s, Euratom institutionalized six European
states' commitment to produce advanced knowledge in the sensitive area of
nuclear energy, mainly for security reasons. However, Europe's techno-
federalist ambitions floundered in the 1960s and 1970s, when the Franco-
German differences caused a stalemate and put a stop to the efforts to achieve
a common design for nuclear reactors. Euratom's troubles during these two
decades showed that the path towards integration was to be a bumpy one.

Science and technology again attracted much political attention in the early
1980s. This was the time of the Euroforia and of Delors' new integrationist
agenda, but it was also the time of deep industrial restructuring in the
aftermath of the 1970s oil crises. The rapid internationalization of production
structures and their concomitant division of labour pushed governments to
focus on technological development as an instrument of growth. Moreover,
the failure of most national public initiatives to redress the industrial crises
made politicians turn their eyes to Europe. Jacques Delors successfully
grasped this momentum by putting forward a whole package of initiatives,
among them the large technology programme (the so-called Framework
Programme (FP)). This had two effects. One was that of enshrining further the
EU involvement in scientific technological matters (the new programme
extended well beyond the Euratom field of nuclear energy, making a serious
commitment to 'Europeanize' the production of advanced knowledge). The
second effect was that of enshrining the pursuit of competitiveness, which has
since become a major 'raison d'être' of the Union.

Since the mid-1990s, a new approach to public action in this field has
gained a firm foothold. Not that science and technology have vanished, but

innovation is understood as a broader and more flexible term that embraces other issues such as intellectual property rights, education and training, organizational change, institutional framework, standards, and so on. 'Innovation' has expanded the agenda of EU action, at a time when the member states want the EU to be the 'most competitive knowledge-based economy in the world by 2010' (following the Presidency conclusions of the Lisbon Summit, 2000). The innovation agenda has broadened substantially the goals of political action at EU level. Concerns now are not just security, as in the old days of Euratom, nor technological development for industrial advance, as during the establishment of the framework programme in the 1980s. The major concern today is how to shape an institutional context that enhances the innovation process as a whole, and that responds to the emerging risks and social consequences of scientific advances. This requires an entire reconceptualization of the functional borders of already existing policy areas, and the development of new ones at EU level.

The goal of this book is to analyse the major transformations and dynamics of EU innovation policy over recent years, and to critically address the emerging issues that policy-makers have to face to generate a positive context for innovation in the EU. Throughout the last two decades, the European Union has gradually been perceived as a key authoritative figure, which should address these matters. The transfer of powers from national to supra-national level that came along with the EU research programmes in the mid-1980s has expanded rapidly in the 1990s into the innovation areas mentioned. Far from being an automatic process, the notorious re-focusing, re-packaging and expansion of European Union involvement in this field ushers in a change of political strategy. Most importantly, it exhibits a novel understanding of the relationship between public action and the innovation process, and between national and supra-national domains. Rather than going over the factors and causes of this transformation of policy goals, this book aims at analysing the complexity and fluidity of governing innovation policy in the European Union. It addresses the strategic choices that are facing the EU in this rapid process of reshuffling policy competences between the national, supra-national and global levels, and of revamping the relationship between public and private spheres.

INNOVATION POLICY IN THE KNOWLEDGE-BASED ECONOMY

The transition from a science and technology policy towards an innovation policy at EU level has been taking place in a context of accelerated change, not just of EU politics but, most notably, of the modes of economic dynamics, namely the so-called 'knowledge-based economy'. This notion rests on the view that in the last two decades the role of knowledge has acquired a central position in the dynamics of the advanced capitalist economies. It has been asserted that the modern capitalist economies are based less on capital and labour, and more on knowledge, which has already become the key factor of production (Druckner 1998). Yet, looking back into the annals of history, we can see that knowledge has always had a prominent role in the economy, and in the historical transformations of the modes of production. What is new about knowledge in the contemporary economy? Why is there so much fuss about knowledge today?

One of the first arguments supporting the idea that we live in a 'knowledge-based economy' is the acceleration of the production, appropriation, exploitation and consumption of new knowledge. The life cycles of nearly all manufacturing products have become notoriously shortened, irrespective of whether they are high-, medium- or low-tech. This means that the knowledge input these products embody is one of the driving forces behind this acceleration. A second argument has to do with the rapid expansion of the frontiers of knowledge. In previous times, substantial production of knowledge in just one area of science and technology was enough for a whole new wave of products or modes of production. Today, we witness the simultaneous rapid expansion of knowledge in many areas, such as information and communication technologies, biotechnology, new materials, nanotechnology and so on, all of them having a significant impact on the dynamics of the economy. Last, but not least, a third argument supporting the idea of a shift to a 'knowledge-based economy' has to do with the expansion of the 'non-manufacturing' sector. The growing importance of the service sector, the increase in the stock of intangible assets, and the relationship between education and employment, all of which point to the economic relevance of competence-building and learning abilities beyond the world of manufacturing.

Another, slightly different, vision of the change in the economic structure is the so-called 'learning economy'. The emphasis here is not so much on the advancement of knowledge per se, or on its increasingly central position in the modes of economic production, but on the social dynamics related to it (Lundvall 1998; Lundvall and Borrás 1998). Learning relates not to the acquisition of new knowledge, but essentially to the organizational adaptation that it accompanies. Therefore, the learning economy stresses the organizational changes concomitant to the expansion of new knowledge, and concludes normatively that the clue to economic success rests on the ability to adapt to the rapidly changing context. Learning combines the acquisition of new capabilities and competences, with organizational adaptation. Regardless of the differences, proponents of both the 'knowledge-based economy' and the

4 The innovation policy of the European Union

'learning economy' point to the centrality of the production, appropriation, exploitation and consumption of knowledge in the contemporary advanced economies, and its concomitant social–organizational dynamics. We can see this knowledge production–appropriation–exploitation–consumption chain as the innovation process, which is essentially a social process.

What is the role of public action in all this? The centrality of knowledge and the acceleration of the innovation process in economic dynamics are a challenge to public action. The pervasiveness of innovation and the broadness of knowledge require a new mode of thinking about policy. Public action can no longer be a reduced set of instruments, generally involving the transfer of public monies or specific regulatory areas, for fostering technology. Policy needs to redress its role in a more contextual form, where the objective is to generate a positive framework for innovators. Most European countries undertook the transition from the technology policy to the innovation policy paradigm in the mid- and late-1990s (Shapira et al. 2001; Biegelbauer and Borrás 2003; OECD 2000). This is not to affirm that these countries are unidirectionally converging, since there are important differences as to how this transition has been undertaken, and how innovation policy instruments and goals are defined. The diversity of policy solutions is relevant, valid, and desirable. Nevertheless, the innovation agenda has emerged in almost all of them, along with the awareness that innovation is a complex social phenomenon. This understanding brings with it a partial reconsideration of public action, no longer focused on research and technological development alone, but increasingly paying attention to the larger picture of structural reform and the institutional set-up that fosters innovation. As we will see in the next chapter, this conceptual expansion poses some problems regarding the precise delimitation of what is, and what is not, innovation policy.

INNOVATION IN EUROPE: COMPETITIVENESS AND SOCIAL DYNAMICS

One could study the innovation policy of the European Union as if it was one more among other innovation policies at national level. But the question of level is analytically too significant to be discarded. Quite the contrary, 'level' represents a whole analytical dimension. This is so because innovation policy is inserted within a complex and ambitious political project of economic integration at international and regional level. European integration is essentially a process of institutionalizing a new political and economic order, which means that all policies aim at addressing their functional goals as much as at 'building' this new political and economic order. In other words, all the economic policies are instruments for this macro goal of system-building, which earmarks any political initiative.

The process of European integration has breathtakingly accelerated over the last two decades, and its political system today has a special nature, having state-like functions in the regulation of the economy. When economic development became the dominant issue of the EU agenda in the 1980s, the rationale for economic integration was not just the opening of markets to gain economies of scale or reduce transaction costs. It was also the creation of a common economic space for stimulating growth and job creation. In other words, the logic of EU action was not just the breaking down of trade barriers among its member states. The EU was paying just as much attention to the creation of incentives and the development of competences in the European economy in order to keep up with the growing pressures of competition coming from the world economy.

Competitiveness is the driving leitmotif of EU innovation policy. Time and again economists have argued that the European economy is losing ground to the more dynamic US and Japan. This was the case in the 1980s, and still is in the 'new economy' (Fagerberg et al. 1999; Soete 2001). Such statements have powerful effects on policy-makers. The intensification of EU efforts in the innovation field, and its notorious centrality in the Prodi agenda of the late 1990s, is the result of this fear of being 'left behind' in the technology race. Unemployment has been a related issue in this regard. European countries face the paradox of enduring high unemployment ratios at the time that some productive sectors, most notably the ICT (information and communication technologies) sector, lack qualified labour. New technologies are a source of job creation, but this has to be tuned with a more flexible and job-oriented educational and training system. Innovation policy looks systematically at the elements that shape the institutional set-up for innovators; namely, the educational system, research facilities, business and patent law, and more. The barriers in Europe are not so much between states and between legal and economic systems, but are found in an institutional set-up that is still not as sufficiently innovation-friendly as it could be.

Beyond the concerns of competitiveness, the EU innovation policy has gradually introduced another important focal point in recent years. This is the question of social trust and social values in relation to science. The dramatic cases of BSE (or 'mad cow disease'), dioxine and GMOs (genetically modified organisms) put on the table the question of food security. Something similar took place in relation to bioethics, where the dust of the fierce debates about biological patents and cloning has not yet settled. These examples are the tip of the iceberg of a much deeper social dynamics, the so-called 'risk society' (Beck 1992). Today there is widespread public concern about what scientific progress brings. And in contrast with some previous decades, there is a much more critical attitude from the people towards scientific advancements. Scientific and technical progress are not accepted with complacency, especially when they touch on sensitive issues such as the limits of human life or the unknown effects of some substances in the human body. This affects the design of innovation policy, which can no longer assume naïvely that all scientific and technological progress is automatically accepted by society. The recent social backlashes have opened up a new era in the governance of science and innovation at EU level.

THE SCOPE OF THIS BOOK

This book wants to provide a clear and concise picture of the development, dynamics and nature of EU innovation policy in recent years. There are two main reasons why this is needed. The first is that so far the studies of EU policy in this field have concentrated on the RTD (research and technological development) aspect and hence have partly failed to address the 'innovation turn' that EU policy has recently experienced. The overwhelming attention that the RTD framework programme has received has tended to obscure a whole set of other innovation-related areas where the EU has been extremely active lately. I refer to, among others, the areas of intellectual property rights regulation, standardization, the information society, education and training, regional policy, bioethics and environmental/consumer protection, all of which affect the institutional context for innovation. Consequently, there is a need to broaden the analysis of the innovation policy to these areas, at a time when the innovation policy agenda is so doing.

The second argument is that such a broad perspective will support the policy considerations developed in more specific economic studies. Admittedly, there is today an endless amount of literature about the EU's innovation and economic performance. Studies have focused on different industrial and technological sectors, or on specific geographical areas. Almost invariably this literature has tended to develop a normative approach to public action in the form of 'policy implications' and 'policy options' stemming from empirical findings. However, this has typically been done without a parallel analysis of the public initiatives already in place. This book aims at providing a succinct but critical analysis of the rapid development of EU innovation policy over recent years, by giving a background analysis for anyone working in innovation studies.

It is important to remember that this book has a 'top-down' analytical perspective, in so far as it looks at the political processes and their effects on building an innovation-friendly context for firms and innovators. This contrasts with a more bottom-up analysis of the behavioural patterns of innovators and their daily shaping of informal institutions through market and other social interactions. This means that I look at formal rules, norms and policy instruments, their political effects and the rationale on which they have been established, and not at the innovative performance of some sectors, firms or geographical areas. With this purpose in mind the book studies in detail the most recent developments of EU innovation policy in some of its most important areas. These include: research and knowledge production, intellectual property rights, the information society, standardization, and risk and social sustainability of innovation.

The book proceeds as follows. The first chapter sets up the analytical framework for the study of the EU's innovation policy. It defines the analytical parameters of the entire book in a way that gives coherence to the study of the different areas under the EU 'innovation policy' agenda. It first discusses the contents of 'innovation policy', and its emergence as a political agenda within the EU level. The 'governance' perspective of the following chapters focuses on three matters. First, the division of tasks between the EU and its member states, and the questions and problematiques related to the 'Europeanization' of these areas; secondly, the international position of the EU, in particular the role of the EU in the global regulatory context; and finally, the changing nature of public–private interaction in innovation and the influence of the EU in this regard.

Chapter 2 is devoted to EU public actions towards research and knowledge production. How is the production of knowledge related to innovation policy? How have governments traditionally approached this issue, and formulated their research and technological development (RTD) policies? What are the changing features of knowledge production, and how is this affecting public action? This chapter examines all these questions in relation to the EU's RTD policy. Science and technology have always been a central element in European integration. However the division of tasks between the EU and its member states has been constantly changing in what now is a multi-level structure. Likewise, the tremendous internationalization and globalization of knowledge production that has taken place over the last decade puts some pressure on national and regional policies, as previous boundaries are becoming blurred. Another issue of the chapter is the changing relationship between public and private spheres, not just in terms of financing knowledge production, but also how 'public' this knowledge is.

Chapter 3 takes up one of the most exciting areas related to innovation at EU level: the changing regime of intellectual property rights. The domain of intellectual property rights (IPRs) is a crucial regulatory framework for innovation, technological development and industrial activity, especially in the so-called knowledge-based economy. This regulatory framework has been changing very rapidly and deeply in the European Union since the beginning of 1990s. Chapter 3 addresses these transformations by asking about the nature of the emerging regulatory system and its impact on the innovation process. The main argument is that the Europeanization of IPRs complements the logic of the single European market. However, some important effects of the regulatory regime for the appropriation of knowledge need further attention, particularly the trends towards a strong and broad regulatory system, the high degree of legal uniformity, and the social legitimacy related to the re-conceptualization of private property at EU level.

Chapter 4 deals with the building and governing of the information society at EU level. The rapid development of ICTs has generated new opportunities to be grasped by firms and individuals, and this was declared the most dynamic sector in the 'new economy'. These opportunities might be enhanced by policies that address and create a new context for these technologies. This has been the main purpose of the wide array of EU regulatory efforts since the mid-1990s. This chapter examines the division of tasks between the EU and its member states in the area of information society and e-Europe, the position of EU initiatives in a world-wide context, and the reorganization of public-private spheres.

Chapter 5 is devoted to standardization. Economists working in the field of innovation have long asserted the crucial role that the definition of technical standards has for the innovation process. Standards are semi-public, semi-private agreements shaping technological paths. With the advent of the single European market project in the 1980s, issues concerning standardization have been moved from national to EU level, without apparently any major upheaval. However, alternative modes of enforcing this semi-regulatory function have been tried along the way. Standardization is also an important issue at global level. Here the role of the EU is less clear, but no less important for trade. A final aspect that this chapter examines is the interaction between public and private spheres. This is a complex matter in the case of standardization, however, several authors already stress the need to give more voice to consumers and the public in general in the standardization process.

Chapter 6 looks at risk and the social sustainability of innovation at EU level. The cases of BSE, dioxine and GMO have recently shaken the governance of science at EU level. The strong social distrust that these cases generated touched not just the political elite, but also the role of scientists. This has prompted a rapid reorganization of scientific advice in food safety matters. However, this is just the tip of the iceberg. These cases have shown, together with the overall social considerations about the limits of biotechnology, that the innovation process needs to be socially sustainable. This is particularly evident in the current risk society. This chapter examines these trends, through the three lines of analysis indicated; namely, the dynamics of Europeanization and internationalization of these issues, and the changing relationship between the public and private realms.

The conclusion identifies the governance patterns of the innovation policy of the EU in the past decade. This chapter also addresses the challenges and opportunities ahead in two interrelated ways. First it analyses two practical consequences arising from the dynamics; namely, the limits of EU action and the issue of democratic accountability. And, secondly, this chapter elaborates on the theoretical consequences of these dynamics both in terms of the theory about systems of innovation, and the recent debates about the EU as a competition state.

REFERENCES

Beck, U. (1992), *Risk Society – Towards a New Modernity*. London, Sage.

Biegelbauer, P. and S. Borrás (eds), (2003), *Innovation Policies in Europe and the US: The New Agenda*. Aldershot, Ashgate.

Druckner, P. (1998), 'From capitalism to knowledge society'. In *The Knowledge Economy*, D. Neef. Boston, Butterworth-Heinemann.

Fagerberg, J., P. Guerrieri and B. Verspagen (eds), (1999), *The Economic Challenge for Europe*. Cheltenham, Edward Elgar.

Lundvall, B.-Å. (1998), 'The learning economy: challenges to economic theory and policy'. In *Institutions and Economic Change*, K. Nielsen and B. Johnson. Cheltenham, Edward Elgar.

Lundvall, B.-Å. and S. Borrás (1998), *The Globalising Learning Economy: Implications for Innovation Policy*. Brussels, European Commission.

OECD (2000), *Science, Technology and Innovation Policy in OECD Countries – a Review of Recent Developments*. Paris, OECD.

Shapira, P., H. Klein and S. Kuhlmann (2001), 'Innovations in European and US innovation policy'. *Research Policy* **30**(6): 869–72.

Soete, L. (2001), 'The new economy: a European perspective'. In *The Globalising Learning Economy*, D. Archibugi and B.-Å. Lundvall. Oxford, Oxford University Press.

1. Analysing the innovation policy of the European Union

Technology works in Europe as a double engine: an engine for growth and an engine for integration.

John Peterson and Margaret Sharp (1998),
Technology Policy in the European Union. London, Macmillan.

INTRODUCTION

This book postulates that the transition from 'technology policy' to 'innovation policy' for the EU in the mid-1990s did not just mean an expansion of the number of issues under the new agenda; more importantly, it started to unleash a reorganization of policy-making at EU level. This was a transition from a mode of policy-making that was functionally compartmentalized, hierarchically managed and had limited accountability, to a new, emerging, mode of 'governance' where the areas are gradually becoming explicitly interconnected, there is no obvious hierarchy, there are substantial pressures to enhance transparency and participation, and public action is increasingly self-reflexive. In other words, the 'contents' of innovation policy are changing as much as the 'form' of conducting public action, and both 'contents' and 'form' are the cornerstones of a public action that is increasingly becoming a centrepiece of EU politics. Innovation policy, as the means of encouraging technical progress and sustainable socio-economic growth, has been recently upgraded from a rather obscure position amid the host of EU policies to an increasingly strategic status within the EU. Competitiveness, growth, job creation and social progress are nowadays key elements in the EU's own 'raison d'être', and innovation policy has a lot to offer in this regard.

This chapter has two purposes. The first is to present, in a nutshell, the history of the EU's involvement in this domain of public action. The argument is that the EU has developed its policy about these matters in three stages; namely, science policy, technology policy and innovation policy. The second purpose is to elaborate the analytical framework for studying the changing trends and dynamics of the EU's innovation policy, the topic of the rest of the book.

FROM GOVERNMENT TO GOVERNANCE IN THE EU

The concept of 'governance' has gained a great deal of acceptance among political scientists over the past decade, spawning an endless literature. Used in different contexts (local, national, EU policy-making, and international politics) and with diverse focuses (actor-based approaches, a regulatory approach, or a more institutional approach), this notion is widely used to portray currently changing modes of political action and public administration. These different uses point to the fact that there are a number of issues at stake, such as the transfer of competences from the state upwards to international and supra-national entities, and downwards towards powerfully decentralized local/regional governments; the emergence of new forms of partnership between public and private actors in public policy-making; or the more horizontal manner of public action. Essentially, the new modes of governance entail new ways of designing and enforcing public action.

Halfway between conventional public administration and international politics (Christiansen 1994), the EU studies have also embraced the 'governance agenda' (Hix 1998). The 'sui generis' nature of the EU as a political system in the making requires an analytical apparatus so that we can address the dynamics and processes that characterize European policy-making and its gradual construction as a new political arena (Kohler-Koch and Eising 1999). This has also been labelled 'supra-national governance' (Sandholtz and Sweet 1998; Jachtenfuchs 1997; Wallace and Wallace 2000).[1] Some authors have pointed to the blurring of boundaries between sectoral politics at EU level, where agenda setting is able to re-shuffle and re-package issues in novel and unexpected ways (Wallace 1996; Peters 1994). Other authors have focused on the multi-level nature of EU policy-making where different arenas and levels of government are deeply intertwined in the daily process of policy-formation, decision-making and implementation (Marks et al. 1996; Christiansen 1997), or have examined the nature of public–private interactions in decision-making, most notably by policy networks, new forms of participation/interaction (direct consultation, comitology) and new socio-economic dynamics (Richardson 1996; Schneider et al. 1994; Weiler 1999). Finally, some scholars have discussed this supranational governance in the context of the EU's ability to work as a unitary actor in the arena of international politics (Jørgensen 1998; Cafruny and Peters 1998).

Common to all these strands of thought is that they give the strong impression of a policy-making process in the EU that is in constant flux, that advances and changes rapidly, and that is quite fragmented. Therefore it is an object of study that is not at all easy to grasp, as it is a sort of a 'moving target'. As indicated above, some of these trends can be traced in recent developments of the EU's innovation policy. Indeed, the expansion of the EU's innovation policy turf is the result of a gradual policy evolution during the last couple of decades – an evolution that can be portrayed as the transition from science policy, to technology policy, and finally to innovation policy, in truly paradigmatic changes. Each of these three policy paradigms has been anchored in a distinct policy rationale that has provided the logical basis for the design of public action. The next section examines this in an abstract form, before considering how this paradigmatic transition has taken place at EU level.

POLICY EVOLUTION THROUGH POLICY PARADIGMS

The Second World War profoundly transformed the relationship between scientific research and politics. In the 1940s, a rather unknown and discreet scientific discipline such as theoretical physics, was able to produce the most powerful weapon ever constructed by human kind. The birth of the nuclear age took place in a turbulent international scenario, and it reaffirmed the role of science in two ways. First, it consolidated and strengthened the alliance of science with the state, an alliance still tangible and visible today. And secondly, it forever transformed its social status: science was never to regain its previous aura of purity and innocence. After the war, though, science was also perceived as a central contributor to the reconstruction process. In particular, nuclear energy was regarded as a new source of cheap and renewable energy. Consequently, science became 'the endless frontier', a resource that could unleash security, prosperity and progress – a vital element for the continuity and wealth of the state. In the aftermath of World War II, the 'Bush report' in the USA expressed this élan, shaping a new rationale for governmental intervention, the commencement of the contemporary 'science policy' (Elzinga and Jamison 1995).

This policy rationale was, however, modified a few decades later. The oil crises of the 1970s put a heavy strain on the production structures of industrialized countries, inducing a long and distressing process of industrial adjustment. Against this backdrop, national governments were anxious to use more tangibly scientific knowledge to help regain economic growth and jobs. They moved from science policy, that only contemplated the generation of scientific knowledge, towards technology policy, that fostered more actively the industrial application of that knowledge. The spotlight turned towards issues like technology transfer, bridging institutions between research and industry, industrial standards, and inter-firm RTD collaboration. Most notably, this decade placed a lot of attention on 'strategic industries', in what turned out to be a rather national protectionist attitude, particularly in relation to large industries (Sharp 1990).

Yet, by the early to mid-1990s 'innovation' was introduced as a new concept. The attitude was that the overtones of technology policy were too linear and deterministic, and were inadequate for the complex process of innovation. This new policy vision stems directly from new theories about the nature of the innovation process that challenged the hitherto dominant neo-classical economic understanding of technology as an economic externality (Coriat and Dosi 1998). Particular attention was given to the concept of 'national systems of innovation' that was developed within institutional economics (Freeman 1987; Lundvall 1992; Nelson 1993). The main postulate was that differences in the innovative performance of states could be explained on the basis of the diverse, historically developed, sets of formal and informal institutional arrangements that form the context for innovation. Following this new understanding, the role of public policy was transformed in an important way. On the one hand, the systemic and institutional perspective allowed a wider vista of the elements that are at play in the innovation process. Policy-makers started acknowledging, in the 1990s, that if innovation is so deeply embedded in social institutions, the fields of public action that have an impact on it are more than those covered by technology policy. Innovative performance lies at the crossroads of a much wider set of functional areas. Policy-makers no longer recognize the 'horizontal' nature of innovation, but its 'systemic' nature. On the other hand, theoretical economists have been actively involved in the normative formulation of specific policy rationales (Andersson 1998; Lipsey and Fraser 1998). In this sense, they have advocated public action that enhances diversity (Cohendet and Llerena 1997) and learning processes (Dalum et al. 1992), that supports the technology paradigm's own evolution (Llerena and Matt 2000), and that focuses on other type of failures which go beyond the mere 'market failures' of previous policy rationales (Malerba 1996; Smith 1996). All in all, the innovation policy paradigm has opened up a new way of thinking and designing public action in this domain. The domain now takes into account issues such as the building of the overall system's capabilities, intellectual property rights, social values and norms in science (bioethics, food safety, environmental protection), and reducing socio-economic disparities.

Figure 1.1 visualizes this three-step evolution of policy, based on Dodgson and Bessant (1996). It is worth noting that there is a cumulative process, since the new policy paradigm encompasses the previous ones. That is, innovation policy encapsulates the objectives and instruments of both science and technology policies.[2] This said, two remarks should be made at this point. First, this ladder is an analytical model for heuristic purposes. Historical developments of specific national or regional innovation policies might not have followed this pattern strictly, and might even have different stages, depending on their institutional political peculiarities. Secondly, in our

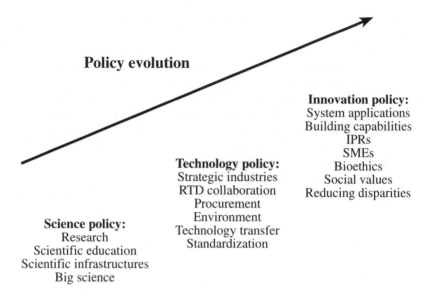

Figure 1.1   Science, technology and innovation policy evolution

understanding, policy evolution is a 'stylized fact' of the transformations taking place through history. In this evolution there is not necessarily an overall pre-determined rationality constantly improving it, as if there was an 'end of history' where policy achieves a perfect, ultimate, formulation. Policy changes are the fruit of many complex factors, which are socially, politically, and economically embedded, and that are not necessarily improvements of one single possible course of history.

Hence, there is no single or perfect 'evolutionary path'. Instead, evolution can be defined as the constant adaptation of policy action to the ever changing societal dynamics, in what is the governmental willingness to respond to a new situation in an effective way. Policy evolution is a cognitive–institutional transformation where political action is shaped by a policy rationale in a more or less explicit manner. Ideas and institutional transformations are inserted in larger political processes, which have distinct socio-economic impacts.

A BRIEF HISTORY

The European Union has followed this policy evolution. At the onset, it engaged in science policy in its goal to generate collective scientific knowledge among its member states. This was, though, undertaken in only one scientific area, namely nuclear energy, which was very sensitive for economic and military security. The Euratom materialized this political wish in the Joint Research Centre (JRC), a common research organization, operative since the 1960s. Yet, as we examine in detail in the coming chapter concerning 'research and knowledge production', these expectations held true only until the JRC stalemate at the end of the 1960s, with the subsequent 'failure [of the Communities] to implement a nuclear techno-industrial federalism' (Carocostas and Soete 1997).

The 1980s brought a fresh breath of air into the EU. The creation, in 1984, of the EU Framework Programme saw the introduction of a new policy area: research and technological development, formally adopted in the Single European Act.[3] The FP introduced some interesting novelties in form and content. Regarding the form, its multi-annual programmatic nature, combined with its co-financing terms, and being based on strictly cross-national and collaborative projects, meant that the EU had learnt the lessons from the past, especially the stories of failure (Peterson and Sharp 1998). Concerning the content, though, it can be argued that the FP inaugurated a new policy paradigm, moving away from the science policy of the JRC towards a technology policy. The dominant element was technological development. Despite its ambiguously implemented 'pre-competitive' nature, a more decidedly industrial dimension was introduced, by encouraging the participation of firms in RTD projects.

Yet, by the mid-1990s, a new policy paradigm superseded this eminently technological approach: the so-called innovation policy (Metcalf and Georghiou 1998). The transition from one to the other was based on a new rationale widely shared among the experts and elites, most significantly among evolutionary institutional economists, and national and European civil servants (Sanz and Borrás 2000). The emergence of the new policy paradigm has to be understood in the specific socio-economic and political context of the European Union at the beginning of the 1990s. At that time, the successful completion of the single market and the commitment towards a single currency were a reality. Nevertheless, the ambition to foster European competitiveness was faltering, given the relative poor economic performance and soaring unemployment rates. Ten years of technology policy had not managed to reverse this situation substantially, keeping politicians in readiness for new courses of public action. The 1994 White Paper on 'Growth, competitiveness and employment' (Commission 1994), where technology and innovation acquired a prominent role, was the political legacy of Jacques Delors. The notion that innovation was partly the solution to the economic problems of the EU indicated the extent to which the new cognitive parameters – insisting on a wider and more 'systemic' vision of innovation as opposed to the previous linear expectations of technology – had penetrated the

EU's political strategic thinking. This was to be the starting point for more specific EU initiatives in the field. The first of those was the 1995 Green Paper on innovation (Commision 1995). Elaborating on a systemic approach, this document identified the deficiencies of European, national and regional public action towards the attainment of a positive and incentive context for innovativeness, in a similar vein to the Cecchini report and 'the costs of non-Europe' a decade earlier. The three lines of action envisaged were:

1. to foster a genuinely innovative culture (training, education, exchanging best practices in industrial performance and public policies);
2. to establish a framework conducive to innovation (European patents, help for start-up firms, financial accessibility); and
3. to articulate better research and innovation (flexible RTD programmes, foresight, more international collaboration).

Most recently, the Prodi Commission has taken up the innovation issue, putting it again in a central position among the EU's general political goals. This coincided with the consecutive Finnish and Portuguese presidencies of the Council of Ministers,[4] which made innovation a flagship for the Union's strategy towards economic growth. As was expressed at the Lisbon Summit:

> The Union has today set itself a new strategic goal for the next decade: to become the most competitive and dynamic knowledge-based economy in the world capable of economic growth with more and better jobs and greater social cohesion. (Presidency Conclusions, Lisbon, 23–24 March 2000: 2)

Three more specific activities related to this thrust are the 'European Research Area',[5] the Communication 'Innovation in a knowledge-driven economy',[6] and the benchmarking and innovation scoreboard exercises in the early 2000s. These three initiatives follow, generally speaking, the spirit of the 1995 Green Paper, but have introduced some interesting novelties and policy instruments. This is particularly true for benchmarking and best practice studies, instruments that fall under the so-called 'open method of coordination', which is now considered as a newly emerging pattern of EU governance (Wallace and Wallace 2000; Borrás and Jacobsson 2004).

There is no risk in claiming that the Green Paper and its related initiatives represent the EU's explicit political agenda of building an innovation policy, but what are the precise boundaries of this new EU policy? Does the Commission's official definition of boundaries provided in the Green paper and the 2000 Communication fit into the actual development of innovation-related initiatives at the EU level? And how is this book going to tackle the key matter of definitional borders?

DIFFICULTIES IN DEFINING POLICY BOUNDARIES

The rapidly growing economic literature about innovation has, so far, produced different interpretations of what the contents and boundaries of innovation policy are. Even if there is wide support for public action that moves beyond the strict technology policy, there is still a certain vagueness as to what constitutes its functional limits. Two interpretations co-exist. On the one hand, some authors argue for a wide agenda of innovation policy. On the top of policy instruments like 'provision of finance' and 'support for networking', Metcalfe and Georghiou include 'information and advice' to innovators, and 'technology foresight programmes' (Metcalfe and Georghiou 1998: 88). Another wide interpretation of innovation policy is provided by Lundvall and Borrás, and this includes, among other things, competition policy, education and training, and organizational change (Lundvall and Borrás 1998). This exercise has however recently been criticized. 'Broadening the perspective is the right approach, but in doing so there is a risk of enlarging the issue to the extreme that innovation policy becomes too pervasive' (Sanchez 2000: 5). On the other hand, a narrow agenda of innovation policy seems to have gained ground among civil servants, wanting to keep the focus on the role of public action. In this sense, the Green Paper of innovation follows this narrow approach, and so does the 2000 Communication from the Commission about innovation in a knowledge-based economy. In this later document there are five policy objectives, as shown in Table 1.1.

As can be seen in Table 1.1, the Commission suggests a definition of innovation policy at EU level that is rather narrow – narrow not in terms of political ambitions, but mostly in terms of functional limits; that is, what lies inside and outside the scope of innovation policy. It is well known that areas such as education and training, telecom infrastructures or competition regulations, fall outside these borders. This makes innovation policy an operable policy area for two reasons. First, because EU action is focused on these particular areas and not others, which are perceived to be the real 'problems' for innovation processes that the EU can tackle selectively. Secondly, because the areas of action fall, generally speaking, within the formal competences of the DG enterprise, and hence do not challenge the hitherto functional division of tasks of other DGs, particularly with regard to DG research.

With this strategic document the Commission seems to have anticipated Edquist's advice that innovation policy design has to be based on a double principle, namely, the existence of real problems hindering innovativeness of an economy, and the ability of public agents to proactively solve or mitigate them (Edquist 2001). The analysis of the system of innovation is supposed to

Table 1.1   Innovation policy objectives of the EU Commission

Objectives	Policy instruments at EU level
Coherence of innovation policies	• Benchmarking and coordination of national innovation policies
A innovation-friendly regulatory framework	• Intellectual property rights
	• Standardization
	• European accounting standards
Creation and growth of innovative enterprises	• Networking activities and directories
	• Support services with a European dimension
	• Encourage participation of SMEs in public tendering
Improve interfaces in the innovation system	• European networks of research institutions and universities
	• Diffusion of good practice of local networking
	• Transnational technology partnerships
A society open to innovation	• Technology foresight at EU level

Source: Author's elaboration from EU Commission Communication 2000.

provide such in-depth knowledge on which public authorities develop general and specific courses of action.

But is this the case? My argument is that even if the EU has formally expressed this narrow functional definition of innovation policy, the truth is that important transformations in strongly innovation-related policy areas have de facto left this official definition without real content. In other words, that actual EU policies towards enhancing innovativeness in the European economy go far beyond the five lines defined in Table 1.1. A myriad of instruments and initiatives have, in recent years, in different policy domains, partly 'converged' in their objectives of fostering innovation processes at supranational/transnational level.

Therefore, there are two arguments here supporting a wider definition of innovation policy at EU level. First, EU innovation policy shows some signs of gradually becoming a sort of an umbrella policy, where different functional dimensions and traditional policy areas partly come together on the basis of their contribution to enhancing innovative processes in society and the economy. Arguably, this responds to the Council of Ministers' appeal and vision for Europe 'to become the most competitive and dynamic knowledge-based economy in the world'. This has turned out to be a meta-objective of the

EU defining the political aspirations which are intrinsically linked with innovation and knowledge production/utilization in their widest sense. Secondly, a broader definition of innovation policy is better suited to understanding the rapid transformation of the boundaries and nature of public action, and to analysing the consequences for the EU. These transformations refer to the transfer of powers between the EU and member states, to the increasing internationalization and globalization of the economy and innovative activities, and to the boundaries between the private and public realms, which are being rapidly recast.

Figure 1.2 shows how the innovation policy is an umbrella policy, and links it with the policy areas already existing at EU level. It clusters these policy areas under three broad goals for enhancing innovativeness and under the dominant tools available for each domain.

The goal of building competences for innovativeness has been quite important in EU policy activity, with intervention in the areas of scientific research and knowledge production (the RTD framework programme), programmes enhancing education and vocational training (mainly mobility), emphasis on EU-wide infrastructure building (particularly in telecoms), special attention to small and medium-sized enterprises' (SMEs) dynamics, regional policy and its objective of building competences and innovation in poor regions (the RIS/RTT initiatives), a focus on bridging institutions (for

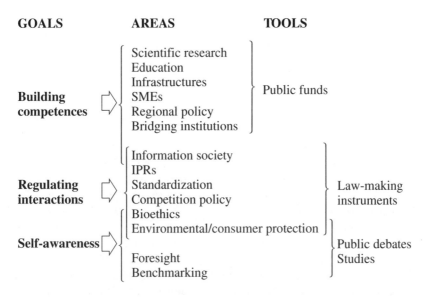

Figure 1.2   Governing the innovation policy of the EU

example the technology transfer network in the EU), and finally, the objectives of an information society maximizing the potentials offered by ICTs. The RTD framework programme and the 'innovation-oriented' initiatives under regional aid are the largest budgetary allocations in this context.

Similarly, the EU has been very active in the regulatory field relating to innovation. This refers equally to deregulation, regulation and regulatory control.[7] The deregulation of ICT markets in the EU comes under the 'information society' and is a significant move for innovation. Similarly, the EU regulations concerning intellectual property rights and standardization (with the semi-regulatory nature of the latter), have paramount importance for the innovation process at large. The same can be said about the regulatory control of competition policy, and the surveillance of 'fair competition' practices, which have an impact on the innovation process by shaping technological trajectories and their commercial exploitation. Last but not least, regulations in the fields of bioethics, food safety, and environmental/consumer protection reflect common social values and shape the borders of technology and its use.

Beyond these specific goals and instruments, the EU policy actions have a reflexive/self-awareness dimension. This is to be found in the lively debates concerning the social values and ethics that are involved in the production of new scientific knowledge and its application. This has been the case for biotechnology, particularly in the field of genetics, and for food safety. However, the dynamics of self-awareness in EU innovation policy can also be related to some new initiatives, namely the tentative foresight and benchmarking exercises in 2001–02. Both aim at developing collective visions of the EU in relation to innovation, technology and competitiveness.

ANALYSING HOW THE INNOVATION POLICY OF THE EU IS GOVERNED

Having argued for a wider definition of innovation policy, the question is how best to analyse all the transformations that have taken place in recent years and what areas to select on this basis. The rapidly changing dynamics of the EU's innovation policy in the 1990s poses the problem of how to analyse it in an orderly manner. Starting with the question about what areas to select, the introduction of this book identified five; namely, research and knowledge production, intellectual property rights, the information society, standardization, and risk and social sustainability of innovation. The criteria for selecting them has been that they represent different dimensions of the goals and tools at EU level, they correspond to the 'hard' nucleus of innovation policy (especially research and knowledge production, IPRs and standardization), and they raise important questions about the social dynamics underlying the use of new technologies (particularly the areas of information society and risk) which have traditionally been regarded as being on the margins of innovation policy. Unfortunately, other relevant areas like competition policy, regional policy, or education and training, are not covered in this book. There are three reasons for this. The first and most mundane is the need to set some sensible limits to this book. The second reason is that some of these areas are partly covered by some of the selected issues. This is the case, for example, of competition policy and the considerations in this regard in the chapter about intellectual property rights, or the case of regional policy instruments used in the area of information society. The last reason, particularly relevant in the case of education and training, is that EU policy action has been rather limited, given the division of competences between the EU and its member states in this field. There are interesting EU policy initiatives in the field of education and training, however, they are not substantial enough to make up a whole chapter.

Related to the analytical strategy of these areas, the book follows a threefold perspective, as indicated in Figure 1.3. First it examines the division of tasks between the EU and its member states: the rationale that has characterized the Europeanization and the current nature of the division of tasks. Secondly, it studies the internationalization/globalization of the corresponding area, looking particularly at the issue of the EU's profile as a unitary actor in the global scene and the blurred borders of EU action in an increasingly internationalized polity context. Thirdly, each chapter investigates the changing nature and relationship between the public and private realms. This is an important aspect, since in most of the areas there are significant transformations in this regard, particularly regarding the scope of individual/ private rights and public participatory channels. Last but not least, some of the chapters have a fourth analytical dimension, namely, disparities and diversity in the EU. These will analyse schematically recent socio-economic trends and recent EU policy initiatives, which also fall under the scope of innovation policy.

---

1. Europeanization: the current division of tasks between the EU and member states.
2. Internationalization: the current international arrangements and the EU acting (or not) as a unitary actor.
3. The changing nature of public and private realms.
4. Disparities and diversity within the EU.

Figure 1.3   Strategy for analysing the innovation policy of the EU

NOTES

1. 'Supra-national governance' contrasts sharply with the intergovernmentalist approach that denies the 'sui generis' 'polity' nature of EU politics.
2. See Caracostas and Muldur for another interpretation of the relationship between science, technology and innovation policy (Caracostas and Muldur 1998).
3. Articles 163–73 (ex. Art. 130F–130P).
4. Finland 2nd half of 1999, and Portugal 1st half of 2000.
5. European Commission (2000): 'Towards a European Research Area', Com (2000) 6, 18 January 2000.
6. Communication COM (2000) 567 final.
7. With this regulatory focus, we back Hart's contention that regulatory policies, traditionally outside the conventional instruments of science and technology policy, need to be recognized as essential elements of contemporary innovation policies (Hart 2001).

REFERENCES

Andersson, T. (1998), 'Managing a systems approach to technology and innovation policy'. *STI - Science Technology Industry Review* **22**: 9–29.

Borrás, S. and K. Jacobsson (2004), 'The open method of co-ordination and the new patterns of EU governance'. *European Journal of Public Policy* **11**(1), forthcoming.

Cafruny, A. and P. Peters (eds) (1998), *The Union and the World: The Political Economy of a Common European Foreign Policy*. The Hague, Kluwer Law International.

Caracostas, P. and U. Muldur (1998), *Society, The Endless Frontier*. Luxemburg, Office for Official Publications of the European Communities.

Caracostas, P. and L. Soete (1997), 'The building of cross-border institutions in Europe: Towards a European system of innovation?' In *Systems of Innovation, Technologies, Institutions and Organizations*, C. Edquist. London, Pinter.

Christiansen, T. (1994), 'European integration between political science and international relations theory: The end of sovereignty'. Florence, EUI. RSC 94/04.

Christiansen, T. (1997), 'Reconstructing European space: From territorial politics to multilevel governance'. In *Reflective Approaches to European Governance*, K.E. Jørgensen. London, Routledge.

Cohendet, P. and P. Llerena (1997), 'Learning, technical change and public policy: How to create and exploit diversity'. In *Systems of Innovation. Technologies, Institutions and Organisations*, C. Edquist. London, Pinter.

Commission, European (1994), *Growth, Competitiveness, Employment. The Challenges and Ways Forward into the 21st Century*. Luxembourg, Office for Official Publications.

Commission, European (1995), Green Paper on Innovation. Com 95 (688) final. Brussels.

Coriat, B. and G. Dosi (1998), 'The institutional embeddedness of economic change: an appraisal of the "evolutionary" and "regulationist" research programmes'. In *Institutions and Economic Change. New Perspectives on Markets, Firms and Technology*, B. Johnson and K. Nielsen. Cheltenham, Edward Elgar.

Dalum, B., B. Johnson and B.Å. Lundvall (1992), 'Public policy in the learning society'. In *National Systems of Innovation. Towards a Theory of Innovation and Interactive Learning*, B.-Å. Lundvall. London, Pinter.

Dodgson, M. and J. Bessant (1996), *Effective Innovation Policy: A New Approach*. London, International Thomson.

Edquist, C. (2001), 'Innovation policy - a systemic approach'. In *The Globalizing Learning Economy*, D. Archibugi and B.-Å. Lundvall. Oxford, Oxford University Press.

Elzinga, A. and A. Jamison (1995), 'Changing policy agendas in science and technology'. In *Handbook of Science and Technology Studies*, S. Jasanoff, G. Markle, J. Petersen and T. Pinch. London, Sage.

Freeman, C. (1987), *Technology Policy and Economic Performance. Lessons from Japan*. Cambridge, Cambridge University Press.

Hart, D.M. (2001), 'Antitrust and technological innovation in the US: Ideas, institutions, decisions and impacts, 1890-2000'. *Research Policy* **30**: 923-36.

Hix, S. (1998), 'The study of the European Union II: The "new governance" agenda and its rival'. *Journal of European Policy Process* **5**(1): 38-65.

Jachtenfuchs, M. (1997), 'Conceptualizing European governance'. In *Reflective Approaches to European Governance*, K.E. Jørgensen. London, Macmillan.

Jørgensen, K.E. (1998), 'The European Union's performance in world politics: How should we measure success?' Aarhus, Department of Political Science, Aarhus University, working paper.

Kohler-Koch, B. and R. Eising (eds) (1999), *The Transformation of Governance in the European Union*. New York, Routledge.

Lipsey, R.G. and S. Fraser (1998), 'Technology policies in neo-classical and structuralist-evolutionary models'. *STI - Science Technoloy Industry Review* **22**: 30-73.

Llerena, P. and M. Matt (2000), 'Technology policy and cooperation: A paradigmatic approach'. Druid working paper no. 00-2.

Lundvall, B.-Å. (ed.) (1992), *National Systems of Innovation: Towards a Theory of Innovation and Interactive Learning*. London, Pinter.

Lundvall, B.-Å. and S. Borrás (1998), *The Globalising Learning Economy: Implications for Innovation Policy*. Brussels, European Commission.

Malerba, F. (1996), 'Public policy and industrial dynamics: An evolutionary perspective'. ISE.

Marks, G., L. Hooghe and K. Blank (1996), 'European integration from the 1980s: State-centric v. multilevel governance'. *Journal of Common Market Studies* **34**(4): 341-78.

Metcalfe, S. and L. Georghiou (1998), 'Equilibrium and evolutionary foundations of technology policy'. *STI-Science Technology Industry Review* **22**: 75-100.

Nelson, R.R. (ed.) (1993), *National Innovation Systems. A Comparative Analysis*. Oxford, Oxford University Press.

Peters, G.B. (1994), 'Agenda-setting in the European Community'. *Journal of European Public Policy* **1**(1): 9-26.

Peterson, J. and M. Sharp (1998), *Technology Policy in the European Union*. London, Macmillan Press.

Richardson, J. (1996), 'Actor-based models of national and EU policy making'. In *The EU and National Industrial Policy*, H. Kassim and A. Menon. London, Routledge.

Sanchez, P. (2000), 'The design of a European innovation policy: issues and problems'. Paper prepared for the European Commission.

Sandholtz, W. and A.S. Sweet (eds) (1998), *European Intecration and Supranational Governance*. Oxford, Oxford University Press.

Sanz, L. and S. Borrás (2000), 'Explaining changes and continuity in the EU technology policy: The politics of economic ideas'. In *The Dynamics of European Science and Technology Policies*, S. Dresner and N. Gilbert. Aldershot, Ashgate Press.

Schneider, V., G. Dang-Nguyen and R. Werle (1994), 'Corporate actor networks in European policy-making: Harmonizing telecommunications policy'. *Journal of Common Market Studies* **32**(4): 473–98.

Sharp, M. (1990), 'The single market and European policies for advanced technologies'. *The Political Quarterly* **61**: 100–120.

Smith, K. (1996), 'System approaches to innovation: Some policy issues', ISE.

Wallace, H. (1996), 'Politics and policy in the EU: The challenge of governance. In *Policy-making in the European Union*, H. Wallace and W. Wallace. Oxford, Oxford University Press.

Wallace, H. and W. Wallace (eds) (2000), *Policy-making in the European Union*. Oxford, Oxford University Press.

Weiler, J. (1999), 'Epilogue: Comitology as a revolution – infranationalism, constitutionalism and democracy. In *EU Committees: Social Regulation. Law and Politics*, C. Joerges and E. Vos. Oxford, Hart Publishing.

2. Research and knowledge production

> The process of European integration is not based on a customs union, a common agricultural policy and a single currency only: it is also based on circulation of knowledge among individual member countries.   (Archibugi et al. 2000: 1)

INTRODUCTION

The production of knowledge has always been an important element of the European integrationist project. In the reconstruction period there was an understanding that science had to be harnessed collectively, becoming a building block for peace, stability and prosperity. Until then, science had had a prominent role in the two great wars, deploying new weapons of mass destruction. No wonder then that the Europeanists' preoccupation was to enforce collective control of advanced knowledge. An entirely new solution was born, European states were not just to exchange their knowledge: they were to produce it collectively. As time went by, scientific cooperation extended to a larger number of areas from what initially was only collaboration in nuclear energy. Consequently, Archibugi's assertion – that European integration deals with the free exchange of knowledge – nicely links science to the market-building rationale of the Communities. Nevertheless, it falls short of explaining the political ambitions behind it. The EU is more than a space for economic transactions. It is a new post-national political-economic order, and in this order, the collective production of advanced knowledge epitomizes the pooling of national sovereignty.

In the last two decades, scholars of innovation and science studies have been reporting significant changes in the patterns of knowledge production. The transition from a 'Mode 1' to a 'Mode 2' of knowledge production, the blurring boundaries of the triple helix (government–industry–university) or the 'new social contract for science' are among the most acknowledged notions of these transformations. In one way or another, they all depict the fact that the traditional institutions that command the process of knowledge production are undergoing rapid transformation.

Likewise, the role of public authorities is changing. The advancement of the 'knowledge-based economy' has brought knowledge production to the forefront of political action aimed at achieving competitiveness and growth.

This has resulted in increased political efforts to improve the institutional environment for knowledge production, but also in increased pressure to see the knowledge outputs in the rates of economic growth.

This chapter explores the changing patterns of governing knowledge production in the EU. As such it focuses on EU policy action regarding this issue, pointing to the emerging trends and challenges ahead, in the globalizing knowledge-based economy. The first section deals with some general matters on the role of knowledge production in the innovation process, and about policy actions towards it. The second section examines the political process of Europeanizing policies for knowledge production. This section will answer two questions, namely, whether the EU is emerging as a federal-like research structure as Sharp has argued (Sharp 1997), and whether the growth of cross-national research endeavours is affecting traditional (national) patterns of research organization. The third section looks at knowledge production at international level. The rapid internationalization and globalization of knowledge since the early 1990s have invariably put some pressure on national and EU policies, as the previous boundaries are becoming blurred. Why support the production of public knowledge if its benefits are uncertain to be located within the EU? How 'European' should European research be? What is the emerging role of the EU level of knowledge production in the global scene? What should be the boundaries for European research? The fourth section focuses on the changing relationship between the public and private spheres of knowledge production. The new 'social contract of science' has put pressure on the rates of return of publicly financed research at a time when universities and public research centres are seeing their roles rapidly transformed. This is also the case at EU level, where there is an increasing focus on the private financing of research. How far are all these trends blurring the previous distinction of public–private realms of research? What are the emerging patterns at EU level? Finally, this chapter examines the disparities and diversity within the EU, especially in regard to the coming enlargement eastwards.

KNOWLEDGE PRODUCTION AND INNOVATION

How is the production of knowledge related to innovation? How have governments traditionally approached this issue? What are the changing features of knowledge production, and how is this affecting public action? Knowledge has always been important in the production process. It can be approximately defined as the amount of expertise, know-how, and scientific and technical aptitudes that a given society has. This 'stock of knowledge' is constantly expanded and modified by social interactions leading to new knowledge and the acquisition of new aptitudes. In both its static and dynamic dimensions, knowledge is an essential element of innovativeness. The different modes in which a system produces, diffuses, appropriates, and exploits knowledge affect the path and forms of innovation trajectories. As this section deals with knowledge production, we will first examine what the features of its production are. After that we will look at the role of public action. The purpose is to point out the constitutive effects that the generation of knowledge has on systems of innovation, and hence provide a starting point for addressing the issue of EU involvement in research and knowledge production.

The Features of Knowledge Production

For some years now it has been commonplace in any book or article about RTD to start discussions with the distinction between 'science' and 'technology'. In conventional wisdom science is a 'pure' and 'basic' form of knowledge, produced through specific rules (the scientific method) and by a selected social group: the scientific community. Technology, on the other hand, is knowledge which is essentially applied, having more technical than scientific elements, and produced by another group of people, namely engineers and technicians. Nevertheless, this distinction is far from clear in reality and has lately come under siege almost unanimously by a large number of scholars. As sociologists and historians of science have stressed, the relationship between science and technology is complex and diverse, and consequently muddled up (Sanchez-Rón 2000). Economists too have criticized this distinction as unrealistic. Some argue that the problem in this traditional view is that knowledge is equivalent to a flow of information, and that this does not represent the dynamics of knowledge production in contemporary economies (Cohendet and Joly 2001). Others argue along these lines, stating that innovation is not a linear process from science to technology, but rather a social learning process where both are deeply intertwined (Lundvall 1998).

Economists' interest in knowledge production and the innovation process in general has grown since the early 1980s, when Nelson and Winter's book opened up a new research agenda under evolutionary and institutional economics (Nelson and Winter 1982). Since then, the literature dealing with the nature, dynamics and position of knowledge in the economy has grown rapidly and parallel to the political concerns about the central position of knowledge for economic development. Most of these economists have a broad understanding of knowledge, including simultaneously scientific/ technical knowledge, and organizational capabilities. In this book, though, we follow the first notion of knowledge, referring to the knowledge associated with scientific research and technological development. This responds to the empirical limits of this book, as it has set aside 'organizational change'.

Amid the current, lively, debates among economists about the nature and dynamics of knowledge there seems to be a common agreement about three key features of knowledge production. First, the production of scientific and technical knowledge is intrinsically related to the *institutional context* where it is produced. This context is formed by formal institutions (laws, individual rights, procedures) and informal institutions (values, unspoken norms of behaviour). As Foray has put it:

> In fact, institutions and norms of behaviour have a certain degree of suppleness, which means that a knowledge product generated in a given organization (say a university) can be expressed in a broad range of forms (scientific papers, patents, shared expertise, restricted or delayed access, etc), depending upon the incentive structures and the institutional compromises that characterize the organization considered. (Foray 1997: 70).

As in this quotation, 'institutional context' can be interpreted in a narrow sense (the firm, the laboratory, the university department), but it can also be interpreted in a wide sense (a locality or a scientific discipline). Within this latest and widest meaning, the notion 'system of innovation' came into view with particular strength in the early 1990s (Nelson 1993; Lundvall 1992; Edquist and Johnson 1997), currently being used widely in economic geography (Storper 1997; Olazaran and Gómez-Uranga 2001). Prominent variants of this concept are 'social system of innovation', which stresses the social and informal aspect of the institutional context (Amable et al. 1997); and 'technical systems of innovation' (Breschi and Malerba 1997), which focuses on the industrial/scientific sectors. Common to them all is the fact that the particularities of the institutional set-up (formal and informal), which has evolved historically and piecemeal, shape the unique features of each system of innovation, working as its linchpin.

A second feature generally acknowledged by evolutionary-institutional economists is that there are different types of knowledge, namely tacit and codified knowledge (Abramowitz and David 1996; Lundvall 1999). Tacit and codified knowledge are important for the innovation process in different ways. Codified knowledge is knowledge that has been disembodied from its generator as it has been conveyed into a common language (mathematics, conventional language, visualized, etc), and consequently can be exchanged with other people. The advancement of information and communication technologies has reduced the costs and improved the accessibility of this type of knowledge, fostering, indirectly, greater codification. Tacit knowledge is quite different. Following Lundvall: 'tacit knowledge is knowledge that has not been documented and made explicit by the one who uses and controls it' (Lundvall 1999: 8). Consequently, tacit knowledge is 'sticky' in nature; 'sticky' in an organizational and territorial sense. Given the fact that knowledge is never fully codifiable, the production of new knowledge will always generate capabilities and abilities for those involved in its production process, even if part of this new knowledge is finally codified. Contesting this, Cowan, David and Foray have recently expressed their doubts about the interest that tacit knowledge has for economists. They distinguish between three categories of knowledge: 'articulated', 'unarticulated' and 'unarticulable', pointing out that conventional wisdom about tacit knowledge has failed to differentiate between the second and the third, considering tacitness to be expressed by both terms. These authors insist that tacitness should be interpreted as unarticulability, and hence left aside in economic enquiries. The relevant questions for social scientists are then, what are the economic conditions under which knowledge is articulated or remains unarticulated, and what are their respective economic consequences? Counterbalancing the rows that these statements have generated in the circle of scholars devoted to these matters, Cohendet and Steinmueller insist that Cowan-David-Foray's view is perfectly reconcilable with the hitherto conventional understanding of codified tacit knowledge, with the virtue that the theoretical question about increasing returns will again come under the spotlight (Cohendet and Steinmueller 2000: 198). Furthermore, it is argued here that tacit knowledge remains an essential economic element, since in many cases tacit and codified knowledge are deeply linked to each other in the innovation process (Archibugi and Lundvall 2001).

A last feature of knowledge production, regarding which most economists seem to be of the same mind, is that knowledge shows a certain degree of cumulativeness. The advancement of knowledge is a process of integrating new pieces of knowledge within the already existing base, so expanding and transforming it (David and Foray 1998). This has been portrayed as 'path dependency' in the evolutionary progress of knowledge advancement, and 'technology trajectories' within specific techno-industrial sectors. Both notions are however related not just to the production of knowledge, but to its application and exploitation. The cumulativeness of knowledge production has also been related to the 'stickiness' of knowledge in geographical and organizational terms, as we have seen. Those firms and localities that have already developed a substantial knowledge base are most likely to continue producing and adapting it, as knowledge is embodied in human resources.

In the past few years some scholars, mainly sociologists of science, have insisted on the fact that there are important new dynamics in the production of scientific knowledge. This correlates with the discussions about the current knowledge-based economy that have lately hit the headlines.

The New Dynamics of Knowledge Production

In their 1994 book, Gibbons et al. developed one of the most successful ideas in contemporary studies of science: the notion that we are approaching a 'Mode 2' of knowledge production (Gibbons et al. 1994), which supplements 'Mode 1' (see Table 2.1).

Table 2.1   Mode 1 and Mode 2 of knowledge production

Mode 1	Mode 2
Produced in strict academic environment	Produced in relation to its application
Disciplinary	Transdisciplinary
Homogeneous	Heterogeneous
Hierarchical organization	Non-hierarchical organization
Not socially accountable	More socially accountable
Produced by academics or technicians	Produced by a wide set of actors

Table 2.1 summarizes the features of each mode of knowledge production. These authors' most important message is that the emerging Mode 2 is related to a whole new socio-economic and political context for knowledge production.

> The core of our thesis is that the parallel expansion in the number of potential knowledge producers on the *supply side* and the expansion of the requirement of specialist knowledge on the *demand side* are creating the conditions for the emergence of a new mode of knowledge production. (Gibbons et al. 1994: 13)

This market approach to the production of knowledge is certainly novel. The expansion of the supply of knowledge links to the emergence of many different knowledge-producer institutions beyond the traditional role of universities. Hence, this change in supply reflects the relative diminishing position of universities as knowledge-generators. By the same token, the expansion of the demand for knowledge is related to three factors. First, firms increasingly need technological and scientific knowledge in order to keep up their competitive position in the more and more internationalized markets. Secondly, there has been a new demand for knowledge from a set of diverse institutions, interest groups, and individuals who want to know more about particular (social and politically related) scientific matters. And thirdly, governments at all levels also have an increasing need for scientific knowledge in order to address and prevent social risks. These arguments have not gone uncontested. Pestre has, for example, criticized Gibbons et al., asserting that both modes of knowledge production have always co-existed in history (Pestre 1997). Nevertheless, most academics seem to assume that the dynamics towards Mode 2 are actually taking place, especially when related to the wider panorama of the knowledge-based economy. As mentioned in the first chapter of this book, the notion of a 'knowledge-based economy' asserts that the modern capitalist economy rests less on capital and labour and more on knowledge, which is already the key production factor (Druckner 1998). Institutional and evolutionary economists have supported the validity of the 'knowledge-based economy' with conflated lines of reasoning. The main point is that knowledge today has a qualitatively different and more central role in economic production than before. Indeed, the image of a knowledge-based economy has successfully permeated international, EU and national levels of policy-making (OECD 1996a, 2000), most recently placed at the forefront of EU political discourse in the EU Lisbon Summit, 2000. Despite the increased pressure for increasing rates of social return, RTD policies have regained most of their lost political shine. We will now examine the political and governing aspect of knowledge production.

Innovation Policy and the New Social Contract of Science

As examined in detail in the previous chapter, the production of scientific and technical knowledge is at the centre of science and technology policies' rationale. Is this still the case for innovation policy? Is the production of research and scientific knowledge still at the heart of innovation policies, or has it been displaced by new areas of public intervention? Answering these questions is not easy, mainly because there is a sort of irony in current arguments about innovation and knowledge. While innovation policy comes up with a new rationale for public involvement beyond the mere production of knowledge, the dominant understanding that we are living in a 'knowledge-based economy' reinforces the role of knowledge as a centrepiece of any strategy for socio-economic development. The irony is that knowledge is simultaneously portrayed as an 'insufficient' focal point and as a 'key element' of contemporary economy. How has this been translated into a single and coherent policy rationale? What have been the battles about 'basic science' and RTD within the new innovation policy paradigm?

The notion that the 1990s brought about a 'new social contract for science' has been gaining ground among scholars, particularly among sociologists. This idea underlines the changing expectations from funding authorities as to what contribution science should make in relation to some socially/politically defined issues. The recognition that massive public investment in new forms of knowledge was not producing the expected results in terms of the competitive position of the economy, and that the public involvement in this area had to diminish along the liberal–conservative governments' overall budgetary retrenchments, put significant strain on RTD allocations in most industrialized countries. The 'value for money' approach, which started in the UK in the 1980s and extended later to the continent, has entailed a new political culture demanding clearer and more accountable results than before from research that is publicly funded. This change of mind has been particularly notorious for 'basic science', and perhaps less for 'applied' research (Martin and Salter 1996; Salter and Martin 2001). What makes this trend confusing is the fact that the new social contract of science has coincided with the advent of the 'innovation policy rationale' and with the knowledge-based economy.

It is not reasonable to expect that all European or industrialized countries have followed simultaneous and identical patterns of change in this matter (Biegelbauer and Borrás 2003). There are two significant reasons for that. First, because there are large differences in terms of the historical and institutional set-up of RTD policies and research systems in general and, secondly, because the 'new social contract' is surely different within each national context. There are as many different types of RTD policies and institutional set-ups for research as there are countries. Diversity is historically contingent. Traditional instruments for the production of scientific and technological knowledge include the establishment of knowledge production centres (like public research centres, laboratories and universities/technical schools), the direct support of knowledge production (directly financing scientific research projects through funding agencies/programmes and/or procurement contracts), or the establishment of 'bridging institutions' between public–private producer–users of knowledge. Each system of innovation shows unique features in producing knowledge, with more or less public–private components, intra-organizational connectedness, or autonomy-politically harnessed scientific activities. This is what has been defined as a 'national research system'. However, there is contradictory evidence as to what characterizes these dynamics in collective terms. Thus some authors show that there are signs of diverging trends among European research systems (Amable et al. 1997; Freeman 1997), whereas others indicate that despite diversity there are some identifiable converging trends (Rip and Meulen 1997; Solingen 1993; Biegelbauer and Borrás 2003).

This chapter deals with the EU level of policy action. The rapid transfer of powers and resources from member states to the EU on RTD matters that has taken place since the mid-1980s means that the EU has developed its own mode of public action based on three pillars, namely, the JRC, the framework programme and lately the 'European Research Area' (ERA). Each of those denotes different historical rationales of RTD policy action, but above all they foreshadow the political compromises on the division of tasks between member states and this supra-national level on knowledge production. Hence, from the policy perspective we can ask how this is currently organized. Can we identify, like Margaret Sharp, elements of a federal-like research structure (Sharp 1997), or is the division of tasks less clear-cut as the EU only fills some gaps in national knowledge-production deficits? The Europeanization of research production brings about another principal question. How far is this form of knowledge production underpinning the convergence of member state research systems? The growing cross-national nature of research endeavours within EU borders is generating meeting points for diverse national research-organizational cultures. From this point of view, we should not underestimate the ability of EU RTD policy to trigger some changes in research organization, not least because of the use of cross-national benchmarking exercises. The next section deals with this.

EUROPEANIZING (FEDERALIZING?) RESEARCH AND KNOWLEDGE PRODUCTION

There has always been an inherent tension in the Europeanization of RTD matters. The costs and benefits of joining forces in the production of collective scientific/technical knowledge depend to a large extent on the expectations and views of the different national industrial-scientific elites. After all, RTD is not a regulatory area where collective action is easily justifiable in terms of the single market project. This is a distributive policy where economic resources are allocated on the basis of pre-established political priorities, and hence is subject to potential high national sensitivities. Yet, the picture emerging from today's EU RTD policy involvement is a multi-level structure. What has been the logic underpinning this far-fetched supra-national involvement?

Jean Monnet's dream of a European Technological Community was partly fulfilled with the creation of Euratom and the Joint Research Centre in the 1950s (Sharp 1989). Much has happened since then. After some uncertain decades, the EU's involvement in research and technological development gained a firm foothold in the mid-1980s, with the launch of the framework programmes. Today, RTD constitutes the third largest recipient of EU budget financial allocations in what seems to be a rather uncontested policy domain of EU involvement. It is not the purpose here to provide a detailed account of the history of the EU RTD policy for which better studies are already available (Sharp 1991; Guzzetti 1995). Instead, the coming sections provide a succinct picture of the course of events, showing that the rapid Europeanization of this area has to be understood in terms of the power of ideas and proactive role of the Commission. The section closes with some considerations about the multi-level nature of research and the production of knowledge in the EU.

The First Steps and the Competitiveness Issue

In the aftermath of the Second World War, science had not only lost its innocence,[1] it also had become a central concern of state politics. Science was a highly sensitive matter in military and security terms, as the opening of the atomic age took place on the eve of the Cold War. Moreover, science was also a sensitive matter in industrial and economic terms. The prospects for post-war economic recovery were mainly based on new forms of industrial organization, energy sources and technological development. It is hardly surprising then that science had a relatively prominent role in Europe's reconstruction, both at national and at EC/Euratom level.

Despite the differences in how each country did (re)construct its research system, most European states shared a preoccupation with their own technological capabilities, especially in relation to three questions; namely, the USA's and USSR's emerging technological hegemony, the 'brain-drain' of European scientists during and after the war, and the lack of appropriate laboratory and experimental facilities/equipment. This triple concern spearheaded the initial European collaborative efforts, which were concentrated on nuclear energy research under the Euratom (one of the three European Communities). Hence, at the onset, the EC involvement in knowledge production was limited to nuclear energy, and was organized in a single instrument: the Joint Research Centre. However, this limited functional approach did not prevent political turmoil in relation to the increasing national sensitivities in the 1960s in nuclear and industrial affairs (Dumolin 1997). As a result, the JRC reached a deadlock in its development, which was only partly resolved by the launch of the Joint European Torus (JET) in 1979 – a large programme concerning fusion, a potential alternative energy source (Peterson 1992). The JRC of the 1960s and 1970s was above all a good illustration of how science policy was devised at that time, assuming a smooth transition from scientific research to industrial development, concentrated in few scientific-technical areas, and involving large public installations (big science).

Understandably, the member states did not grant the European Community additional significant competencies in the field of science and research during the 1960s and 1970s. At that time, their efforts were devoted to consolidating national research capabilities, and international collaboration was undertaken on other than an EC basis. However, the oil crises of the 1970s were to become a watershed for national-only policy endeavours. The drastic fall of growth levels, the severe reduction of industrial production ratios and the rise in unemployment, showed that the crisis was not a transient phenomenon, but the start of a deep industrial readjustment with long-lasting effects on industrial organization. To improve the rapid loss of competitive position of their industries, most European governments launched large national RTD schemes supporting 'strategic' industrial sectors. This has been termed the 'national champions strategy' of the 1970s and early 1980s (Sandholtz 1992; Lawton 1997). In times of uncertainty, technology was the flagship of governmental action against economic deterioration, and the emphasis was no longer on scientific matters as such, but on their potential economic and industrial application.

Incipient voices supported the idea of EC involvement in the technology area (Layton 1969; Moonman 1969; Pavitt and Patel 1971). However, political events evolved piecemeal, as it took more than a decade for the opinion of national governments to tilt in favour of direct EC action.[2] Several authors have stressed the pivotal role of the European Commission in this regard, mostly by aligning large firms' interests in persuading national governments (Mytelka and Delapierre 1987; Peterson 1991; Grande and Peschke 1999) and the resulting 'technology corporatism' (Parker 2000; Nollert 2000). This 'purposeful opportunism' of the Commission (Cram 1997) was successfully combined with the lessons that national governments had learnt in early experiments of European collaboration in the nuclear, space and aviation sectors. The lessons were, namely, the need for institutional flexibility, for industry's involvement and for a focused functional scientific-technical approach (Peterson and Sharp 1998).

It is important to note, though, that whereas the dire straits generated by the oil crises, the support shown from large firms, the lessons learnt from the past, and the active role of the Commission were important factors triggering member states' acceptance of the EC's involvement, all of them took place within a given cognitive background. This background can be defined by two prominent ideas, namely, the existence of a pressing 'European technology gap' (lately to become the 'European paradox') demanding the EC's collective action; and a policy rationale focusing on the technological and industrial effects of research.

The 'European technology gap' is the political cornerstone of the EU's involvement in RTD. No wonder then that the Commission has overused it as a mantra justifying the need for European concerted action. The 'European technology gap' includes two intertwined arguments. The first says that 'one of the major weaknesses (of the EU) lies in its inferiority in terms of transforming the results of technological research and skills into innovations and competitive advantages' (Commission 1994). The second points to the fact that overall EU15 expenditure on RTD as percentage of aggregated GDP (2 per cent in 1993) has continuously been inferior to that of its major world competitors, the US (2.7 per cent) and Japan (2.8 per cent), during the same year (Commission, 1994).

The arguments put forward in the 'European paradox' have been partly contested. Despite the fact that a recent study of the ICT sector confirmed the gap in this specific industrial area (Tijssen and van Wijk 1999), some authors have made critical remarks about the political use of this notion. As Pavitt has argued, in the 1970s 'many of these concerns were misplaced, since sales, productivity and R&D expenditures in European (and Japanese) firms were all growing faster at the time than in the US firms' (Pavitt 1998: 560). Nevertheless, this trend towards convergence changed significantly in 1989, when the aggregated share of European R&D expenditure and patenting decreased in relative terms from the US. It was first in the 1990s that Europe truly had a 'gap' to fill in. Furthermore, this author states that intra-EU differences in RTD performance and expenditure are so great that the aggregated vision provided by the 'European paradox' invariably has an element of political distortion.

Irrespective of the appropriateness or otherwise of the 'European paradox', the EC's involvement in research and technology matters in the mid-1980s expressed a change of mind: the understanding that public action could no longer focus on the generation of generic scientific knowledge, but had also to support its transition to industrial applications (the technology policy approach); that supra-national action in this area complemented national efforts; and that involvement should be focused on 'strategic industries', in areas like information and communication technologies, new materials, or biotechnology, as key sources for competitiveness, job-creation and growth. The European politics of high-tech had changed substantially: Europeanizing the problem of competitiveness meant Europeanizing knowledge production and technological development too.

The Framework Programme: A Criss-cross of Compromises

The result of all this was the creation of the framework programme for RTD in the mid-1980s. Since then, this programme has grown exponentially, in terms of both economic allocations and political expectations. As for the first, Table 2.2 does not require further explanation, just that this represents around 4 per cent of the EU's own annual budget. As for the second, the next section on results and returns elaborates on the difficulties of matching political expectations and reality.

Notwithstanding this spectacular increase, the EU's allocation of funds is just a meagre sum when seen against the overall governmental expenditure by member states: the FP accounts for approximately 5.5 per cent of national RTD expenditure of the 15 member states taken together. This puts in bold

Table 2.2   Allocation in million euros to the different framework programmes, at given prices

	FP 1 1984–87	FP 2 1987-91	FP 3 1990-94	FP 4 1994-98	FP 5 1998-2002	FP 6 2002-06
EU allocation	3.750	5.396	6.600	13.100*	14.960	17.500**

Notes:
* In 1995 an addendum of 115 million ecus was approved after the membership of Austria, Finland and Sweden, which is not included in this amount.
** Amount for the framework programme and Euratom treaty, as accepted by the Council in its Common Position with the European Parliament, 30 January 2002.

Source: Various EU documents.

relief one of the principles on which EU RTD involvement has been politically articulated: complementarity. EU funds should not substitute those public funds that were to be allocated at national level on the basis of national political preferences, nor those private funds that were to be allocated by industry anyway. Hence, the division of tasks between the EU and its member states has been based on non-substitution and additionality.

A second important principle guiding the EU's involvement is that the FP only supports research that is pre-competitive in nature. This principle was the political compromise between those advocating an industrialist-interventionist approach to EU RTD policy in order to respond effectively to the loss of competitiveness; and those advocating a liberal–market approach so that the EU's involvement should be confined to the single market regulatory framework (Sharp 1991). The pre-competitive solution sought to satisfy, in part, both ideological positions, but even if it seems the logical and balanced solution, it has turned out to be difficult to manage. Moreover, this principle has been constantly challenged in political terms, as it is difficult to link with the objectives of enhancing European competitiveness.[3]

The criticism of managerial rigidities and lack of overall strategy of EU-funded research projects expressed in the highly influential Davignon report (Commission 1997a) was the triggering factor for a two-step reorganization of the FP in the late 1990s. The first, piecemeal, reforms came with the Fifth Framework Programme (5FP; 1998–2002) (Küppers et al. 2001). This was carried out essentially by selecting a series of 'key actions' and priorities (Cannell 1998; Caracostas and Muldur 1998). Some authors have expressed doubts about how far the 5FP represented a real breakthrough from previous practices (Sanz and Borrás 2000). In any case, truly far-reaching changes have arrived with the recent Sixth Framework Programme (6FP; 2002–06),[4] where novelties are abundant and ambitions high. This programme notably increases the managerial flexibility and autonomy of research activities, and concentrates research efforts into larger networks and projects. New instruments have been put forward, namely, 'integrated projects', 'networks of excellence' and the 'article 169 instrument'. The two first envisage larger groups of researchers, larger EU resources concentrated in fewer projects/ networks, considerable managerial autonomy and longer duration of activities with expected long-term perspectives (Commission 2002). Article 169, in contrast, is ambitious in a different manner. This article states the possibility of Community participation in research projects undertaken jointly by EU member states. Small pilot projects are to be launched in 2002, scouting the potential that this article actually offers. All in all, the new instruments of the 6FP have to be understood in relation to the 'European Research Area', an initiative launched in 2000 by the Commission, with potential federalizing effects, as we will see.

Results and Returns

The results and returns that the FPs have produced have always been a highly political issue. This is partly related to the politics of national 'fair return' (member states controlling how many funds their researchers are able to raise from the EU), and partly related to the mood for greater accountability of publicly funded research. In both cases, the FP has always been under strain to demonstrate its validity and usefulness. These tensions are an illustrative example of Kuhlmann's argument that: 'In innovation policy, the governance system has to deal with two types of distributive conflicts reflecting two different divisions. The first one relates to conflicts among important actors within the system (i.e. scientific or academic versus industrial interests), whereas the second refers to potential conflicts between national states as players in distributive and re-distributive games' (Kuhlmann 2001: 957).

Although the politics of 'fair return' had its peak in the mid-1980s with Margaret Thatcher's renegotiation of the UK's contribution to the overall EU budget, member states have always looked closely at the input–output tables. All national representatives in the field of RTD have a rough idea of how much their research system receives from Brussels, compared with the overall percentage of their budgetary contribution. This has been used in several contexts, not least for electoral purposes. For example, the Danish government has repeatedly stressed that the FP is 'good business' for Danish science, in an attempt to give a positive image of the EU amid an overly Euro-sceptic research community. However, not all is internal politics, the 'fair return' sheet balance has also served for negotiating strategies at EU level. For example, in the early 1990s, Spanish authorities expressed their dissatisfaction with the fact that Spain only received 5 per cent of the FP, given its contribution of 8 per cent to the overall budget of the EU. This opened up a discussion about the research fields that the FP was sponsoring, and how far the 'cohesion' aspect should be taken into account when distributing funds. We will examine the matter of cohesion later. Suffice to say here that the politics of 'fair return' have always underlain the distribution of EU RTD funds.

Apart from national scrutiny, there is also the question of the overall results and benefits. Several authors have pointed out that despite the massive number of evaluations and studies, it is still rather difficult to assess precisely how far the FP has contributed to improving European competitiveness. First, there is the question of the ambiguity between the overall objective of improving competitiveness while funds go only to pre-competitive research funding (Larédo 1997). Secondly, most evaluations have been carried out at micro-level, analysing research networks and firms, with subsequent aggregative difficulties when assessing improvements in competitiveness (Luukkonen 1998). Thirdly, another problem is how to assign specific value to the 'additional' contribution that EU funds have made to the research project. Luukkonen has found that additionality has not always been fully achieved (Luukkonen 2000). Despite all this, several authors have stressed that the EU programmes seem to have affected positively a whole set of other important issues, like the creation and negotiation of standards, sharing risks and costs of uncertainty related to innovative activities, fostering long-term rather than short-term strategies in firms' research, enhancing the acquisition of new skills and knowledge, and helping to create a cross-border community of professionals and research networks (Metcalf et al. 1991; Commission 1997b; Larédo 1998; Peterson and Sharp 1998). That is, a host of indirect results and benefits. This led Luukkonen to conclude that:

> 'The observation that the impact of EU research programmes is on the promotion of infrastructural matters rather than on the promotion of competitiveness leads us to question whether expectations as to the role of the programmes as a promoter of competitiveness in European industries are not misplaced. (Luukkonen 1998: 609).

With this remark we can now see that the rising expectations about FP results, the politics of fair return, and the difficult balancing act of implementing the 'additionality' and 'pre-competitive' principles, have all contributed to make the FP a complex EU policy instrument, moved by the heavy mechanisms of inter-state politics.

New Trends, New Times for EU Involvement

Two interesting novelties in EU RTD policy, namely, the 'European Research

Area' (ERA) and the 'innovation 2000 initiative' (i2i), are opening up a third generation of EU policy involvement. Launched in 2000, in conjunction with the Lisbon Summit, both are in a way bringing new winds of political change towards knowledge production at EU level.

Starting with the first, the European Research Area initiative (Commission 2000b) is rather large-scale as regards the topics and the means it envisages (see Figure 2.1).

---

1. Material resources and facilities for research
    a. Networking centres of excellence
    b. Access to research facilities
    c. Electronic networks
2. Public instruments
    a. Coordinating EU and national research programmes
    b. Coordinating pan-European cooperation
3. Private investment
    a. Improving indirect aid to research
    b. Protecting intellectual property rights
    c. Fostering risk capital investment
4. RTD for policy-making
    a. Research for political decision
    b. Common system of scientific reference
5. Human resources
    a. Greater mobility across the EU
    b. More female researchers
    c. Young researchers
6. Other
    a. Research in regions
    b. Integrating Eastern and Western researchers
7. Values and ethics
    a. Science and society
    b. Ethics

Source: Own elaboration from Commission (2000b).

Figure 2.1   Topics covered by the ERA initiative, 2000

As Figure 2.1 shows, the range of topics is rather impressive. It denotes that the Commission has wholeheartedly embraced the 'systemic approach', making the production and dissemination of knowledge the cornerstone of a truly EU 'research system', well beyond the delimited framework programme.

In the document, the Commission criticizes the 'compartmentalization of public research systems [in Europe] and the lack of coordination in the manner in which national and European research policies are implemented' (p. 9), all this resulting in 15+1 RTD policies. The ERA initiative decidedly strikes a note in the EU's willingness to build up a single trans-national research system, establishing a wide array of formal institutions that allow knowledge production to be generated more freely within EU borders. Given such a level of ambition, it is not adventurous to affirm that the ERA initiative represents to knowledge production in the EU what the 'Delors plan' represented for the accomplishment of a single currency in the late 1990s.

Nevertheless, ambitions have to face the reality of implementation. Here ERA might encounter some hurdles. First, the Commission does not hide its intention to maximize the potential offered by the Treaty in terms of conventional policy instruments such as regulations, exchange of information (working groups, task forces) or financial resources. This idea of 'stretching' existing tools invariably means a reinterpretation of the subsidiarity principle, which is, as we know from the experience of the framework programme and the EU regulation of intellectual property rights, not an easy task. Secondly, the new and promising 'open method of coordination' might not be as smooth as expected (Borrás and Jacobsson 2004). This new policy instrument uses 'benchmarking' and 'mainstreaming' of national policy actions/cases in the undisguised expectation that member states will learn from each other when confronted with 'best practices' (Eberlein and Kurwer 2002).[5] This is certainly something new in EU policy-making. The political course is in principle steered by national governments on an open and voluntary basis, setting some common goals. In spite of this, we should not underestimate the potential of 'best practices' and 'mainstreaming' to generate political tensions. The eagerness and diversity of institutional traditions in the 15 (soon 25) national research contexts does not render this an easy task from a top-down perspective. Moreover, some signs of scepticism have been already expressed (Cordis 2000). After all, learning is not an automatic process, it depends entirely on the willingness of national politico-administrative and scientific elites to ponder and make use of the suggestions. This is not to undermine the value that the 'open method of coordination' has in political terms, and in terms of being an intelligent tool of public administration. It is just to underline that its success is far from secure.

The second interesting novelty in EU RTD policy is the innovation 2000 initiative (i2i). With a financial endowment as large as the FP (12–15 b€ 2000–03), i2i is managed by the European Investment Bank. The Lisbon Summit endorsed this initiative, which is in many ways a new approach towards the EU role on knowledge production. One important element is the financing form: long-term loans; a second is its high operational flexibility;

and a third is its emphasis on venture capital funds. The initiative's areas of action are education/human capital, research and development, SMEs and venture capital, ICTs, and diffusion of innovation. Most interesting is venture capital. Is the EIB/EIF initiative the policy instrument of the future? In many respects, the answer is positive. Lending is certainly a flexible and low-cost mechanism of public action in a context where conventional public subsidies are becoming contested in several ways including, among others, the new social contract of science, public expenditure retrenchments, and the limits of subsidiarity–complementarity principles of the EU RTD programmes. Lending is perfect for projects which have a direct, short-term investment return, and for which other sources of capital are difficult. However, it is not so appropriate for those without such features, namely more 'basic' 'pre-competitive' projects where pay-offs are not so short-term. Parallel to this is the question of venture capital. The EIF lends money to venture capital funds, and by this encourages the emergence of a high-risk capital market in the EU. Hence, it is not unreasonable to expect that in due time the EIB lending function will be slowly taken over by a dynamic pan-European financial market. These two arguments support the idea that the FP and the EIB might complement each other.

Towards a Multi-level System of Knowledge Production

The rich history of EU RTD policy can be categorized into three generations of policy rationales and instruments; namely, the period of Euratom and nuclear energy research in the JRC, the FP and the concerns about European competitiveness, and finally, the ERA time with its 'grand' view and flexible policy tools. In all these stages of EU involvement, the collective production of knowledge at a supra-national level has been the driving force, far beyond the mere 'exchange' of knowledge. Yet, as the EU has become more integrated through time this involvement has assumed different forms. The far-reaching political ambitions of ERA deserve especial attention here, as they *might perhaps* represent a qualitative difference in the historical division of tasks between the EU and its member states. The political agenda envisaged in the European Research Area expands notably the role of the EU in the collective production of knowledge. With initiatives like European centres of excellence, open access to national research facilities or a common system of scientific reference, EU involvement moves far beyond the previous limits of the FP. This implies that the collective production of knowledge is no longer activated through EU funding of specific projects, but essentially as a cross-border endeavour that entails pooling national resources and the creation of new collective nodal points with strong inter-organizational effect (industry and universities). This invariably has structural effects on the way in which national and EU tasks are divided. How can we characterize this political structure?

This question, once posed by Margaret Sharp about the framework programme, seems particularly relevant today (Sharp 1997). This author compares the division of tasks between the EU and its members in the 1990s with those existing in the US and Germany. In a nutshell, these two federal countries divide their tasks as follows. In the US the federal government supports basic science while the states, more concerned with industrial development, support more application-oriented RTD. In Germany the division of tasks is more complex, as the Länder have extended competences and co-finance some scientific endeavours with the Federal level, in a model where both levels are deeply interrelated and the Länder finance approximately two-thirds of the total costs. The EU FP, concludes Sharp, evolved piecemeal on a rather ad hoc basis without any neat ex ante design of task division, other than the member states' willingness to avoid too much power transfer to Brussels. Nonetheless, the federal nature of the EU FP, continues this author, is undeniable, and it is a system closer to the German model than to the US model. However, in my opinion, it is precisely this piecemeal development in the absence of clear *ex-ante* political design combined with the meagre EU budgetary allocations (as compared to national RTD efforts), which indicate that the EU is not a federal structure. Admittedly, the political systems of knowledge production in the EU show elements of lowering previous national boundaries, becoming gradually interconnected and interdependent in the collective production of knowledge. On this basis, it is more appropriate to talk about the emerging trends towards a multi-level knowledge production system in Europe, where the supra-national, national, regional and local levels have become gradually more interrelated. However, this is a trend that has not been fully developed, since, as Kuhlman indicates: 'A "governance gap" emerges here: the presently applied "division of work" in innovation policy between regional, national and EU political levels and institutions is not yet systematically structured and determined. The subsidarity principle has been working only as quite an abstract rule for practical policy decisions and their implementation yet' (Kuhlmann 2001: 965).

After the advent of the ERA initiative, the question about what type of system of knowledge production is emerging in the EU seems even more pertinent. The expansion of EU involvement does not affect the previous arrangements, since the FP continues to follow the principle of complementing national RTD endeavours. However, if successfully implemented, the ERA might affect the role of the EU in a subtler manner, namely enhancing its role as soft coordinator with the objective of articulating the national research systems. As Cannell has put it: 'ERA presents the major challenge of

European Union research policy, not as the implementation of research action on the Community's behalf, but as *the development of greater coherence between national frameworks for action*' (Cannell 2001: 210).[6] As we examined earlier, this will not be achieved by further funding involvement of the EU, but rather through new instruments, particularly the benchmarking and open method of coordination. This is obviously intrinsically an inter-governmental instrument, however it is capable of having significant integration effects in terms of a long-term and much wider rapprochement of national organizational and policy structures.

So far, this is the formal perspective on the organization of RTD policies in the EU. Another important matter is its own dynamics of research, which has a much more bottom-up and informal form. The question at stake is whether the significant number of cross-border, cross-institution and cross-disciplinary research projects in Europe are fostering new styles and new forms of knowledge production. Several authors have pointed out that by supporting this type of scientific endeavour the EU enhances the 'Mode 2' of knowledge production (Solingen 1993; Sharp 1997). In this sense, the EU awards European researchers an advanced mechanism to keep ahead in the flexible patterns of knowledge production. Hence, we might well be experiencing the gradual emergence of a 'new generation of European researchers' operating on this basis. Not that heterogeneity and diversity in the 'modes of doing science' will be homogenized in the EU, but they represent new mutual sources of institutional and scientific learning, especially for the less developed countries (Pereira 2001). All this indicates that the micro-level implications that the increased cross-European mobility and collective production of knowledge, that ERA wants to strengthen, should not be underestimated in the bottom-up construction of a decentralized and increasingly interdependent system of knowledge production in the EU.

THE INTERNATIONALIZATION OF RESEARCH AND TECHNOLOGY

The evolution of EU RTD policy can hardly be accurately understood without looking at the general trends of international cooperation in knowledge production, both in Europe at large and in global terms. This is important for two reasons. First, to understand how much the history of EU RTD policy links with the evolving patterns of international cooperation. Secondly, to see that since the 1990s a much faster process of internationalization has been taking place. After briefly looking at the position of the FP within the other pan-European collaborative schemes, this section will devote special attention to the new trends of European and global scientific cooperation. The rapid internationalization trends, both from the public and private sectors, are partly redefining the conventional boundaries of national and regional knowledge production. This poses several interesting questions. One of them being what role the EU has to assume in the heavily internationalized scenario of the coming decades.

The Scientific and Technological Architecture of Europe

EU involvement in RTD matters has run parallel to a series of other pan-European collaborative schemes of inter-governmental nature. This is what we will term here 'the scientific and technological architecture of Europe', whose patterns have evolved along the changing macro-political and economic trends in the Old Continent, and the cognitive parameters associated with science and technology policies. The first of these collaborative schemes is CERN. Founded in 1954 and dedicated to basic nuclear research, CERN is the twin brother of the JRC. The European Laboratory for Particle Physics has today a world-class system of particle accelerators (an impressive and costly installation near Geneva) and has been awarded several Nobel prizes. CERN's success story contrasts sharply with the political turmoil that the JRC suffered in the 1960s–70s, and it is partly the reason why CERN had a tremendous influence in European collaborative schemes to be developed in the decades after.

The real thrust of pan-European cooperation came though in the 1970s, with agreements in a panoply of different scientific fields, like molecular biology, space research and aviation. Based mostly on 'big science' and large investments, these initiatives were the first building blocks of the current European scientific and technological architecture. The collaborative patterns at that time were characterized by four features: (1) their scientifically oriented nature (rather than technological development nature); (2) the direct involvement of public financing (rather than private financing); (3) their non-military nature; and (4) the creation of large installations and laboratories. In other words, European cooperation arrangements were based on big science, and in inter- rather than supra-national political structures. Obviously, there are some exceptions. Of the eight organizations in place by the mid-1970s, CERN,[7] EMBO[8] and ESO[9] strictly followed these parameters in the areas of nuclear research, molecular biology and astronomy, respectively. ESA[10] and Airbus[11] have a more technological and industrial orientation, whereas the ESF[12] and COST[13] have a more multi-disciplinary approach. Last, the Joint Research Centre has a supra-national rather than inter-national structure, following the Community method of the EU Treaty.

Whereas the first building blocks of the European scientific architecture were well established by the end of the 1970s, the next decade experienced a significant expansion and widening of European collaboration in these matters. Eureka and the framework programme were a new generation of European collaboration schemes, both marking the 1980s. Their multi-sectoral, multi-annual, and their well-endowed economic resources placed them at the core of the current European architecture.

Figure 2.2 represents the European scientific architecture in 2001, showing the year of establishment and the number of member states that currently take part. Since the early 1990s, this European scientific architecture has been experiencing a significant geographical expansion. There are two reasons for this. One is that the end of the Cold War has opened up these collaborative schemes to the Eastern European countries. Some organizations have accepted new members, while others have signed bilateral cooperation agreements with them. Another reason is that other Western European countries have shown an interest in these organizations, in the face of increased market competition and their willingness to generate collectively scientific knowledge.

Quite naturally, this spur to intra-European scientific collaboration has again turned the eyes of policy-makers towards how to ensure better coordination at European level. 'Again' because coordination has been a sort of mantra since the inception of the framework programme. History has shown how difficult it has turned out to be, especially in the case of Eureka (Georghiou 2001). The recent 'European Research Area' initiative strikes a

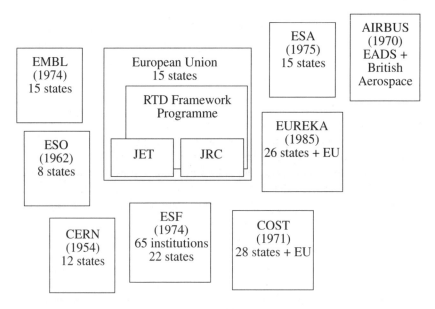

Figure 2.2   The scientific and technological architecture of Europe, 2001

note in this direction, renewing this old political goal (Commission 2001a). Nevertheless, and independently of ERA's future accomplishments, the emerging pattern of European scientific architecture in the early 2000s is a highly integrated pan-European cooperation, where previous East–West and EU–non EU borders are becoming increasingly blurred. This is the expression of increased political and managerial flexibility, and the fact that security concerns no longer dominate the agenda of international scientific cooperation in Europe the way they did during the Cold War.

Global Science in the 2000s?

At the same time as these transformations are taking place in the European scenario, a whole new wave of knowledge production at international level is currently starting. As such, international collaboration in RTD matters has long existed since the post-Second World War period (Ancarani 1995). What we are witnessing now is that the number of public and private cooperation schemes and the trans-national generation of knowledge has grown significantly since the 1990s.

Referring to international and global RTD knowledge generation, Georghiou has developed a triple typology of informal, formal and big science cooperation (Georghiou 1998).[14] The first, informal international RTD, refers to the host of technological alliances between private firms across national borders, the amount of private RTD that firms conduct abroad, and scientists' cooperation more broadly. Most recent studies coincide in pointing out that informal internationalization thrived in the 1990s, especially for large firms. It was not just that the number of alliances increased rapidly, but the difference from the 1980s is that in the 1990s firms had more focused and strategic emphasis than before (Meyer-Kramher and Reger 1999: 763). Another important trend identified in these studies is that alliances and foreign RTD are carried out overwhelmingly within the 'triad' of US–Japan–EU. 'Less than 1 per cent of these firms' foreign innovative activities are located outside the "triad" countries, showing that the process of internationalization of technological activities can at best be described as "triadization" rather than "globalization"' (Patel and Pavitt 1999: 221). Similarly, there is strong evidence that European large firms are more international in their scope than their Japanese and American competitors (Patel and Vega 1999). With regard to the scientific community, the growing internationalization can be detected by bibliometric analysis of co-authored publications. Here too, the growth among industrialized countries has been explosive, probably due to the massive use of ICTs in this community (Georghiou 1998: 614). The policy advice coming from all these economic studies is that 'it is much more important for a country to become a junction of exchange of knowledge and technical expertise than to secure returns from each exchange' (Archibugi 2000: 13).

The category of 'formal public international cooperation' corresponds to the myriad of bilateral RTD agreements between countries. Few studies have been conducted about this matter, but the limited data available tend to indicate a certain decrease, at least in European and North American countries (Georghiou 1998: 615–17). This needs further empirical analysis. Bilateral agreements are inclined to support small research activities, most typically exchange of students and scientists. Therefore, if this decreasing tendency is confirmed it might have two consequences: one would be that public efforts at internationalizing RTD are increasingly focused on big science and large projects; another might be that the putative thrust of international mobility of researchers is mainly related to these large public facilities or to firms' internationalized RTD activities, or that it has simply been exaggerated.

Also, international cooperation in big science grew significantly in the 1990s. Table 2.3 (pages 50–51) gives an account of a succession of large-scale cooperation agreements, but it is not an exhaustive listing. From what we can see, most of these were launched in the 1990s, and some in the late 1980s. The topics vary greatly, as do the numbers of countries involved. Yet, common to them all is the fact that, as we saw earlier, the countries involved belong to the industrialized world, with a core of triad countries. The growth of big science underlines two phenomena. One is that it has followed the globalization and internationalization trends of contemporary politics and economy since the end of the Cold War. The other is that the accretion of big science cooperation is the result of a substantial learning process as to how to set up and manage such large-scale projects. The OECD has had a prominent role in this respect, providing useful insights from different big science cases. Its objective in the 'megascience forum' has precisely been to extract the lessons and foster the learning process among national representatives (OECD 1995). Five points for success in these large-scale scientific endeavours have been put forward:

> 1) the need for a foresight process, 2) the need for a forum outside government to carry out foresight and to advance projects, 3) the need for the support of national governments, 4) the significant role of champions, 5) the need for forward planning. (Tegart 1995: 39)

What International Role and What Boundaries for the EU?

There is an apparent contradiction in the EU's relation to RTD. On the one hand, the EU has been gaining relevance since the 1990s as an international partner in RTD matters. This relates to the bilateral and multi-lateral agreements at international level where the EU is directly represented, occasionally being a nodal point, as in the case of pan-European agreements.

On the other hand, the boundaries of what is and is not EU RTD are becoming increasingly blurred. The increasing openness of the FPs and the growing internationalization/triadization/globalization of knowledge production, we have just examined, contribute to these unclear borders.

There is little doubt that the EU has lately acquired an autonomous political profile in international RTD matters. This is related to four events unfolding through the 1990s and early 2000s. First, the EU has gradually become a centrepiece within the European scientific architecture. This has to do with the opening up of the FP to other European countries, almost all of them now 'association countries' participating on the same basis as EU partners. Similarly, the ERA initiative is an attempt to link, more effectively, all the European research organizations in a single forum, envisaging tighter cooperation at European level. Secondly, the EU has conducted a series of bilateral and multi-lateral agreements on RTD since the early and mid-1990s. Hence, the openness of the framework programme 5 was organized as shown in Table 2.4. Thirdly, with regard to the Triad (EU–USA–Japan), the US–EU RTD agreement in force since 1998 has given political positioning to the EU, while responding to the political pressures to open further the FP to US firms. Several studies have pointed out that European firms prefer cooperation with US partners rather than with Japanese partners (Meyer-Kramher and Reger 1999: 755; Caracostas and Muldur 1998). This means that in the Triad, the link between the EU and Japan is relatively weaker than the US–EU and US–Japan. Finally, since the FP4 the EU has devoted a special budgetary line to international cooperation for less developed countries. The successive INCO programmes, INCO1 (575 m€) and INCO2 (475 m€), have been specifically designed with this purpose.

On the basis of these four events, the accusations of a 'fortress Europe' in the RTD realm (Väyrynen 1998) seem at best poorly founded, particularly since the mid-1990s, when the EU opened up the FP to foreign participants in a rather flexible way. Yet, this has gone hand in hand with the fact that the external boundaries of EU knowledge production are becoming more difficult to identify than before. With the increasing internationalization in public and private agreements, previous borders of knowledge production (and its appropriation) are rapidly becoming blurred.

What international role for the EU RTD is most appropriate? The opening up and flexibility of the FP, and the efforts to build a network of cooperation with non-EU countries and organizations are positive trends that need to be reinforced in the future. Whereas the focus on the 'technology gap' put emphasis on competitive attitudes towards other international knowledge producers, this has been now complemented with a cooperative attitude that recognizes the increasing internationalization of knowledge production. This denotes an important change of mind of EU policy-makers: no longer looking

Table 2.3 Large-scale international cooperation in RTD, 2001

Name	Established	Countries involved	Contents
International Space Station (ISS)	Assembly began in 1998	United States, Russia, Canada, Japan, ESA[a]	Build, develop and operate a permanently orbiting space station for scientific research and exploration of space
Human Genome Project (HGP)	Formally begun 1990	At least 18 countries have HGP programes. Human Genome Organization helps coordinate the international effort by scientists	To map and determine the chemical sequence of the three billion nucleotide base pairs that comprise the human genome
International Thermonuclear Experimental Reactor (ITER)	1988: start phase 1992: engineering design activities (current phase)	Euratom, Japan, and the Russian Federation. Canada and Kasakhstan have joined through association with Euratom and Russia	Joint project by leading fusion energy programmes, to demonstrate the technological feasibility of fusion energy for peaceful purposes
Large Hadron Collider	1994: go-ahead agreement 2005: expected completion	CERN member states[b] Japan has made a contribution of 8.85 billion yen Agreement with India in 1996 Agreement with Canada in 1996 US agreement in 1997	Build an accelerator to collide protons and ions, thus creating immense amounts of energy, and allow the study of the structure of matter
Human Frontier Science Program (HFSP)	1989	Management Supporting Parties (MSP): Canada, France, Germany, Italy, Japan, Switzerland, UK, USA and the EU	Programme aimed at supporting international cooperation in neurosciences and molecular biology

Hubble Space Telescope	1981: Space Telescope Science Institute (STScI) built 1990: Hubble deployed	USA and ESA member states (HST is a cooperation between NASA and ESA. STScI operates HST)	The first step in establishing a permanent observational capability for astronomy in space
'Very Large Telescope' (VLT)	Go-ahead given by ESO council in Dec. 1987	ESO member states[c]	Astronomy project to provide for a ground-based, optical and infrared telescope, to be built at the facility of European Southern Observatory at Paranal observatory in Chile
Science and Technology Centre in Ukraine (STCU)	1993	Uzbekistan, Ukraine, Georgia, Sweden, Canada, United States, EU	Aims to support research and development activities for peaceful applications by Ukrainian, Georgian and Uzbekistani scientists and engineers, formerly involved with development of weapons of mass destruction, as part of the general process of conversion from a military to a civilian, market-oriented environment
International Science and Technology Centre (ISTC)	1992	European Union, Japan, Russian Federation and United States	Coordinates the efforts of numerous governments, international organizations, and private sector industries to provide weapons scientists from Commonwealth of of Independent States (CIS) countries with opportunities to redirect their talents to peaceful science

51

Notes:

[a] ESA member states: Austria, Belgium, Denmark, Finland, France, Germany, Ireland, Italy, The Netherlands, Norway, Spain, Sweden, Switzerland, United Kingdom, Canada (participating country)

[b] Austria, Belgium, Czech Rep., Denmark, Finland, France, Germany, Greece, Hungary, Italy, The Netherlands, Norway, Poland, Portugal, Slovakia, Spain, Sweden, Switzerland, UK, Israel, Russia, Turkey, Yugoslavia

[c] Belgium, Denmark, France, Germany, Italy, The Netherlands, Sweden and Switzerland. Portugal has signed an agreement about membership and will join shortly. UK has expressed interest to join.

Table 2.4   Participation of non-EU countries in FP5,[1] 30 October 2001

ASSOCIATED STATES may participate WITH COMMUNITY FUNDING	CANDIDATES FOR EU MEMBERSHIP	Bulgaria, Republic of Cyprus, Czech Republic, Estonia, Hungary, Latvia, Lithuania, Malta,[2] Poland, Romania, Slovakia, Slovenia: In force. For Turkey, please see footnote 3.
	EFTA-EEA	Iceland, Liechtenstein, Norway: In force.
	OTHERS	Israel: In force.
	OTHER EUROPEAN	Albania, Bosnia-Herzegovina, Croatia, Federal Republic of Yugoslavia, Former Yugoslav Republic of Macedonia, Switzerland[4] Turkey[3] is also shown under Mediterranean Partnership Microstates and Territories in Europe[5]
THIRD STATES[6] may participate WITHOUT COMMUNITY FUNDING (exceptionally with Community funding when duly justified as being essential	EUROPEAN NIS	Armenia, Azerbaijan, Belarus, Georgia, Moldova, Russia, Ukraine
	MEDITERRANEAN PARTNERSHIP	Algeria, Egypt, Jordan, Lebanon, Morocco, West Bank and Gaza Strip, Syria, Tunisia, Turkey[3] All above countries may participate project by project if in conformity with the interests of the Community and on a self financing basis.
	COUNTRIES WITH COOPERATION AGREEMENT	Argentina, Australia, Canada, China, Russia, South Africa, USA: In force. India: Agreement signed. Brazil, Chile: Negotiations under way. Ukraine: Negotiation mandate given by the Council. The above countries may participate in the fields covered by the Co-operation Agreement, once in force, and on a self financing basis.

for achieving the
objectives of the
project)

| ANY OTHER COUNTRY | May participate project by project if in conformity with the interests of the Community and on a self financing basis, only if its participation is also of substantial added value for implementing all or part of the specific programmes in accordance with its objectives. |
| INTERNATIONAL ORGANIZATIONS[7] | May participate project by project if in conformity with the interests of the Community and on a self financing basis. |

Notes: Participation from third States and of International Organizations must take place together with the minimum number of legal entities from the Community and any Associated States.

1 Different rules apply for the specific programme 'Confirming the international role of Community research' (except for Associated States) and the EURATOM Framework Programme.

2 Association agreement with Malta entered provisionally into force on 1st March 2001. For latest information, please also consult http://europa.eu.int/comm/enlargement/pas/ocp/ocp_index.htm.

3 Turkish research entities participate to the activities of FP5 as 'other European' as well as candidate countries non associated in FP5. They are still also shown under Mediterranean Partnership. For latest news see also http://europa.eu.int/comm/enlargement/pas/ocp/ocp_index.htm.

4 This association agreement is expected to enter into force sometime in 2002. Once associated, that status shall take precedence over any other and Switzerland shall not be considered as an 'Other European' country anymore. For more information on Swiss participation, http://www.cordis.lu/inco2/src/p-swiss.htm.

5 Andorra, Monaco, San Marino, Vatican City State (Holy See), Faeroe Islands (DK), Channel Islands (GB), Isle of Man (GB), Svalbard and Jan Mayen Islands (NO).

6 In the case of a country becoming associated to FP5, that status takes precedence over any other.

7 Community funding may also be granted if it is foreseen to use the facilities of an international organization that is based in a third country, should this use be essential for achieving the objectives of the project.

Source: Cordis website – http://www.cordis.lu/fp5/src/3rdcountries.htm.

at the individual results from each single international arrangement/project, but seeking to become the natural 'point of reference' or 'conjecture' for certain types of knowledge production (Archibugi 2000). This new policy rationale recognizes that beyond immediate benefits, knowledge always has a degree of stickiness to the territory, which has a mid- to long-term perspective, and that EU partners can successfully learn a lot from non-EU partners. 'Open European programs have the potential to bring very important "soft" technology transfer and managerial learning to firms in this region' (Mowery 1998: 651). Nevertheless, there are still some areas that need further diplomatic effort, most notably Japan and other Asian countries, where few relatively formalized RTD agreements at EU level have been established so far.

PUBLIC AND PRIVATE DIMENSIONS

With these considerations we have arrived at another important issue, namely the changing relationship between the private and the public realms in the production of knowledge. This is becoming a central concern in the contemporary politics of science and technology, not least at EU level. As we saw earlier in this chapter, the advent of the knowledge-based economy has put forward a series of new challenges for governmental action that have triggered the re-conceptualization of RTD policies, widening their scope of action. However, this has not simply meant more government and less private action. Parallel to these new considerations about the role of science in society, the increased requests for greater accountability of governmental expenditure have resulted in a 'new social contract of science'. Paradoxically enough, though, experts point at the glowingly blurred boundaries between governments, firms and universities, in what seems an important reorganization of the domains of public and private action.

From the EU's point of view, two issues are worth discussing here. The first is the issue of what levels of public–private research financing are best for the EU. Secondly, considerations about how the public research centres should contribute to the innovative performance and knowledge creation. We start with the first.

Too Much Public, Too Little Private RTD in Europe?

It has become commonplace to assert that in Europe research activities are mainly financed publicly, and that the levels of private involvement are unsatisfactory. Yet, does this hold true when confronted with the available indicators? A rapid examination soon gives a nuanced picture, stressing large diversity from country to country. Examining in detail the aggregate data at national level as regard to how much the gross domestic expenditure on R&D is distributed along the public–private dimension, great differences emerge. One general conclusion is that for those countries where the overall expenditure is highest (notably Sweden, Finland and Germany) the largest proportion of research by far is in the business sector. On the contrary, for those countries showing the lowest record (Greece, Portugal and Spain) public financing tends to dominate over the meagre business expenditure. This is hardly a surprise. Less favoured countries have made significant efforts to enhance the knowledge production of their national research systems, mainly by a rapid growth of public fund allocations, and the role of public funds has been to 'push' in this direction. In contrast, for countries with a strong tradition of industrial innovativeness, the role of public expenditure has been of 'matching' the strength of the private sector in generating human resources and fostering knowledge production in less directly commercial domains.

Despite the large differences between high and low performers, the average for European countries shows that business expenditure leads the overall efforts with 1.2 per cent of GDP, as against 0.7 per cent of government and high education expenditure together (see Figure 2.3).

Another question is, though, whether there is an adequate level of private financing of research in Europe. Again, the picture is very different from country to country, yet, at an aggregate level, since the mid-1990s Europe has been experiencing a breath-taking development of the venture capital industry and of nationally and pan-European technology-based equity markets. The Nasdaq stock exchange has a solid position within the US mechanisms of private RTD financing. In contrast with this, the European experience of creating such markets (also called second-tier markets or tech-markets) is relatively recent, and arguably is still in a start-up phase (Partners G.B. 1996). Whereas in the early 1990s almost all European stock exchanges had parallel or unlisted security markets, it was only in the mid-1990s that more far-reaching initiatives like Euro.NM, AIM, and Easdaq were launched. Let us have a close look at each of these. Euro.NM is an alliance of second-tier exchange markets operating at national level (Paris, Frankfurt, Milan, Amsterdam and Brussels), of which Frankfurt has always dominated. With 310 listed companies and 65 billion euro joint capitalization in 2001, Euro.NM is a strong player in these markets. The rapid transformation of national stock exchanges these days might perhaps push Euro.NM to move beyond a mere alliance of national exchanges. Another important tech-market in Europe is AIM, the London Stock Exchange's Alternative Investment Market, which has been rather successful with a total listing of 545 companies in 2001. The third market operating in Europe, Easdaq has tended to be somehow weaker vis-à-vis the two others. Operating at a truly pan-European rather than a

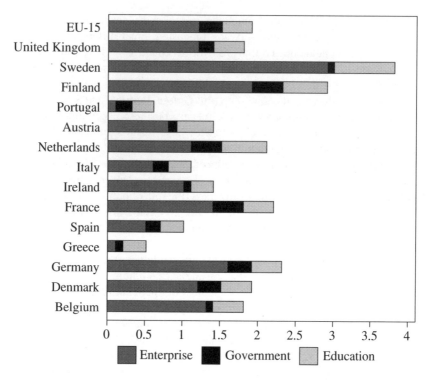

Source: Key figures for science, technology and innovation (Commission 2000b).

Figure 2.3   Gross expenditure on RTD (GERD) by GDP, divided by sources, 1999

national basis, this market has 171 companies listed and a total 20 billion euro capitalization. In March 2001, Easdaq was taken over by the US based Nasdaq, and re-named Nasdaq-Europe. Consequently, the European tech-market context is changing rapidly. First, the creation of the single currency might enhance further pan-European operations. However, the battle for attracting new listing companies is far from over. With more than 1000 small companies now being traded, the market has grown sharply during the last five years. Despite the recent downturn of Nasdaq index in the 2000–01 crises, it is still likely that the volume of these tech markets in Europe will grow in the future. This is due to their relative under-development as compared with the US, and to the current surge of share culture and higher-risk investment profiles of private and corporate portfolios in Europe.

   In spite of the advancement of tech markets, corporate venture capital is still the most prominent way for European firms to obtain high-risk capital. The private equity industry in Europe grew spectacularly in the 1990s, as shown in Figure 2.4. This figure also shows the 'bubble burst' of late 2000 and early 2001, which had dramatic effects on high-tech investment rates.

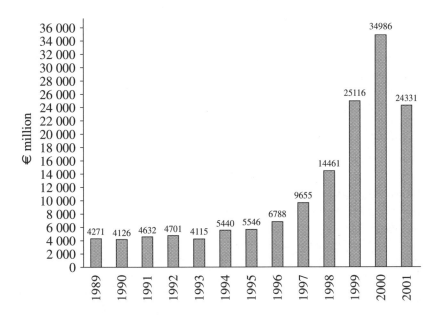

Source: EVCA (2002) and EVCA (2000).

Figure 2.4   Annual European private equity investment, million euros, 1989–2001

Venture capital (representing three different types of capital: seed, start-up and expansion capital) is quite outstanding among the different types of capital offered by this industry, representing 55 per cent of the total amount invested in the first half of 2000 (see Table 2.5).

The interesting thing about Table 2.5 is that it shows how venture capital reached a large number of companies. 'The average investment per company was shown to be: €0.9m in seed, €1.3m in start-up, €2.5m in expansion, €4.2m in replacement capital and €11.8m in buyout investments' (EVCA 2000: 1).

From what has been seen, the recent evolution of the venture capital industry and of technology stock markets in Europe has been astonishing. However, it is still quite small when compared with the US. Is European private financing of innovation still faltering? This is the underling question in almost all studies of European performance. Determining the optimal level of

Table 2.5   Distribution of European investment per m€, first 6 months 2000

	Amount	%	Number of companies	%
Seed	385	2.9	431	9.3
Start-up	2,124	15.8	1,623	35.0
Expansion	4,762	35.4	1,883	40.7
Replacement	1,116	8.3	263	5.7
Buyout	5,081	37.7	430	9.3
Total amount invested	13,470	100	4,630	100

Source: EVCA (2000: 651).

private financing is a thorny matter for two reasons. First, financial institutions/markets function as selection mechanisms, hence this might mean that the problem is not on the supply side of capital but rather on the demand side, as SMEs' business plans are not good enough to pass close examination. Secondly, there is rarely a clear separation between financing innovation and financing the firm as a whole (Christensen 1997). In any case, we have seen that there has been considerable dynamism in Europe since the mid-1990s, and this is unleashing more capital for high-risk enterprises. Nevertheless, this greater supply should not overshadow the fact that important national patterns still persist in Europe, especially in the way the venture capital industry operates (Kluth and Andersen 1999).

What is the role of public policy in this regard? A whole panoply of national and sub-national public policies in the 1980s–90s have been directed to this (most notably, tax incentives, loan guarantees, government loans and government equity investment) (OECD 1996b: 7), with different success stories. All of them have tried to address the so-called equity gap, or the gap for small firms trying to gain high-risk capital financing. This is a key area for an active industrial policy aimed at generating dynamic entrepreneurship by enabling markets to work more effectively. Three main lessons can be learnt from previous policy experiences; namely, that government involvement has to be flexible and progressively less visible as financing structures become more sophisticated, that the emphasis of policy action should be on growing business rather than on growing venture capital itself, and that it should be done in close partnership with the private sector (Harding 2000: iii–iv).

In recent years, the European Union has been quite active in fostering the emergence of a venture capital industry in Europe. The rather stealthy

European Investment Bank has granted loans to emerging European venture capital funds through its instrument, the European Investment Fund. These operations were reinforced in 2000 by the large i2i initiative (seen earlier). Until early 2002, the fund had invested in around 80 different venture capital firms, with a participation ranging from 3 to 20 m€, and without exceeding 25 per cent of each fund's total capital. All these funds should be directly involved in providing high-risk capital to European based SMEs.

Public incentives and initiatives are welcomed. In any case, the main burden for change lies with the private sector itself, and there are signs that this is already taking place. On the one hand, the increasing convergence of the financial systems in Europe and the single currency in the Eurozone are reducing the barriers for cross-border operations of this kind. This is backed up by the gradual convergence of the high-tech stock markets (Easdaq and NM), and the growing cross-border operations of the venture capital industry in a more open financial sector environment. On the other hand, the late 1990s experienced an increasing popular interest in equity investment in all European countries. There has also been an increasing high-risk profile in large and small portfolios. Despite the recent high-tech bubble and the drastic fall of high-tech index values in 2000–01, European investors' interest in this type of firm has come to stay.

What Role for Universities and Public Research Centres?

Since public efforts are accountable to tax-payers, in recent decades Europe has experienced considerable political attention being paid to the results of research carried out at higher education and public research centres. This has developed within much larger discussions about the role and future of universities, higher education centres and public laboratories in relation to the provision of education and production of knowledge. Since the inception of the universities in medieval times, there have been different types of university, those focused on the 'pure' production of knowledge for the sake of it, and those with a more industrial-productive focus. Both types have been co-evolving in their function and structures, showing great adaptability in history (Martin and Etzkowitz 2001). The advancement of the 'Mode 2' of knowledge production seemed to suggest the relative diminishing role of universities and public centres of research in the face of a growing number of other 'knowledge producers' (hence the expansion of the supply side of knowledge production) (Gibbons et al. 1994). This statement has been rather controversial among scholars, since not everyone agrees that the growing diversification of knowledge production necessarily pushes aside universities and research centres within the overall system (Godin and Gingras 2000).

The triple helix model has provided another interesting perspective regarding universities and public research centres. This metaphor stresses the fact that the increasingly close links between universities, government and industry are reshaping their roles, and indirectly inducing a new form of cognitive parameters about what science is (Etzkowitz and Leydesdorff 1997, 2000). The emergence of the 'entrepreneurial university' relates to this and to the 'new social contract for basic science' (Martin and Etzkowitz 2001), a university where researchers operate as entrepreneurs raising funds and establishing fluid contacts with the 'external' world.

The question of public research centres and universities has also reached EU level in at least two clear ways. First, the political considerations about the role of the Joint Research Centre in the EU; secondly, the new efforts under the ERA initiative in this respect, mainly by networking centres of excellence and by benchmarking national public research centres. The JRC, the research centre of the EU, is currently in a process of reorganization along three lines: concentration, user orientation and cooperation with external partners (Commission 2001b). This is still in the process of political decision, but all indicates that the JRC has to find its place within the vision framed by the European Research Area initiative, under growing pressure to be more effective and accountable. The interesting thing is that the JRC's central role will be to provide scientific support for EU policies, and it has to do so in a more focused way, and by exploiting the resources generated in a wider network of expertise; that is, as an increasingly 'networked' and more concentrated centre. As to the benchmarking of national public research centres, a first exercise has identified six areas for success and best practices from each case studied (Commission 2000a).[15] The overall picture is rather intelligent, as there is a relatively large variety of issues and of good practices, and the report systematically avoids pointing at one single model. Yet, among the six issues identified, three relate to networking with external partners, showing its centrality in the new role assumed for public research centres.

DISPARITIES AND DIVERSITY IN THE EU

An underlying issue all through this chapter has been the large diversity and disparities with the EU. The unspoken treatment of the EU as a homogeneous and unitary system needs to be refuted in the examination of the multiplicity of modes and dynamics of knowledge production. This section looks briefly at the issue of disparities and diversity in the EU, first along its north–south axis, and later along its west–east axis on the eve of the eastern enlargement.

The North-South Divide

Since Greece, Portugal and Spain joined the EU in the 1980s, the Community has no longer shown the relatively homogeneous level of socio-economic development it used to have in previous decades (Borrás 1999). The southern enlargement increased intra-EU disparities in all socio-economic indicators, including knowledge infrastructures and production dynamics. In this sense, Figure 2.5 needs almost no further comments. The 'champions' of RTD expenditure (Sweden, Germany and Finland) more than double the efforts of the 'laggards' (Greece, Portugal and Spain), which do not even reach the threshold of 1 per cent of national GDP. Quite obviously, these differences date back to long historical trends for the aggregated efforts for producing knowledge. As we saw earlier in this chapter, the recent growth of expenditure has been mainly on the public side.

Two of the most interesting EU policy initiatives trying to build up the

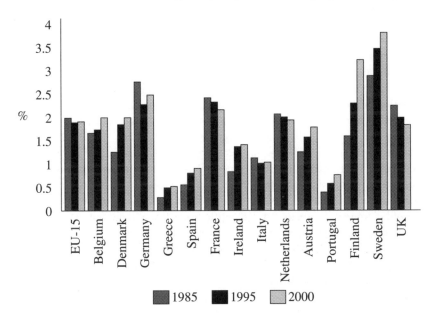

Notes:
Notions to the reference year 2000: B, DK, I, P, FIN and S: 1999; NL: 1998; EL and IRL: 1997.
Notions to the reference year 1985: EL and P: 1986; F: 1991.

Source: Own elaboration from Eurostat (2001a) and Eurostat (2001b).

Figure 2.5   Gross domestic expenditure on R&D as percentage of GDP, 1985-2000

knowledge production system in weak regions have been the RIS and RTT (Regional Innovation Strategy and Regional Technology Transfer, respectively), both under the EU regional policy. Started in 1994, they have engaged more than 40 regions in launching their own regional strategies in accordance with regional stakeholders. Taken as a whole these two initiatives have been successful, fostering strategic thinking, socio-economic dialogue and a broader understanding of innovation in these regions (Covers 2000). The RIS and RTT initiatives have openly followed the innovation system approach, in the understanding that regional actors have to mobilize themselves by articulating a common strategy to address the question of how to boost innovation-generating activities in the territory (Landabaso 1997; Cooke et al. 2000). Therefore, they can well be considered as a 'second generation' of policy initiatives, where the role of the EU is mainly a sort of catalyst, encouraging regional actors to set up their own RTD strategy on a systemic perspective. This contrasts with the 'first generation' of EU policy actions, with a more 'hands-on' strategy, where the EU allotted funds for raising physical RTD infrastructures in poor regions, either by the STRIDE programme or within the large multi-annual development programmes of the Structural Funds, typically involving solely the acquisition of research facilities and equipment.

An issue that generated a degree of political unrest in the mid-1990s was the question of how far the EU framework programme had to take account of partners from less developed countries/regions. In other words, whether adding the 'cohesion' principle into EU RTD policy involved special treatment for these partners in the allocation of funds. The debate was connected with Spanish political pressure to get more from Brussels, in the politics of 'fair return' (Robles 1991). The turbulence came to an end when a panel of independent experts recommended in the Caraça Report that the FP should continue to focus on 'scientific excellence' and not be used for redistributive purposes (Commission 1991, 1993).[16] Inter-state and inter-regional disparities continue to be large in participatory terms, but recent studies reveal that in aggregate terms the cohesion countries (Greece, Spain, Portugal and Ireland) have benefited greatly from EU funding in the 2FP and 3FP in proportion to their own RTD capacity (Sharp 1998; Sharp and Pereira 2000), and those regions that are 'economic catchers-up' and 'technological catchers-up' show clear patterns of convergence and an absorptive ability for EU funds (Clarysse and Muldur 2001).

Enlargement: A New Triangle

There is no doubt that the coming eastern enlargement of the EU will exacerbate the question of disparities within the Union. As the number of less well-off countries increases, political pressures to combine the scientific excellence and cohesion principle are likely to re-emerge. Yet, what are the prospects for these newcomers? What new patterns of the EU political

Table 2.6   R&D expenditure in EU member states and candidate states, 1998

	R&D expenditure as % of GDP
EU-15	1.86
Belgium[1,2]	1.84
Denmark	1.93
Germany	2.29
Greece[1]	0.51
Spain	0.90
France[2]	2.19
Ireland[1]	1.40
Italy[2]	1.02
The Netherlands[1]	2.04
Austria	1.80
Portugal[1]	0.63
Finland	2.89
Sweden[2]	3.77
United Kingdom	1.82
Luxembourg	–
Candidate countries	
Bulgaria	0.59
Cyprus	0.23
Czech Republic	1.27
Estonia	0.62
Hungary	0.68
Latvia	0.45
Lithuania	0.57
Poland	0.73
Romania	0.50
Slovak Republic	0.86
Slovenia	1.42

Notes:
[1] 1997 data.
[2] Provisional data.

Source: Eurostat (2000).

economy and of knowledge production will emerge in the aftermath of the first round of eastern enlargement?

The first point to mention is the fact that Central and Eastern European Countries (CEECs) show large differences between themselves. This heterogeneity does not only reflect historical features of socio-economic and political systems, but also their evolving situation since 1989. It seems then that central European countries (most notably the champions among the countries in the first enlargement wave, particularly Poland, the Czech Republic, Slovenia and Hungary) are converging rapidly to EU levels through higher growth rates than the EU average, whereas some other Eastern countries (Bulgaria, Romania and Slovakia) have had difficulties converging (Grabbe et al. 1999).

Common to them all, however, is that they are relatively well endowed with human resources, skills and scientific capabilities, compared with the deindustrialized poor regions of Southern Europe. This is the result of the emphasis of the Soviet era on scientific and skill development, combined with a process of rapid industrialization after the Second World War. Hence, the newcomers are relatively well placed with regard to scientific abilities and human resources. Table 2.6 shows for example that Poland, Hungary, the Czech Republic, Slovenia and Slovakia outperform Greece and Portugal in overall expenditure on R&D per GDP.

Table 2.6 reinforces the view that the challenge for the CEECs is not to build knowledge competencies, but rather to use them more efficiently. The long decades of a centrally-planned economy institutionalized a system of knowledge production based on hierarchical scientific organizations and an almost complete detachment between scientific and technological endeavours. Addressing these two points is the fundamental challenge of these systems of innovation and knowledge production.

Consequently, it is most likely that the eastern enlargement will generate a sort of a triangular pattern of knowledge production in the future EU25, where the 'south' still struggles to build up its infrastructure and knowledge competencies, whereas the 'east' is more focused on strengthening the 'connectivity' of its system and exploiting optimally its already existing competencies.

CONCLUSIONS

Summing up these discussions, we can observe that the Europeanization of knowledge production in the EU has followed a three-step evolution (first with the JRC, second with the Framework Programme, and third with the ERA and i2i initiatives), in what seems to be a multi-level type of interaction between member states and the EU. The European Research Area initiative explicitly aims at overcoming the division of powers defined in the 15+1 system, and a move to a more open, flexible and fluid cross-national dynamics of knowledge production beyond the strict limits of the FP endowments. The success of this initiative is far from clear. First, the number of areas that ERA deals with is rather large. This breadth of scope is interesting as it aims at governing the production of knowledge in a more 'contextual' way, rather than by providing only direct public funds for RTD. It also renders policy action more diffused and with several simultaneous goals. Secondly, the success of ERA depends on how far national administrations will embrace and pursue the common goals. Benchmarking and mainstreaming are interesting tools, but they are still much to be proved in EU politics.

Parallel to this, EU RTD has unequivocally gained a higher profile in the international arena. This has to do with the centrality of the FP in the European scientific architecture, its recent openness to non-EU partners, and the embryonic participation of the EU in large international and global research schemes. Yet, partly because of all this, the boundaries of what is 'EU' and what is not 'EU' knowledge production are becoming increasingly blurred. In any case, the times of a 'fortress Europe' are already over, and the very recently pursued rationale of becoming a 'junction' of knowledge production rather than focusing on exact monetary returns, is fortunate given the current globalization trends of the knowledge-based economy.

A third aspect that this chapter has examined is the relationship between public and private realms of RTD. The notion that RTD in Europe has been essentially driven by public financing was partly contested on the basis of two sets of evidence. First, the fact that private expenditures in RTD are higher than public ones in the EU average, and proportionally much more in those countries with the highest RTD expenditure. Secondly, the rapid advancement of pan-EU technology stock markets (like AIM, Euro-NM, and Esdaq) in the 1990s and the growth of the venture capital industry, support the idea of much more dynamic private finance capabilities than assumed hitherto. Another dimension of the interactions between public and private realms that is changing is the increasingly demanding attitude towards the publicly financed centres of knowledge production (such as universities, public laboratories or public research centres) for improving their performance. Admittedly, the EU has had a low profile in these two dynamics of public–private interactions in RTD. However, it has more openly promoted greater capital mobility, and has launched political debates about these issues. The challenge ahead, not just for the EU but for all public administrators on the continent, is to address seriously the question of generating an optimal environment for private investment in knowledge production.

The fourth and last aspect examined was the question of disparities within the EU. This chapter showed that disparities in terms of aggregated knowledge production performance and outputs are rather high in the current north–south division of the EU. Most economic studies agree, pointing out that this trend is likely to persist, making still valid the double EU political goal of cohesion and competitiveness. Another interesting point is the question of the Eastern enlargement. The candidate countries from Central and Eastern Europe show an important intensity in human resources and scientific capabilities with an overall strength in knowledge production but these overlie difficulties in linking it to the manufacturing sector.

Given these overall trends, the picture emerging is one of a complex, diverse and dynamic system of knowledge production in the EU. Complex because the division of tasks between the EU and its member states, and the borders between the EU and non-EU produced knowledge have become less clear-cut than before, at a time when a new panoply of indirect (EU/national) policy initiatives to boost knowledge production has been launched. The system is diverse, because knowledge production in the EU shows a rich pattern of national and inter/supra-national institutional and organizational settings. Even if scholars still discuss whether there are or are not signs of converging national models, and without underestimating the connectivity effect of the EU initiatives, diversity is a reality in the EU. Furthermore, at an aggregated level, performance ratios are rather different, and disparities large. Once enlarged, the EU will become even more diversified as the knowledge production structures of the candidate countries have some peculiarities inherited from the previously centralized regimes. Finally, dynamic, because the knowledge production system of the EU, as any other, is subject to very fast development. Not just from the political scenario, but also from the inner dynamics of knowledge production in the current Mode 2, and from the globalized knowledge-based economy.

Emerging issues for the governance of knowledge production at EU level are as follows.

- Maximizing the value of diversity. The diversity of knowledge production structures and institutions in the EU is a factor for richness and capability for the economy. Diversity however should not mean atomization and compartmentalization. Creating fluid and trans-border knowledge production in the EU should be driven by the goal of generating a single space where there is a certain degree of specialization on a European scale. Specialization ensures synergy while preserving diversity, and gives a good platform for the objective of cohesion. In other words, a diverse system that does not foster further the existing disparities.
- A complex policy structure that comes with flexible solutions. The

dynamics of knowledge production are changing rapidly. This needs new and flexible public action, able to maximize the adaptability of the research and knowledge production systems at national and EU level by responding rapidly to the new challenges, and new institutions that by breaking down traditional organizational barriers are able to open up to new possibilities and new modes of producing knowledge collectively. This requires a public administration that goes beyond a 'subvention' culture, and a 'nationally exclusive' oriented attitude looking mostly at direct economic inputs–outputs. Complexity should be creative and flexible, and policy-makers must be aware of building a positive environment for knowledge production in a diversified manner.

- This leads to a third issue; namely, the need to foster the dynamics already present in the current mode of knowledge production. This should be done through a more consistent and determined approach from policy-makers in Europe to involve further private capital and partners in the knowledge production process. The private financing of innovation and knowledge production is particularly important in those areas and countries where public financing has so far dominated. This is a particularly important challenge, since the rising costs of knowledge production can no longer rest so heavily on public shoulders. The benefits and risks coupled with knowledge production offer interesting investing opportunities in an economy increasingly driven by the development of competences and abilities generated by advanced knowledge. It is then a central future issue for the EU to give a stronger signal in this direction, aligning the private financing of knowledge production to the overall strategy of integrating further and having more risk-oriented capital markets in Europe.

NOTES

1. Following the famous dictum of Oppenheimer, the nuclear physicist who developed the first nuclear bomb in world history.
2. In the Paris 1972 and Copenhagen 1972 summits, national chiefs of government agreed on moving EC matters in science technology. As a result, the first embryonic resolutions for action were adopted in 1974 (OJ L 29 January 1974). But it took ten years, before the first EC RTD Framework Programme saw the light of day in 1984.
3. The French have traditionally been among those questioning the political appropriateness of this principle, pushing for a more industrial approach. In a sense, the higher political profile that employment and competitiveness gained in the mid-1990s has underpinned this approach. In 1995, the Commission launched eight 'task forces' and more targeted research efforts.
4. The Commission proposal for the 6FP is to be found in COM (2001)94 final, Brussels, 21 February 2001.
5. The first results of benchmarking exercises are being made public in 2001/2002. This is the case of benchmarking national research policies (Commission 2001c) and national public

research institutions (Commission 2000a).
6. Cannell's emphasis.
7. CERN: Conseil Européen pour la Recherche Nucléaire, known too as the European Laboratory for Particle Physics.
8. EMBO: The European Molecular Biology Organization; with a large laboratory, EMBL, in Heidelberg, created in 1975.
9. ESO: European Southern Observatory, created in 1962 by five countries to operate an astronomical observatory in the Southern Hemisphere (in Chile).
10. European Space Agency, created in 1975 by ten states, through the merging of ELDO (European Launcher Development Organization) and ESRO (European Space Research Organization).
11. Airbus is a consortium created in 1970, which today consists of the new European giant EADS (after the 1999 merger between the French Matras-Aerospatiale, DASA of German origin, and Spanish CASA) and British Aerospace. It is the largest world producer of commercial aircraft after Boeing.
12. ESF: European Science Foundation, created in 1974, brings together different organizations within different national research councils.
13. COST, European Cooperation in the Field of Scientific and Technical Research, was created in 1971.
14. Other authors provide alternative taxonomies (Archibugi and Michie 1997; Meyer-Kramher and Reger 1999).
15. The six benchmarking issues are market focus and intelligence, culture, internal management and organizational set-up, IPR management, networking and information systems, and entrepreneurship and new business creation.
16. Instead, the report indicated how some indirect measures could help enhance participation of poor members without distorting scientific excellence. These measures were essentially to increase SMEs' participation and to give special treatment to southern researchers on mobility programmes.

REFERENCES

Abramowitz, M. and P. David (1996), 'Technological change and the rise of intangible investments: The US economy's growth path in the twentieth century'. In *Employment and Growth in the Knowledge-based Economy*, OECD. Paris, OECD.

Amable, B., R. Barré and R. Boyer (1997), 'Diversity, coherence and transfomations of innovation systems'. In *Science in Tomorrow's Europe*, R. Barré, M. Gibbons, J. Maddox, B. Martin and P. Papon. Paris, Economica International.

Ancarani, V. (1995), 'Globalising the world: Science and technology in international relations'. In *Handbook of Science and Technology Studies*, S. Jasanoff, G.E. Markle, J.C. Petersen and T. Pinch. Thousand Oaks/London, Sage.

Archibugi, D. (2000), 'The globalisation of technology and the European innovation system'. Paper prepared for the European Commission.

Archibugi, D. and B.-Å. Lundvall (eds) (2001), *The Globalizing Learning Economy*. Oxford, Oxford University Press.

Archibugi, D., J. Howells and J. Michie (2000), *Innovation Policy in a Global Economy*. Cambridge, Cambridge University Press.

Archibugi, D. and J. Michie (1997), 'The globalisation of technology: A new taxonomy'. In *Technology, Globalisation and Economic Performance*, D. Archibugi and J. Michie. Cambridge, Cambridge University Press.

Biegelbauer, P. and S. Borrás (eds) (2003), *Innovation Policies in Europe and the US: The New Agenda*. Aldershot, Ashgate.

Borrás, S. (1999), 'The Europeanization of politics in the southern members of the

EU'. In *Economic Integration in Nafta and the EU*, K. Appendini and S. Bislev. London, Macmillan.

Borrás, S. and K. Jacobsson (2004), 'The open method of co-ordination and the new patterns of EU governance'. *European Journal of Public Policy* **11**(1), forthcoming.

Breschi, S. and F. Malerba (1997), 'Sectorial innovation systems: Technological regimes, Schumpeterian dynamics and spatial boundaries'. In *Systems of Innovation. Technologies, Institutions and Organizations*, C. Edquist. London, Pinter.

Cannell, W. (1998), 'The fifth research and technology development framework programme of the European Union'. *STI Review* **23**: 240–61.

Cannell, W. (2001), 'Afterword'. In *The Dynamics of European Science and Technology Policies*, S. Dresner and N. Gilbert. Aldershot, Ashgate.

Caracostas, P. and U. Muldur (1998), *Society, The Endless Frontier*. Luxemburg, Office for Official Publications of the European Communities.

Christensen, J.L. (1997), *Financing Innovation*. Aalborg, ISE Project.

Clarysse, B. and U. Muldur (2001), 'Regional cohesion in Europe? An analysis of how EU public RTD support influences the techno-economic regional landscape'. *Research Policy* **30**: 275–96.

Cohendet, P. and P.-B. Joly (2001), 'The production of technological knowledge: New issues in a learning economy'. In *The Globalizing Learning Economy*, D. Archibugi and B.-Å. Lundvall. Oxford, Oxford University Press.

Cohendet, P. and E.W. Steinmueller (2000), 'The codification of knowledge: A conceptual and empirical exploration'. *Industrial and Corporate Change* **9**(2): 195–209.

Commission, European (1991), *Evaluation of the Effects of the EC Framework Programme for Research and Technological Development on Economic and Social Cohesion in the Community - The Caraça Report*. Brussels, European Commission.

Commission, European (1993), *Communication: Cohesion and RTD Policy*. Brussels, European Commission.

Commission, European (1994), *The European Report on Science and Technology Indicators*. Luxembourg, Office for Official Publications.

Commission, European (1997a), *Five Year Assessment of the European Community RTD Framework Programme - Report of an Independent Panel chaired by Viscomte Davignon*. Brussels, European Commission - DG XII.

Commission, European (1997b), *Second European Report on S&P Indicators 1997*. Luxembourg, Office for Official Publications.

Commission, European (2000a), *Getting More Innovation from Public Research*. Luxembourg, Office for Official Publications.

Commission, European (2000b), *Towards a European Research Area*. Brussels, European Commission.

Commission, European (2001a), 'The international dimension of the European Research Area'. Communication from the Commission. Com (2001) 346 Final. Brussels, 25 June 2001.

Commission, European (2001b), *The JRC in the European Research Area. Making the Best Use of the JRC's Resources to Fulfil its Mission*. Brussels, European Commission.

Commission, European (2001c), 'Progress report on benchmarking national research policies'. Commission staff working paper SEC (2001) 1002. Brussels, European Commission.

Commission, European (2002), 'Introduction to the instruments available for implementing the FP6 priority thematic areas'. Speaking note from the Commission.

28 February 2002. Brussels, European Commission, DG Research, Unit B.2.

Cooke, P., P. Boekholt and F. Tödtling (2000), *The Governance of Innovation in Europe. Regional Perspectives on Global Competitiveness*. London, Pinter.

Cordis (2000), 'ERA: An idea whose time has come'. *CORDIS Focus* 18 December: 1–2.

Covers, F.B.J.A. (2000), 'How to promote regional innovation systems? Efforts and evidence from the European Union'. Unpublished paper.

Cram, L. (1997), *Policy-making in the EU*. London, Routledge.

David, P.A. and D. Foray (1998), 'Accessing and expanding the science and technology knowledge base'. *STI, Science Technology Industry Review* **16**: 13–63.

Druckner, P. (1998), 'From capitalism to knowledge society'. In *The Knowledge Economy*, D. Neef. Boston, Butterworth-Heinemann.

Dumolin, M. (1997), 'The Joint Research Centre'. In *History of European Scientific and Technological Cooperation*, J. Krige and L. Guzzetti. Luxemburg, Office for Official Publications.

Eberlein, B. and D. Kurwer (2002), 'Theorizing the new modes of European Union governance'. *EIOP* **6**(5).

Edquist, C. and B. Johnson (1997), 'Institutions and organisations in systems of innovation'. In *Systems of Innovation. Technologies, Institutions and Organisations*, C. Edquist. London, Pinter.

Etzkowitz, H. and L. Leydesdorff (eds) (1997), *Universities and the Global Knowledge Economy: A Triple Helix of University-Industry-Government Relations*. London, Pinter.

Etzkowitz, H. and L. Leydesdorff (2000), 'The dynamics of innovation: from national systems and "mode 2" to a triple helix of university–industry–government relations'. *Research Policy* **29**: 109–23.

Eurostat (2000), 'R&D expenditure and personnel in candidate countries and the Russian Federation in 1998'. *Statistics in Focus*, Theme 9-3/2000.

Eurostat (2001a), *Statistics on Science and Technology in Europe: Data 1985–1999*. Luxembourg, Office for Official Publications (Theme 9: Science and Technology).

Eurostat (2001b), *Research and Development - Annual Statistics 1990–2000*. Luxembourg, Office for Official Publications (Theme 9: Science and Technology).

EVCA (2000), *EVCA Mid-year Survey 2000*. Zaventem, Belgium, EVCA.

EVCA (2002), EVCA Yearbook 2002. Annual Survey of Pan-European Private Equity and Venture Capital Activity. Zaventem, Belgium, EVCA.

Foray, D. (1997), 'Generation and distribution of technological knowledge: Incentives, norms and institutions'. In *Systems of Innovation. Technologies, Institutions and Organisations*, C. Edquist. London, Pinter.

Freeman, C. (1997), 'The diversity of national research systems'. In *Science in Tomorrow's Europe*, R. Barré, M. Gibbons, J. Maddox, B. Martin and P. Papon. Paris, Economica International.

Georghiou, L. (1998), 'Global cooperation in research'. *Research Policy* **27**: 611–26.

Georghiou, L. (2001), 'Evolving frameworks for European collaboration in research and technology in research policy'. *Research Policy* **30**: 891–903.

Gibbons, M., C. Limoges, H. Nowotny, S. Schwartzmann, P. Scott and M. Trow (1994), *The New Production of Knowledge. The Dynamics of Science and Research in Contemporary Societies*. London, Sage.

Godin, B. and Y. Gingras (2000), 'The place of universities in the system of knowledge production'. *Research Policy* **29**(2): 273–8.

Grabbe, H., K. Hughes and M. Landesmann (1999), 'The implications of eastward enlargement for EU integration, convergence and competitiveness'. In *The Economic Challenge for Europe*, J. Fageberg, P. Guerrieri and B. Verspagen. Cheltenham, Edward Elgar.

Grande, E. and A. Peschke (1999), 'Transnational cooperation and policy networks in European science policy-making'. *Research Policy* **28**: 43–61.

Guzzetti, L. (1995), *A Brief History of European Union Research Policy*. Luxemburg, Office for Official Publications.

Harding, R. (2000), *Venturing Forwards: The Role of Venture Capital Policy in Enabling Entrepreneurship*. London, IPPR.

Kluth, M.F. and J.B. Andersen (1999), 'Globalisation and financial diversity: The making of venture capital markets in France, Germany and the UK'. In *Innovation Policy in a Global Economy*, D. Archibugi, J. Howells and J. Michie. Cambridge, Cambridge University Press.

Kuhlmann, S. (2001), 'Future governance of innovation policy in Europe – three scenarios'. *Research Policy* **30**: 953–76.

Küppers, G., J. Roth and C. Schlombs (2001), 'Shifting uncertainties: The self-organization of European research policies'. In *The Dynamics of European Science and Technology Policies*, S. Dresner and N. Gilbert. Aldershot, Ashgate.

Landabaso, M. (1997), 'The promotion of innovation in regional policy: Proposals for a regional innovation strategy'. *Entrepreneurship & Regional Development* **9**: 1–24.

Larédo, P. (1997), 'European research policy on industrial competitiveness'. In *Science in Tomorrow's Europe*, R. Barré, M. Gibbons, J.S. Maddox, B. Martin and P. Papon. Paris, Economica International, 145–54.

Larédo, P. (1998), 'The networks promoted by the framework programme and the questions they raise about its formulation and implementation'. *Research Policy* **27**: 589–98.

Lawton, T. (1997), *Technology and the New Diplomacy*. Aldershot, Avebury.

Layton, C. (1969), *European Advanced Technology. A Programme for Integration*. London, Allen & Unwin.

Lundvall, B.-Å. (ed.) (1992), *National Systems of Innovation: Towards a Theory of Innovation and Interactive Learning*. London, Pinter.

Lundvall, B.-Å. (1998), 'The learning economy: Challenges to economic theory and policy'. In *Institutions and Economic Change*, K. Nielsen and B. Johnson. Cheltenham, Edward Elgar.

Lundvall, B.-Å. (1999), 'Knowledge production and the knowledge base'. Unpublished, Dept. of Business Studies, Aalborg University.

Luukkonen, T. (1998), 'The difficulties in assessing the impact of EU framework programmes'. *Research Policy* **27**(6): 599–610.

Luukkonen, T. (2000), 'Additionality of EU framework programmes'. *Research Policy* **29**: 711–24.

Martin, B.R. and H. Etzkowitz (2001), 'The origin and evolution of the university species'. Brighton, SPRU Paper no. 59.

Martin, B.R. and A. Salter (1996), *The Relationship between Publicly Funded Basic Research and Economic Performance*. Brighton, SPRU – University of Sussex.

Metcalf, E.I.S., L. Georghiou, J. Stein, M. Jones, J. Senker, M. Pifer, H. Cameron, M. Nedeva, J. Yates and M. Boden (1991), *Evaluation of the Impact of European Community Research Programmes upon the Competitiveness of European Industry – Concepts and Approaches. A PREST Report*. Luxemburg, Office for the Official Publications of the ECs.

Meyer-Kramher, F. and G. Reger (1999), 'New perspectives on the innovation strategies of multinational enterprises: Lessons for technology policy in Europe'. *Research Policy* **28**: 751–76.

Moonman, E. (ed.) (1969), *Science and Technology in Europe*. Harmondsworth, Penguin.

Mowery, D.C. (1998), 'The changing structure of the US national innovation system: Implications for international conflict and cooperation in R&D policy'. *Research Policy* **27**: 639–54.

Mytelka, L. and M. Delapierre (1987), 'The alliance strategies of European firms in the information technology industry and the role of esprit'. *Journal of Common Market Studies* **26**(2): 231–53.

Nelson, R. R. (ed.) (1993), *National Innovation Systems. A Comparative Analysis*. Oxford, Oxford University Press.

Nelson, R.R. and S. Winter (1982), *An Evolutionary Theory of Economic Change*. Cambridge, MA, Harvard University Press.

Nollert, M. (2000), 'Biotechnology in the European Union: A case study of political entrepreneurship'. In *State-building in Europe. The Revitalization of Western European Integration*, V. Bornschier. Cambridge, Cambridge University Press.

OECD (1995), *Megascience Policy Issues*. Paris, OECD.

OECD (ed.) (1996a), *Employment and Growth in the Knowledge-based Economy*. Paris, OECD.

OECD (1996b), *Government Programmes for Venture Capital*. Paris, OECD.

OECD (2000), *Knowledge Management in the Learning Society*. Paris, OECD.

Olazaran, M. and M. Gómez-Uranga (eds) (2001), *Sistemas regionales de innovación*. San Sebastián, Universidad del Pais Vasco.

Parker, S. (2000), 'Esprit and technology corporatism'. In *State-building in Europe. The Revitalization of Western European Integration*, V. Bornschier. Cambridge, Cambridge University Press.

Partners G.B. (1996), *Making Markets Work. Support Services for Equity Markets for Emerging Growth Companies in Europe*. Brussels, Commission DGIII – EIMS project.

Patel, P. and K. Pavitt (1999), 'National systems of innovation under strain: The internationalisation of corporate R&D'. In *Productivity, Innovation and Economic Performance*, R. Barrel, G. Mason and M. O'Mahony. Cambridge, Cambridge University Press.

Patel, P. and M. Vega (1999), 'Patterns of internationalisation of corporate technology: Location vs. home country advantages'. *Research Policy* **28**(2-3): 145–55.

Pavitt, K. (1998), 'The inevitable limits of EU R&D funding'. R*esearch Policy* **27**(6): 559–68.

Pavitt, K. and P. Patel (1971), 'Technology in Europe's Future'. *Research Policy* 1: 210–73.

Pereira, T.T.S. (2001), 'Collaboration among diversity: The national research systems in Europe and the framework programmes'. In *The Dynamics of European Science and Technology Policies*, S. Dresner and N. Gilbert. Aldershot, Ashgate.

Pestre, D. (1997), 'La production des savoirs entre académie et marché: Une relecture historique du livre *The New Production of Knowledge*'. Revue d'Economie Industrielle **79**: 163–75.

Peterson, J. (1991), 'Technology policy in Europe: Explaining the framework programme and Eureka in theory and practice'. *Journal of Common Market Studies* **29**(3): 269–90.

Peterson, J. (1992), 'The European technology community. Policy networks in a supranational setting'. In *Policy Networks in British Government*, D. Marsh and R.A.W. Rhodes. Oxford, Clarendon.

Peterson, J. and M. Sharp (1998), *Technology Policy in the European Union*. London, Macmillan Press.

Rip, A. and B. v. d. Meulen (1997), 'The post-modern research system'. In *Science in Tomorrow's Europe*, R. Barré, M. Gibbons, J. Maddox, B. Martin and P. Papon. Paris, *Economica International*.

Robles, E. (1991), 'Economic and social cohesion and community R&D policy'. In *Proceedings of the 2nd Annual Workshop STRIDE*, European Commission. Brussels, European Commission.

Salter, A.J. and B.R. Martin (2001), 'The economic benefits of publicly funded basic research: A critical review'. *Research Policy* **30**(3): 509-32.

Sanchez-Rón, J.M. (2000), *El Siglo de la Ciencia*. Madrid, Taurus.

Sandholtz, W. (1992), *High-tech Europe. The Politics of International Cooperation*. Berkeley, University of California Press.

Sanz, L. and S. Borrás (2000), 'Explaining changes and continuity in the EU technology policy: The politics of economic ideas'. In *The Dynamics of European Science and Technology Policies*, S. Dresner and N. Gilbert. Aldershot, Ashgate Press.

Sharp, M. (1989), 'The Community and new technologies'. In *The European Community and the Challenges of the Future*, J. Lodge. London, Pinter.

Sharp, M. (1991), 'The single market and European technology policies'. In *Technology and the Future of Europe: Global Competition and the Environment in the 1990s*, C. Freeman, M. Sharp and W. Walker. London, Pinter.

Sharp, M. (1997), 'Towards a federal system of science in Europe'. In *Science in Tomorrow's Europe*, R. Barré, M. Gibbons, J.S. Maddox, B. Martin and P. Papon. Paris, *Economica International*, 201-18.

Sharp, M. (1998), 'Competitiveness and cohesion – are the two compatible?' *Research Policy* **27**(6): 569-88.

Sharp, M. and T. Pereira (2000), 'Cohesion and RTD policies in the EU'. In *Cohesion and Competitiveness*, R. Hall, A. Smith and L. Tsoukalis. Oxford, Oxford University Press.

Solingen, E. (1993), 'Between markets and the state: Scientists in a comparative perspective'. *Comparative Politics* **26**(1): 31-51.

Stein, J.A. (1999), *External Relations in the European Union, the United States and Japan, and International Research and Technological Development Cooperation*. Brussels, Forward Studies Unit, European Commission.

Storper, M. (1997), *The Regional World. Territorial Development in a Global Economy*. New York/London, The Guilford Press.

Tegart, W.J.M. (1995), 'Generic megascience policy issues. Foresight and forward planning in megascience'. In *Megascience Policy Issues*, OECD. Paris, OECD.

Tijssen, R.J.W. and E. van Wijk (1999), 'In search of the European paradox: An international comparison of Europe's scientific performance and knowledge flows in information and communication technologies research'. *Research Policy* **28**: 519-43.

Väyrynen, R. (1998), 'Global interdependence or the European fortress? Technology policies in perspective'. *Research Policy* **27**(6): 627-32.

3. The changing regime of intellectual property rights

Money's only paper only ink
We'll destroy ourselves if we can't agree
How the world turns
Who made the sun
Who owns the sea.

(Tracy Chapman, 'Paper and ink', 2000)

INTRODUCTION

The regulation of patents, and more generally of intellectual property rights, is a ubiquitous key element of public action towards fostering innovation. The possibility for an innovator to acquire special rights in the form of a patent, a copyright, a trademark or an industrial design, and the way in which these rights are used, defined, enforced and protected have several functions in an innovation system. One of the most important is the creation of incentives to innovate, as the innovator can exclusively enjoy, for a period of time, the fruits of his or her knowledge production. Yet, above all, these rights have a very direct effect on everyday practices, and for many innovative firms the management of their intellectual property rights portfolio is almost invariably a core business issue. Several studies show that in the last couple of decades, the intellectual capital component of firm assets has been soaring both in absolute as well as in relative terms, and that we live in a 'pro-patent era' (Kortum and Lerner 1999; Arundel 2001a) or in an 'intellectual capitalism' (Granstrand 1999).

The EU's political awareness of the issues of competitiveness and growth in the 1990s has given a boost to the idea of common European regulations in the area of intellectual property rights (IPRs). It is as if the attention paid to the production of knowledge has also moved to the issue of knowledge appropriation. As a matter of fact, since the launch of the single market project, the Commission has constantly argued for the benefits of harmonizing and unifying IPRs among member states. Despite some attempts in the 1980s, legislative initiatives had to wait until the 1990s. This means that the EU regulatory framework for intellectual property rights is still under construction, and in this process several questions emerge. How are the tasks between the EU and its member states being distributed? How is Europe tackling and managing the growing internationalization of intellectual property rights' protection? And how is the balance between private and public interests being struck in this EU regulation?

Specifically focusing on patents, this chapter examines these questions one by one. First, however, it devotes some time to discussing more generally the way in which IPRs relate to the overall innovation system and innovation policy. This will serve as a backdrop for the debates that follow. In accordance with the analytical framework established at the onset of this book, the next section looks at the distribution of tasks between national, EU and pan-European levels of government in the regulation, enforcement and protection of these rights. The third section moves the scope of analysis slightly beyond the European scenario, and looks at the rapid process of the internationalization of IPRs. Of special relevance is the TRIPS agreement under the realm of the WTO. The EU position in the WTO negotiations, and the recent ECJ jurisprudence about TRIPS are two important aspects in this regard. The fourth section is devoted to analysing critically how the balance between private and public interests is struck in the different EU IPRs. The regulations of biotechnological patents and software patents, and the highly protective 'élan' of some regulations seem to indicate the emergence of a rather strong and broad intellectual property rights regime in the EU. Finally, the last section looks at the diversity in patenting propensity within the EU and the Triad and the conclusions address the questions of what type of regulatory regime is emerging in the EU, the hurdles of governing a complex and asymmetric IPR regulatory system, and the socio-political and economic effects of re-conceptualizing property.

INTELLECTUAL PROPERTY RIGHTS AND INNOVATION

Since the mid-19th century economists have been discussing the role of IPRs in the economy. Indeed, in recent years, these debates have become livelier. Two central issues are at stake. The first has a theoretical character: institutional–evolutionary economists are currently discussing the nature and process of knowledge appropriability. In particular, their concern is how to consider, theoretically, the role of intellectual property rights in relation to the larger vista of the process (and limits) of knowledge codification and appropriation. A second issue, of much greater and direct political relevance, is the question of what sort of regulatory regime is best for the present economic dynamics and the innovation process. Most particularly, the role of patents has been the object of much consideration between those who support a strong regulatory system, and those in favour of a more lax one. The point for such alternative positions lies in the different understanding of what gives most benefit to the general interest and the economy of a country. We examine these two debates one after the other, introducing the central elements that define the economics of intellectual property rights regulation.

The Constitutive Nature of IPRs

Historians have shown the intrinsic relationship between the creation of the institution of private property and the emergence of the capitalist state. The historical development of IPR regulations follows the organization of other types of property rights, which have been related to national constitutional frameworks since the first liberal constitutions of the 19th century. Therefore, IPRs have so far been essentially national in nature because they have been related to the state exercise of granting property rights. In this sense, IPRs have traditionally followed the territoriality principle of all national legal systems, as national authorities are those that grant the rights and determine the scope and nature of their exercise. By this simple fact, IPRs have become the cornerstone of the relationship between state and society, for it is the regulatory power of the former which shapes the conditions under which transactions and interactions between innovators take place.

> The national regimes of intellectual property rights (and of patents in particular) are the results of historical processes of institutional change. These processes have allowed distinct societies to design gradually specific forms of compromise between individual incentives to innovations (exclusion) and the co-ordination of innovation activities (diffusion-information). ... The spirit of concrete intellectual property regimes cannot be correctly captured outside the coherent relationships linking them to the other components of national systems of innovation. (Foray 1995: 110)

In other words, national IPR regimes are the product of state-specific historical evolutions, and gradual institutionalization processes of public decisions, collective understandings, and social practices.

In this sense, we can see that IPRs are a constitutive element of each national system of innovation because they regulate the forms and procedures for the appropriation of knowledge, which is a crucial aspect of the interactions between actors involved in the innovation process. However, it is important to distinguish, at this point, between the formal and informal dimensions of intellectual property rights, and their role in socio-economic dynamics. In formal terms, the intellectual property rights regime forms part of the overall regulatory regime of the economic and legal order that shapes a state. In this sense, IPRs can be seen as a functional sub-set within the entire collection of legal rules available within a given state jurisdiction. The functional specificity of the IPR regime is defined by the object and subject it regulates; namely, the legal protection of certain concrete pieces of knowledge that have been generated by some agents. At least two crucial aspects have to be considered when examining the formal dimension of the IPR regime. One of them is the nature of the rights that the state confers on the knowledge producer; that is, the type of legal entities available (patents, copyrights, trademarks, etc), their individual and collective scope of protection, and the legal caveats that foresee exceptions to these general rules. A second aspect is the way in which the protection that these rights grant is legally enforced. The legal exercise of these rights is intrinsically bound to judicial practices and jurisprudential doctrines. These, too, are important elements of the formal dimensions of intellectual property rights. Therefore, the formal constitutive element of IPRs has to be addressed in both these questions: how the contents of the law are defined, and how these are effectively exercised by the judicial system and the interpretative tradition embodied in the jurisprudence. One final remark about the formal dimension of IPRs is that the inherent territoriality of the rights depicts a neat borderline of the legal system. Within these borders, the intellectual property rights holder enjoys full protection. Outside them, the endowments of the nationally granted IPRs are withdrawn. As we will see later in this chapter, the increasing internationalization of the economy has posed some challenges to this.

Indeed, the intellectual property rights also have an informal dimension. This is a set of social practices in the form of the recognition of, the collective expectations concerning, and the use and the abuse related to IPRs. Here the regime does not refer to the set of existing legal rules (law and jurisprudence), but essentially to the routines, codes of conduct, habits and other informally institutionalized social practices relating to IPRs. This informal dimension is crucial because it is the cornerstone of the actual relevance that the regime has for innovators. As we will see in the coming section, this informal dimension is related to several aspects of the codified knowledge appropriation process, such as the level of trust among agents, the intra-organizational incentives for agents, and the specific traditions within some scientific and industrial sectors. All these aspects tend to indicate that contextual conditions define, to a large extent, the everyday practices of the use (or non-use) of intellectual property rights.

The formal and informal dimensions of intellectual property rights are deeply interrelated, and can hardly be analytically separated from each other. The point is not so much to determine what comes first, formal or informal; this might turn out to be as fruitless as the chicken and egg question, and equally unsolvable. Instead, social scientists need to examine what sort of dynamics are emerging within each of these dimensions, and how they can be mutually attuned in order to generate a balanced and dynamic innovation process in a given territory. In other words, what sort of intellectual property rights regime is most adequate for the contemporary knowledge-based economy, and how to insert it into a comprehensive innovation policy.

The Theoretical Debates about Knowledge Appropriation

The question of the appropriability of knowledge has long interested theoretical economics, and is an issue that lies at the heart of the policy rationale for intellectual property rights regimes (Metcalfe 1995). Neo-classical economists treated knowledge as being equal to information, implying that knowledge is always easily transferable and that this transfer involves no significant costs. For Arrow, one of the most acclaimed economists within the neo-classical school, knowledge is a 'non-rival good' because it is infinitively expansible without being diminished in quality or quantity, and is a 'non-exclusive good' because it is almost impossible to exclude individuals from using it. These two properties of knowledge pose a severe problem for establishing market incentives to innovate. Since the producer of this knowledge cannot experience the full ownership of its own creation, free-riding is very likely to take place, where competitors appropriate and copy the knowledge generated by the innovator. This is a sub-optimal situation in economic terms for the reason that it discourages individual investments in knowledge production, thus calling for policy action to address this specific market failure.

Institutional and evolutionary economists have repeatedly criticized this view, arguing that knowledge is not the same as information, and that the overall process of knowledge creation and appropriation is more complex than Arrow claimed (Cohendet and Meyer-Krahmer 2001). Tacit knowledge, an essential ingredient of the learning process that characterizes innovation, cannot be transferred directly to competitors. The distinction between tacit and codified knowledge shows that most knowledge is neither fully public nor fully private (Lundvall 1999), and that there are manifold means of appropriating knowledge (Cowan and Paal 2000). Furthermore, these authors underline the fact that the most crucial element defining the innovativeness of a system is its ability to absorb, understand and exploit knowledge effectively (Steinmueller 1994), and not just the appropriation of the knowledge as such. However, beyond these common positions, institutional economists are now producing different views of the relative importance of codified and tacit knowledge. These might have important implications for the policy rationales that drive the regulation of intellectual property rights. A factor that has recently triggered these debates has been the consideration by some authors that if the importance of tacit knowledge is taken to the extreme, then the question of how intellectual property rights are regulated and exercised is entirely indifferent to the innovation process. However, this does not correspond to the actual dynamics of the contemporary economy.

> The notion that the economic case for public support of science and engineering should now be based upon the inherently tacit and 'craft' nature of research activities certainly is rather paradoxical. Taken at face value it would suggest that intellectual property protection is unjustified, since, in the 'natural' state of things, there are no 'externalities' of new knowledge. By implication, the patent system's exchange of monopoly of use for 'disclosure' allows the patentee to retain the tacit knowledge without which the information contained in the patent really is useless. (Cowan et al. 2000: 224; emphasis in the original)

But this is far from being the case.

A new theoretical challenge is being launched here. If institutional economists criticize the neo-classical assumptions that reduced knowledge to mere information, and they equally criticize those who claim that innovation is almost exclusively based on tacit knowledge, what are the economics of codified knowledge? And what is the role of intellectual property protection in the knowledge-based economy? Substantial theoretical efforts are still required in this field, not least in order to define policy implications more clearly. Nevertheless, an important step in this direction has indicated that a 'knowledge-oriented policy' does not invalidate the traditional hypothesis on which the current rationale of public action is based, but that 'the ways to interpret them, the ways to design and implement them, the ways to use them will be different' (Cohendet and Meyer-Krahmer 2001: 1576). What these authors are saying is that real-world examinations reveal complex patterns of use, abuse and non-use of intellectual property, in a manner that goes beyond the strict profit-maximizing assumptions about incentives and behaviour suggested by Arrow. Consequently, they suggest four types of cases of the use of intellectual property rights, where non-economic incentives and trust/distrust are represented (see Table 3.1).

The four cells in Table 3.1 represent different situations extracted from the real world, where the use of patents is more contextually bounded than in previous expectations that foresaw only one possible situation, namely the 'use of patents as pure property rights'. This table allows for different situations, has a more contextual understanding of the use of patents, links nicely with our previous distinction between the formal and informal dimensions of intellectual property rights, and connects with relevant empirical research that shows different patterns of behaviour across industrial sectors (Arundel and Kabla 1998; Eurostat 1999), firm size (Arundel 2001a), industrialized countries (OECD 2000), and European regions (Maursseth and Verspagen 1999).

Table 3.1   Trust, appropriability and incentives in the production of knowledge

	Absence of trust	Existence of trust
Appropriability is the only incentive	Use of patents as pure property rights	Trade-off between using pure property rights and rights of access
Different incentives	Use of patents as property rights, signalling and reputation	Complex use of patents and rights of access

Source: Reprinted from *Research Policy* 2001, vol. 30, issue 9, Patrick Cohendet and Frieder Meyer-Krahmer, 'The theoretical and policy implications of knowledge codification', pp. 1563–91. Copyright 2001, with permission from Elsevier Science.

Notwithstanding these fascinating theoretical debates and the empirical results of economic research, we need to approach the rationale on which intellectual property rights regimes are regulated nowadays, and the emerging trends that are rapidly shaping these traditional policy instruments.

The Regulation of IPRs Today: Current Rationales and Emerging Trends

Among all legal forms of intellectual property rights (like trademarks, copyrights, industrial designs, etc.) patents have traditionally been considered the most relevant for the innovation process. This is so because the new knowledge that patents protect has typically been the outcome of scientific/technological research efforts, with potential or direct industrial application. Patents can be of a product or of a process. They are not obtained automatically, since a public patenting authority grants them on the basis of certain criteria. The three criteria that new knowledge has to fulfil are, generally speaking, the following: novelty (the knowledge should not have been patented before/not publicly available), non-obviousness (not being common sense in the particular knowledge field they relate to) and industrial applicability/usefulness. These are the most generally recognized conditions for patentability in national settings. An additional condition is that the patent application

> shall disclose the invention in a manner sufficiently clear and complete for the invention to be carried out by a person skilled in the art and may require the applicant to indicate the best mode for carrying out the invention known to the inventor. (art. 29(1) of the TRIPS agreement)

This condition ensures that others can exploit the patent after the patent rights have been exhausted (OECD 1997). A further element concerning patent regulations is the time limit of the rights granted – patents generally last 20 years, and are not renewable except in a few cases, such as pharmaceutical drugs.[1]

What are the conventional arguments for the regulation of patents in the first place? What is the current rationale for governmental action in this area? Which functions are they expected to fulfil in both society and the economy? Mazzoleni and Nelson have identified three interrelated functions (Mazzoleni and Nelson 1998). The first and most important one is the 'incentive to innovate' function through granting a temporary monopoly to the innovator in order to allow him or her to capitalize on the fruit of their creation by preventing free access to imitating competitors. Consequently, patents anticipate the inventors' rewards, and are a clear induction for invention/ innovative activities. The second function is the establishment of an 'innovation market', or a market related to the commercialization of such rights through the buy–sell action of the patent itself or of licence rights. This means that IPRs induce the commercialization and commodification of innovative results that otherwise would have been kept secret by the innovator. The third is the 'transparency' function, as the public availability of the databases from national patenting agencies serves two purposes. The first is that they work as a vehicle for disclosure, because the 'claims' of the patent contain accurate information about the technical properties of the new invention. The second is that these databases are an up-dated indicator of the technological capabilities being developed in the given innovation system/ territory they apply to and, hence, allow public authorities to define in approximate terms the scientific and technological competences of the system.

In general terms considerations of these three functions acknowledge the costs related to patenting: both the collective negative effects related to the provision of an exclusive (yet temporary) right, and the individual financial and administrative burden borne by each patent applicant in the process of applying for a patent. However, concerning individual costs, it has to be mentioned that there are different types: those related to getting a patent, those regarding litigation, and those related to the maintenance and management of the IPRs' portfolio (OECD 1997). Whereas the costs of getting a patent are relatively low in most industrialized countries, the costs of litigation, that is, when protection really becomes effective, might be extremely expensive (especially in the US). Likewise, the management costs tend to increase the larger the collection of IPR assets becomes for a single firm. Taken together all these costs point to the risk and uncertainty invariably related to the ownership of these rights.

Much of the substantial legal development of IPRs took place during the second half of the 20th century, along with the increased role that knowledge has been playing in the economic/industrial development since the end of the Second World War. The three functions mentioned earlier refer to the 'market failure' rationale for establishing IPRs, and are the basic elements of the current rationale of public action in this domain. However, to what extent and how do these regulatory features still fit within the current trends of the knowledge-based economy? Policy-makers are looking for answers to questions such as the adequacy of the current intellectual property law to protect new knowledge and the overall dynamism of the innovation process (van der Steen 2001).

Two sets of questions seem to emerge in this regard. The first addresses the optimal level of public action. That is, does the increasing internationalization of economic transactions need to be followed by international regulation of these rights? And how do national and international levels co-exist nowadays? How consistent are the principles of international free trade with the existence of nationally granted rights? The second set of questions regards 'how to regulate' these rights. Here the issues are the optimality of strong or soft proprietary regimes, the homogeneity/heterogeneity of legal forms, the flexibility of the legal exercise of IPRs, who should be entitled to earn them, and the ethical/substantive limits to what is patentable.

This chapter is devoted to European Union policy in the IPR regime. The rapid Europeanization of the IPR regime put in bold relief these two sets of open questions, in a domain that is of central concern to innovation policy and that is experiencing rapid transformations in all dimensions.

> European policy makers have reacted to the apparent rise of 'pro-patent' era with both unease and resolve. The unease comes from a widespread belief that the European 'innovation system' is unable to translate inventions into innovations as successfully as their American and Japanese competitors ... The resolve comes from the belief that new IPR policies could enhance the competitiveness of European firms. (Cowan and Paal 2000: 58)

THE EUROPEANIZATION OF IPRS

In an astonishingly short space of time, the EU has regulated common trademarks, copyrights, industrial designs and plant variety rights, whereas intense debates about a single community patent and the limits of patentability are being held among social groups and the Commission. Common EU regulation will invariably supersede national IPRs, generating one IPR framework that will reinforce the dynamics of the single market. This section presents the historical development, and introduces the general situation regarding IPRs before discussing, in greater detail, the political processes that are currently taking place concerning the regulation of patents in the European context.

How it All Began: Negative and Positive Integration

None of the European Communities' treaties envisaged, directly, the regulation of intellectual property rights as such. Besides the lack of regulation, article 295 (ex. art. 222) provided explicitly for the non-interference of the EU in matters of property at national level: 'the Treaty shall in no way prejudice the rules in Member States governing the system of property ownership'. Taken together, these two facts could from the start have effectively prevented any attempt to regulate IPRs at EU level. But this was not the case. The need for common IPRs has been related to the much wider topic of legal harmonization for the internal market, given the centrality that these rights have acquired in intra-EU trade during the last decades (Groves et al. 1993), and also because article 295 has been politically cast aside.[2]

As early as 1959, the Commission realized the potential hindrance that national IPR regulations might represent to the common market. Consequently, it prompted the creation of several working groups on the matter, which produced reports and drafts of the Community Patent convention and the Community Trade Mark regulation. However, several political pitfalls emerged on the way and neither of these saw the light of day.[3] This represented an abrupt end to the early integrationist attempts in this field. However, it did not represent a major obstacle to the development of the so-called negative integration process; that is, the approximation of national laws through European case law. By virtue of the extensive EU powers in competition policy, the European Court of Justice (ECJ) has long ruled on IPRs when they are abused, violating the principles of free trade and fair competition within the EU borders.[4] This created an interesting situation from the 1960s onwards when the ECJ developed substantive jurisprudence which had harmonizing effects at national level (negative integration) in the total absence of any direct EU regulations on these matters (positive integration). Even if some specialists regard this discrepancy as non-problematic and even perfectly consistent given the pre-eminence of competition law in the EU legal and economic context (Anderman 1998), the gap between negative and positive integration certainly induced a growing political willingness to regulate IPRs at EU level. Thus the political initiatives towards EU IPR regulations arose in 1985 with the thrust of the single market project, and were later wrapped up within the debates about the information society and knowledge-based economy.

The White Paper about the single market envisaged few and relatively unexciting proposals in the IPR field; namely, re-launching the failed

Community patent convention and trademark initiatives, and (as a novelty) the promise of prompt action in the field of biotechnological inventions and electronic microcircuits. These proposals were rapidly overtaken by a further series of legislative initiatives in the areas of copyrights, designs and patents. Since the early 1990s, the Commission has launched a far-reaching agenda for harmonizing IPRs in the European Union.

The General Situation in the EU Today

Table 3.2 provides an overview of the most important EU regulations on the IPR field to date, and tries also to put some order into this apparently disorganized bundle of regulations by relating them to their corresponding generic type of intellectual property rights. At first sight, the most remarkable feature is its relatively large size, and its relative novelty. As mentioned earlier, EU regulations on IPRs have, since the beginning of the 1990s, been in a process of rapid expansion.

Table 3.2 is a selection of the most relevant IPR regulation,[5] the primary aim of which is to offer the reader an overview of EU activity in this area. Therefore, this requires some general remarks about the way in which the EU has so far regulated intellectual property rights. Starting with copyrights, the first fact that strikes one is that this type of IPR has received considerable attention at EU level. Undoubtedly this is related to the new situation in which these rights have found themselves, due to advances in information and communication technologies, reflecting the difficulties and new challenges to the protection of ownership. It is also interesting that the regulation of copyrights seems to have started in the early 1990s with rather limited specific sectors. The functionally narrow regulations on issues such as databases, computer programs, renting and lending, or satellite broadcasting, give evidence of this. This phenomenon might indicate two things. One is the possible intense pressures from the affected sectors to obtain EU regulatory protection in a rapidly changing social and technological context; and another reason might be the more general need to introduce sectoral flexibility in the specific legal form of copyright. With the introduction in 2001 of the directive on copyrights in the information society, which overrides some previous regulations (among them the rental and lending directive), the protection of copyrights in the EU now has a single generic legislative framework.

Contrasting with the functional and sectoral approach to copyrights, the EU has regulated designs and trademarks in a more generic manner since the very beginning. Both legal entities were first harmonized, approximating national regulations in these matters, then were developed more recently as single common EU-wide legal entities in their own right by the creation of 'Community trademarks' and 'Community designs'. These EU legal entities

Table 3.2   Most relevant EU regulations on intellectual property rights, 2002

Generic type of IPR	Area	Regulation	Remarks
Copyrights	Harmonization in the information society	Directive 2001/29/EC; OJ L 167 22.06.2001 p. 10	
	Computer programs	Council Directive 91/250/EEC; OJ L 122 17.05.1991 p. 42	
	Rental and lending rights	Council Directive 92/100/EEC; OJ L 346 27.11.1992 p. 61	
	Satellite broadcasting and cable retransmissions	Council Directive 93/83/EEC; OJ L 248 06.10.1993 p. 15	
	Databases	Directive 96/9/EC; OJ L 077 27.03.1996 p. 20	
Trademarks	Approximation of laws	Council Directive 89/104/EEC; OJ L 040 11.02.1989 p. 1	
	Community trade mark	Council Regulation (EC) No. 40/94 of 20 December 1993; OJ L 011 14.01.1994 p. 1	
Designs	Harmonization	Directive 98/71/EC; OJ L 289 28.10.1998 p. 28	
	Community design	Council Regulation EC/6/2002, OJ L 3, 5.1.2002 p. 1	
Utility models	Harmonization	Commission proposal Com (1999) 309 final	Not regulated yet
Plant variety rights	Community plant variety rights	Council Regulation (EC) No. 2100/94 of 27 July 1994; OJ L 227 01.09.1994 p. 1	
Patents	Community patent	Commission proposal Com (2000) 412 final	Not regulated yet
	Patentability of biological inventions	Directive 98/44/EEC; OJ L 213, 30.07.98 p. 13	Highly controversial
	Patentability of computer-implemented inventions	Commission proposal Com (2002) 92 final	Not regulated yet

Source: Author's elaboration from EU legal database, EUR-lex.

are managed by the Office for the Harmonization of the Internal Market (OHIM), which was created in 1994 and established in Alicante (Spain). This Office operates in a similar way to the European Patent Office (EPO), seeking organizational and budgetary autonomy from the other EU institutions. Something similar took place with 'plant variety rights', a specific form of IPR, when in 1994 'Community plant variety rights' were introduced, managed by the Community Plant Variety Office.

The 'utility model' is another IPR legal entity that is on the way to being harmonized. These are also called 'petty-patents', as they ensure protection for minor technical inventions that have a practical value. Utility models are intended to operate alongside the conventional patent law, and are of special interest for small firms. In Germany they are increasingly used to provide legal protection for inventions that have a patent application pending (Vinje 1995). Last but not least, patent regulations in Europe do not yet have an EU regulatory framework. The story of the Community patent is an interesting and long one, especially when compared with the successful 'European patent'. The next section examines this. Until now the only existing directive applies to the patentability of biotechnological inventions. As we will see later, this topic has turned out to be highly sensitive politically, given the bioethical elements involved in it. Finally, one of the newest Community proposals – the patentability of software – has also generated substantial political uneasiness. The idea of allowing 'software patents' was strongly contested in the informal consultations that preceded the official launch of the legislative proposal.

Before moving beyond this point, it is worth remembering that there are other EU regulatory frameworks directly affecting IPRs. Besides the direct regulations harmonizing or creating Community entities examined in Table 3.2, the EU has long since established the legal framework for the use of these rights in the context of the single market. Technology-related agreements between firms or certain ways of managing intellectual property rights' assets might go against the free and fair competition of the single market. With the purpose of defining the legal framework of technology-related operations, the EU created in the mid-1980s a series of regulations that contained 'block exemptions' to the general competition rules. The most significant of these for the IPR regime in Europe were the regulations on patent licences and know-how licensing.[6] In 1994, the Commission proposed adopting a single 'technology transfer' block exemption, that substitutes and amends both previous regulations into one single legal text, adopted in 1996.[7] The new regulation provides an exemption from article 81.1 (ex. art. 85.1), for know-how and patent licensing, but it also limits this exemption when the licensee has a strong position in the market, with 40 per cent of market share for substitutable products. This was strongly criticized by European industrial groups, which did not agree with the 'market share' limitations (Vinje 1995).

Community vs. European Patent

In spite of the increasing EU competences in IPR regulation, the question about how to regulate patents in Europe is still unresolved. The political debates in the early 1970s about this issue led to the establishment of two (supposedly complementary) frameworks, namely the European patent and the Community patent. The European patent, a legal entity created by the 1973 Munich Convention,[8] has operated successfully ever since, providing a single procedural mechanism for granting such rights in as many of the signatory countries as the patentee wishes to, and pays for. On the other hand, the Community patent as envisaged in the 1975 Luxembourg Convention, and later in the 1989 agreement,[9] was never enforced due to lack of sufficient ratification. The unborn Community patent foresaw a single, unitary, and autonomous protection right valid throughout the EU. In other words, the creation of a truly one-for-all patent within the EU context.

The success of the European patent, with more than 140 000 patent applications per year (EPO 2001), contrasts sharply with the political quarrels that hindered the creation of the Community patent as a legal entity. This raises a very fundamental question as to why the great interest that innovators have shown in European patent procedural advantages has not been able to persuade the political forces blocking the advancement towards a Community patent. It could be expected that innovators would be at least equally interested in it, since the Community patent is a single regulatory mechanism for the overall EU area, reducing the costs of patenting and the legal uncertainty of operating in 15 different regulatory/judicial systems. These two major advantages of the Community patent were put forward again by the European Commission in the second half of the 1990s in a Green Paper on the Community patent (Commission 1997),[10] in what has been a renewed political effort to go ahead with the issue.

The main aim of this Green Paper is to come to grips with two of the political problems that have so far represented the major hurdles for realization of the Community patent: language costs and judicial competences (Commission 1997). The high profile political conflicts about language plagued the failed negotiations of the 1989 Convention, ending with the idea that each contracting state could demand a translation. This means that the three-language solution efficiently working in the EPO (German, English, French) was rejected, excessively raising the costs for individual applicants and patent holders.[11] This decision effectively blocked the implementation of the Convention, as industrial organizations/firms lost interest in it (Doern 1997). However, the five-language agreement on trade marks (German, English, French, Italian and Spanish) in the mid-1990s opened up new prospects in this regard (Krieger 1998). The question of judicial competences is more complex, as it is related to the legal nature the Community patent should have. The failed 1989 Convention on the Community patent envisaged that questions of infringement, validation, and revocation of patents were to be a competence of national judicial authorities. This has long posed the problem of uncertainty related to the territoriality effects of litigation, since 'national judges would have been able to declare a Community patent invalid with effect for the entire territory of the Community' (Commission 2000: 5). The Green Paper prompted a clear division of tasks between the national judicial instances, which would only be entitled to deal with infringement cases, and the bodies operating at Community level, dealing with the final validation/revocation of the patent. In the follow-up to the Green Paper (Commission 1999b), there was a wide acceptance for the idea of including the Community patent within the 'acquis communautaire', rather than through the ratification of the 1989 Convention. However, the problems of language proved more resilient, as some parties insisted on the idea that patent applications should be accepted and dealt with in all the EU official languages.

On the basis of these long-term discussions, the recent proposal for a regulation has presented some interesting solutions, not just concerning language and judicial organization, but also with regard to the relationship of the Community patent in the European patent system (Commission 2000). Starting with this, the Commission envisages a 'symbiosis' of both systems that in reality means the integration of the future Community patent within the well-functioning procedures of the Munich Convention. Therefore, the EU as such has to become a signatory party of the Convention, and the European Patent Office the patent granting agency. As to the language problem, the Commission has suggested the translation of the patent documents into one of the Office's three working languages, and the claims (the technical descriptive part of the patent) into the two others. This, it is argued, would dramatically reduce the costs of patenting. Equally ambitious is the judicial structure foreseen in the proposal. Here the Commission suggests a centralized system in order to guarantee 'Community level legal certainty'. A new Court will be established – the 'Community Patent Court' – with chambers of first instance and appeal. The Commission argues the need for such an independent Court on the basis of the fact that the current Court of First Instance of the ECJ does not have the necessary technical qualifications to deal with such matters. This new Court will have jurisdiction over some categories of actions, most notably infringement and validity of the patent, and preliminary rulings raised by national courts. Other matters, such as the transfer of patents or contractual licences, will fall automatically within the scope of national Courts.

Whereas in the coming sections we will discuss the effects of this proposal in terms of the breadth and strength of patent rights protection in the EU, it is worth remarking that some economic studies seem to demonstrate that the regulatory uniformity of the Community patent will have positive effects in economic terms (Dijk and Cayseele 1995).

THE INTERNATIONAL SCENE

The Europeanization of IPRs has been taking place simultaneously with the enforcement of the most far-reaching international IPR regulation ever: the TRIPS agreement (Agreement on Trade-related Aspects of Intellectual Property Rights). Agreed in the context of the Uruguay Round, TRIPS sets important aspects of IPR matters under the realm of the WTO. There have been two main consequences of TRIPS for the EU, namely, the re-definition of the trade policy competences, as IPRs have become a 'new trade issue'; and issues related to the legal implementation of TRIPS. By examining these two issues, this section will provide evidence that the limits of what is national, European and international have been re-cast since the 1990s, and that the EU is playing a significant part in IPR regulation on the international scene.

Rapid Internationalization during the 1990s

The regulation, exercise and protection of IPRs has traditionally been exercised at national level. Yet, since the end of the 19th century a series of international agreements on the matter have stipulated basic international procedures. The first ever international considerations on the exercise of IPRs were codified in the Paris Convention for the protection of industrial property of 1883, still valid today with 90 signatory states.[12] This Convention is administered by the World Intellectual Property Organization (WIPO), a UN agency based in Stockholm. The internationalization of IPRs took another firm step in the 1970s with the world-wide Patent Cooperation Treaty (PCT), also administered by the WIPO. The PCT provides the basis for international harmonization and integration in the application, search and examination stages of patenting. Something similar for trade marks came in 1994 with the Trademark Law Treaty. A common feature of the international conventions concerning IPRs is that they have set a minimum standard of protection, and they have enshrined two basic legal principles, namely 'national treatment' and 'independence of rights' at world level.

Since the 1990s, there has been renewed interest in IPRs along with the economic internationalization of trade, industrial production, and finance. The conclusion of the TRIPS agreement brought about a new dimension for IPRs at international level, because, for the first time, it directly related questions of trade to the protection of these rights (Maskus 2000b). As Govarere has pointed out:

> The linking of the issue of intellectual property protection with international trade is a relatively new phenomenon and is chiefly inspired by the growing awareness by the industrialised countries of the economic impact of intellectual property rights and their value as trade assets. (Govarere 1996: 37)

What is special about the TRIPS agreement is not just that the set of standards of protection and enforcement is higher than prior international conventions, but that it has the WTO system of dispute settlements.

The conclusion of TRIPS left a number of issues open that were supposed to be tackled in the Millennium Round of the WTO (Seattle, January 2000). These were mainly the questions of enactment, parallel imports and the limits of patentability (Tancer and Tancer 1999). Of these three issues enactment is undoubtedly the most crucial one. Since the signature of TRIPS, several developing countries have expressed their dissatisfaction with the general goals of the agreement, and hence are reluctant to enact it fully beyond the 5–10 year transition period initially granted (Lal Das 1999). Concerns are that an international agreement like TRIPS limits their possibilities for catching up in terms of economic development through 'imitative-copying' practices (Correa 2000). The divide between developed and developing countries is quite large when it comes to issues surrounding IPR. This is because the economically developed countries would like to have a harmonized and strong, protective international regulatory regime, whereas the other countries see this as a barrier to their industrial and economic growth (Smith 1999). The failure of the Millennium Round was partly the result of this gap, which turned out to be diplomatically unbridgeable (Kyriakou 2000; Maskus 2000a), but this situation might be reversing now.

The Doha meeting in November 2001 agreed on a new WTO round of negotiations, and on the fact that the agenda should include IPRs. However, the backdrop of future IPR negotiations is going to be different from that of the Millennium Round. One of the reasons for this is the highly political controversies that arose in 2000 regarding the case of AIDS medicines in South Africa. Social concerns were that TRIPS regulations interfered with the right to access cheap medicines (Skjalm 2001). Once the political turmoil had settled down, the WTO members signed a declaration stating that TRIPS should be interpreted in a way that supports public health by promoting both access to existing medicines and the creation of new ones. Furthermore, the Doha meeting extended the deadline for developing countries to apply provisions on pharmaceutical patents until 1 January 2016. Nevertheless, several important points remain on the table for the future round, among them the enactment of TRIPS and the review of article 27.3(b) dealing with the patentability or non-patentability of plant and animal inventions.

Negotiating TRIPS: One Voice for the EU?

One of the most direct political impacts of TRIPS in the EU context was the question of whether the Commission could negotiate it on the same basis as EU trade policy. Trade policy is one of the most integrated policy areas in the EU, where the EU enjoys exclusive competences. This means that the Commission has a large degree of autonomy in international trade negotiations, where it represents EU member states. In the 1950s, when the EC treaties were signed, IPRs were not considered to be related to international trade. This situation changed dramatically in the 1990s when the IPRs became one of the so-called 'new trade issues'.[13]

The Commission's expectations that IPR matters could equally be subsumed under its exclusive competences together with the 'old issues' of trade policy were not accepted by the member states. The dispute was solved by the European Court of Justice in 1994, which ruled that member states and the EU have 'joint competences' to negotiate and conclude the GATS and TRIPS agreements, and an obligation to cooperate[14] (Govarere 1996; Cremona 2000). Ever since, experts have differed in their approach to this Solomonic ECJ judgement. For some, not least the Commission itself, this opinion has rendered more difficult the ability of the EU to speak with one voice on the international scene. In this sense as Mortensen has pointed out, 'the risk of defection is more credible, and negotiations thus more difficult, when it is uncertain who has the mandate to negotiate' (Mortensen 1998: 225). He also points to the difficulties that the Commission faced in the elaboration of the 'code of conduct' with the Council – the informal practice of coordinating negotiating positions between the EU and all its member states. Other authors have looked positively at the ECJ decision as member states score a clear victory in this 'sovereignty camp', regaining power and control of this highly integrated policy area (Meunier and Nicolaïdis 1999). Cremona, though, emphasizes the legal and political constitutional effects of such a judgement in terms of who has the power to alter Treaty obligations:

> To have extended the scope of article 133 to cover all trade in services and all those aspects of intellectual property rights contained in the TRIPS agreement would have in fact got very close to the re-definition of the CCP (common commercial policy) in terms of a general external economic policy proposed by the Commission and rejected by the Member States at Maastrict. The Court was thus not only recognizing the sensitivity of Member States in relation to the specific subject matter under discussion, but confirming the locus of the political power to aler Treaty obligations. (Cremona 2000: 13)

Celebrated or criticized, scholars agree that the ECJ decision has generated quite a lot of uncertainty as to how this 'shared competence' and 'the duty to cooperate' should be operationalized, particularly in terms of dispute settlement procedures under the WTO. A few years later, the Amsterdam compromise reworded article 133 (ex. art. 113), stating that IPR matters can fall under exclusive EU competence if the Council unanimously agrees (which has not been the case yet). Nevertheless,

> as the Court points out, intellectual property rights are at least as much about internal trade as international trade. We are therefore not only concerned with the appropriate legal base for concluding an international agreement, but also with the implications for the agreement for internal harmonization measures. (Cremona 2000: 20)

The next section examines this.

TRIPS in the EU Legal System

The broad regulatory framework provided by TRIPS is, so far, the most ambitious attempt to harmonize IPRs at international level.[15] Therefore, the question of how to enforce TRIPS within the EU legal system is of great importance. Two major legal questions have emerged in this regard: first, whether the European Court of Justice is competent to rule on TRIPS-related issues; and secondly, whether TRIPS is directly applicable in the EU and its different national regulatory system.

The question of the ECJ's role in relation to TRIPS is interesting in legal and political terms. As a result of the Hermès case (1998), the ECJ has found itself competent to interpret a provision of the TRIPS agreement, despite the doubts raised in this regard by the member states intervening in the case (the Netherlands, France and the United Kingdom)[16] (Desmendt 1998). The ECJ put forward three arguments. First, TRIPS, which was concluded by the EU and ratified by its member states, did not stipulate any direct obligations to member states individually. Secondly, the Hermès case was about trade-marks, and the EU had recently regulated such matters, so implying that this also falls under EU legal competences. Thirdly, there is a common interest in having a uniform judicial interpretation in cases like this where matters fall simultaneously under both EU and national legal competences.

The second legal question, regarding the direct applicability of TRIPS, is also very interesting, mainly because, compared with the general WTO agreements, the TRIPS agreement regulates private rights and is based on the nationality of individuals (Dörmer 2000). Since the early 1970s, the ECJ has consistently argued that international agreements concluded by the EU with third parties under article 300 (ex. art. 228) are part of the EU legal system and bind the EU and its member states.[17] Moreover, the ECJ has also stipulated that the legal provisions of these international agreements have direct applicability in those cases where the nature of the agreement lends itself to it, and the invoked provision is unconditional and sufficiently precise. This did not apply to the GATT, because, the ECJ argued, its provisions were not unconditional, given that dispute settlements were based on negotiation.[18] In the Hermès case, the ECJ refused to rule on the direct effect of TRIPS in the context of the newly established WTO dispute settlement.[19] This was a major disappointment for experts working in this area, given the centrality of this matter for the EU legal order on external relations, and it left the question of binding international agreements unsolved (Dörmer 2000).

However, this issue was raised shortly after in the Dior case.[20] Here the ECJ was openly confronted with the question of the direct effect of article 50(6) of TRIPS, posed by the Dutch High Court. The ECJ ruled that this TRIPS article does not have direct effect because its function is not that of creating rights on which individuals can rely in the Court by virtue of Community law. Nevertheless, the ruling went on to state that national courts were required to apply their national rules 'as far as possible in the light of the wording and purpose of article 50 of the TRIPS Agreement'. As General Advocate Jacobs put it, the Dior judgement reflects the Court's earlier approach to the provisions of GATT,[21] having avoided any significant jurisprudential turning point.

What makes Article 50 of the TRIPS agreement so special and judicially so important? This article is quite atypical in the sense that it regulates some procedural aspects in situations of potential IPR infringement; namely, it sets a restrictive time limit on all provisional measures raised against potential infringers.[22] In other words, the TRIPS agreement aims at delimiting the harmful effects on potential infringers in a more precise manner than some national regulations do. Wisely enough, Jacobs is of the opinion that in those situations where national regulations provide no limits at all, national courts should reflect the wording of TRIPS, which is more restrictive. The paradoxical situation in this regard is that, whereas TRIPS has been fiercely criticized as imposing regulatory measures that benefit IPR owners (Braithwaite and Drahos 2000; Sell 1999), it turns out, at least in this legal caveat, that this is not the case.[23]

All in all, the TRIPS agreement is a significant example of the current trends in the international economic and legal order. Some authors interpret the rapid institutionalization of the WTO trade regime in the 1990s as a building block of a global economic polity with clear constitutionalization elements (Mortensen 2000). This trend has re-opened the issue of how to organize the authority, legitimacy and position of the EU legal order vis-à-vis national and international regulations. Besides the formal question of who is entitled to negotiate and to shape the external policy of the EU, lies the question of who is entitled, and how, to shape the content and interpretation of intellectual property rights and their exercise in the EU, and what sort of regulatory regime is emerging from this. As we saw in the Dior case, in spite of the lack of direct effect of TRIPS articles, some international legal caveats might still result in significant homogenizing effects within the European single market. This is to say that it is not just the conventional boundaries of the legal systems that are currently being challenged in the increasingly multi-layered multi-level legal authority structure, but what might be more important from the point of view of innovation policy, the outcome in terms of the content and exercise of IPRs is being substantially transformed too.

WHAT RIGHTS, WHOSE RIGHTS? PUBLIC AND PRIVATE INTERESTS IN THE EU REGULATIONS

The two previous sections have focused on the relationship between national, EU and international regulatory trends in IPRs, and their rapid Europeanization. However, beyond the question of borders and competences, regulation always entails the enshrinement of specific values and worldviews in a (re)consideration of the nature of what is being regulated. The regulation of intellectual property rights is a matter of striking a balance between public and private interests; that is, between the exclusive rights granted to an individual or a firm, and the public interest of availability of the knowledge/properties embodied in the right. All in all, the balance is the result of (sometimes hard) political negotiations, where not only economic interests are at stake, but also the overall understanding of how patents and other IPRs induce (or not) innovativeness and general welfare. This is a much debated matter, especially in the wake of the trend towards strong and wider IPR regimes.

> Recently, the opportunities and disruptive effects created by technological change itself have set in motion economic and political pressures that are tending to unbalance the innovation systems of many of the world's economies. Greater reliance is being placed on the 'property' solution, by extending the domain of private ownership and strengthening the legal protection of intellectual property rights. (David 2000: 2)

Two matters are of importance here, the first being the extension of the IPR regime; namely, what might be patented, and under what conditions. In the realm of the EU this is being debated particularly in the areas of software and biotechnology. Secondly, how should the contents of these rights be designed? Does strong protection of IPRs enhance innovativeness?

The Limits of Patentability: A Hot Issue

The limits of patentability are a sensitive political issue, mainly because they define, by exclusion, which things might be entitled to become private property, as well as defining the breadth of patents. This topic has hit the headlines in Europe in the last two years in relation to both software and biotechnology patents. Examining the developments in these two sectors will pin down the statement that the emerging EU regulatory regime in IPRs is being conceived in quite extensive terms, and that the difficult balance between public and private interests has been overly weighted in favour of the second.

Information and communication technologies are challenging the conventional intellectual property regime, especially the formal terms under which software products might be appropriable. The question of patenting software is a good example of the difficulties in striking a balance between public and private interests when the object of patentability is extended. Though they are widely used in the US, and to a lesser extent in Europe (by some member states and the EPO), software patents are controversial because they grant a much higher level of protection than copyrights – the legal entity that has traditionally been used for this type of product – and because they are extensively used by large companies but rarely by SMEs, who prefer copyright or secrecy.[24] Some social groups have expressed justified fears that software patents have potentially large anti-competitive effects in the development of the sector due to the easy generation of 'essential patents' that effectively block related knowledge (particularly algorithms), and due to the likely predatory attitude of large companies hindering the development of dynamic SMEs by the threat of unbearable costs of litigation. The latest round of consultation launched in 2000 has manifestly shown the wide gap between the interests of large firms and those of SMEs and open source developers. Nothing daunted, the Commission has put forward a legislative proposal for the harmonization of software patents in Europe, arguing that there is a clear case for such legal action, since the economic interests of large companies have a special significance for the overall European interest:

> Thus although the responses [of the consultation process] in this category [in favour of software patents] were numerically much fewer that those supporting the open source approach, there seems little doubt that the balance of economic weight taking into account total jobs and investment involved is in favour of harmonisation along the lines suggested in the paper. (Commission 2002: 4)

With such an argument, the Commission has followed the signals of large industrial groups, in the belief that extending the scope of protection will foster economic development in this sector. The equation is simple: more IP protection will generate more innovation. The new regulation will probably affect innovators asymmetrically, in such a way that SMEs will suddenly be confronted with new legal requirements and boundaries that will have a direct impact on their daily management of innovative activities. Aware of this large–small firm dilemma, the Commission has attempted to address it by actively promoting the use of patents among SMEs. But this is based on a rather unrealistic and simplistic expectation that SMEs can easily reap the benefits and bear the costs involved in patenting and litigation. As a qualified commentator has noted: '[the] EU institutions are pursuing the goal not only of harmonizing intellectual property legislation, but also, and at least as vigorously, of strengthening it at the same time' (Vinje 1995). Following some legal experts, the proposal seems to assume implicitly that algorithms and business practices are not patentable (Raasteen and Skibsted 2002). If this is the case, then it means that the Commission has partly responded to the fears of a broad patent regime. However, since this is only assumed implicitly, an explicit legal formulation prohibiting the patentability of both (algorithms and business practices) would be desirable in order to generate an unequivocal legal understanding on the matter, and to avoid the real threat of anti-competitive effects in this sector.

Indeed, if the defining limits of patentability seem to be difficult in the software sector, they are even more complex in biotechnology, given their ethical dimension and the unclear boundary between inventions and discoveries. It is not surprising then that the European directive on biotechnological inventions passed in 1998 has been highly controversial.[25] This directive aims at clarifying the question about the patentability of biotechnology inventions at EU level by seeking uniform approximation of national laws. However, it has run into trouble due to the high stakes at play, the large differences in national regulations and the extended practice of the EPO granting biotechnology-related patents[26] (Vinje 1995).

Another author reminds us that whereas TRIPS has given free hands to signatory states to exclude patentability of biotechnological inventions on the grounds of public morality, it is the European Convention on Human Rights (ECHR) which represents the ultimate legal basis for the interpretation of what constitutes morality (Ford 1997). Predictably enough, the political debates related to the EU directive in this question have turned out to be quite hard and convoluted. The Commission's first proposal was launched in 1988, but the European Parliament made full use of its powers in the co-decision procedure and, in March 1995, rejected the conciliation committee agreement, vetoing the proposal. Shortly after, the Commission launched a second attempt with a new legislative proposal, which was finally accepted by the European Parliament in 1998 on the basis of several amendments that clarify further the prohibition to patent the human body. However, the story has not finished here since the directive on biotechnology patents it is still provoking much political and social concern. The very same year the directive was passed, the Netherlands presented a case to the ECJ for its nullification on several grounds, namely that it:

> (i) is incorrectly based on Article 100a of the Treaty; (ii) is contrary to the principle of subsidiarity; (iii) infringes the principle of legal certainty; (iv) is incompatible with international obligations; (v) breaches fundamental rights; and (vi) was not properly adopted since the definitive version of the proposal submitted to the Parliament and the Council was not decided on by the college of Commissioners.[27]

While waiting for an ECJ decision, the opinion of General Advocate Jacobs was against nullification because the Dutch arguments are of a technical character. Despite the understandable concerns of Dutch authorities that 'irresponsible pursuit of biotechnological research may have consequences which are ethically unacceptable', the directive is concerned with the patentability of biotechnological inventions and not their use.[28] In the meantime, most EU members have avoided implementing the directive.

Are Broad Patents Good for Europe?

The breadth of patents goes beyond previous questions about the limits of patentability, and includes another dimension worth exploring. In the US, the debate about broad patents has lately become very intense. This has not just involved the question of software patents, with 'business practices' and algorithms being widely patented (Ratliff 2000), but also the nature of patents being granted to 'basic science' knowledge, most typically held by universities and research centres. Some leading economists have argued that the US tendency to award broad patents grants disproportionate market power to the corresponding rights holders, with noticeable anti-competitive effects on the overall economy, and limited proved positive effect on the innovation process (Mazzoleni and Nelson 1998; Jaffe 1999; Mowery and Ziedonis 2000). Is Europe moving in the same direction? This is not an easy question to answer. On the one hand, the Commission does not seem to be cautious about constraining the patentability of software products. On the other hand, the rows about biotechnological inventions indicate that much wider limits have already been granted there. The breadth of the regime, however, depends also on other factors such as, for example, the type of patent owners (large firms, small firms, or universities, etc.) and the way in which the legal system reacts to the bottlenecks emerging from that.

Economists have been discussing the optimal breadth of patents and the essential dilemma between the private appropriation of knowledge and its public diffusion. Some recent theoretical advances in this issue have emphasized that the trade-off between diffusion and appropriation should not be understood in terms of a binary choice for policy-makers. Rather, 'a set of modalities and arrangements do exist that would ultimately allow for a reconciliation of both goals' in different national innovation systems (Foray 1995: 122). Diffusion for example, takes place to a larger or lesser extent through the disclosure/transparency function of the IPR system.

When regulating Community patents, the EU should seriously address the matter of 'broad patents', and consider two facts: the potentially distorting effects of the competitive dynamics of the single market through the innovators' use of excessive market power; and the potentially sub-optimal social effects of 'privatizing' large areas of knowledge. As ETAN has recently put it: 'social benefits are not necessarily increased by more patenting'[29] (ETAN 1999: 12). One regulatory way of approaching this might be to state in a precise manner the terms by which the principles for granting a patent, namely 'non-obviousness', 'innovation' and 'industrial application', should be interpreted. This alone would provide a satisfactory legal mechanism to avoid over-broad patents, a trend already put into practice by the EPO, which has recently been dismissing broad patent applications through strict interpretation of the legal principle of 'innovativeness' (rather than based on the 'sufficiency' argument, as it was doing before) (Karet 1996).

The report of the expert group ETAN and other authors has indicated the existence of another type of problem; namely, the situation of 'patent-blocking', also called 'anticommons property' or 'patent thicket' where many patents cover small and very interdependent parcels of knowledge in a way that means none of the owners can exploit them adequately and that makes commercialization a very complex matter (Foray 2001; David 2000). This results partly in a similar situation to that of broad patents, since there is an effective blockage of patent exploitation. The incremental nature of most current technical knowledge aggravates this situation (Foray 1995), where coordination problems arise despite the wide practices of cross-licensing (Shapiro 2001). The ETAN recommendations listed in Figure 3.1 suggest a precisely balanced regulatory approach to the public–private interests in this particular matter.

Is a Strong IPR Regime Good for Europe?

Closely linked to the issue of the expanding domain of IPRs (in terms of both patentability and broad patents), the emerging EU regime conceives of IPR protection in quite a strong manner. A strong regime means that the private rights granted have few restrictions and it entails high levels of protection to the private owner, but this might have negative effects on the public interest.

- More effective filtering of insignificant patents by raising the standards of non-obviousness and usefulness, steepening the renewal fee schedule, and implementing more efficient patent examination procedures;
- Using a two-tier structure with patents and utility models;
- Improving mechanisms for technology markets and transfer, including more liberal attitudes towards patent pooling and technology sharing; schemes for collecting rights and clearing-house procedures; cross-licensing and block-licensing incentives;
- Control of monopolistic abuse by reducing the scope and length of protection and/or more consistent use of compulsory licensing;
- Reduction of legal uncertainty by faster and cheaper validation of rights and dispute resolution.

Source: ETAN (1999: 22).

Figure 3.1   ETAN recommendations for avoiding the 'patent-blocking' problem

Three examples to illustrate such trends are the Directive of copyright protection of databases (1996),[30] the harmonization of copyrights in the information society,[31] and the compulsory licence caveats in the 2000 proposal for a Community patent.

To start with the EU databases copyright regulation, David's analysis identifies some legal novelties that made it notoriously strong. These legal innovations have broken with long-established traditions of national copyright regulations. For example, the EU directive discards the distinction between 'original expressive matter' and 'pre-existing expressive matter' with the result that '[it] will allow a database maker to qualify for renewal of the 15 year term of exclusive rights over the database as a whole' (David 2000: 27). Another novelty refers to the question of licences: 'investors in database production can always deny third parties the right to use pre-existing data value-added applications, even when the third parties are willing to pay royalties on licences for such use' (p. 27). The notorious lack of compulsory licensing provisions implies that 'the directive opens the door for the construction of indefinitely renewable monopolies in both non-regeneratable and regeneratable scientific data' (p. 27). Furthermore, free access and use of data can only be for purposes of 'illustration in teaching or research' rather than the conventional legal formula of 'fair use for research'. The shallowness of the term 'illustration' renders this caveat unclear and possibly unusable for scientific activity. Furthermore, this creates a twofold risk for public sector-funded research programmes:

> one is the threat to data quality in the separating of the database creation and maintenance from the scientific expertise of the research community that creates and uses the data; the other is the resulting squeeze on public research resources, as already restrictive appropriations would have to be spent on purchasing data and database licenses. (David 2000: 28)

A second example of an unnecessarily strong EU IPR regulation is the recently passed directive on the harmonization of copyrights in the information society. As the European Commission recognized in the proposal, the balance between private and public interests has not been easy to strike (Commission 1999a). However, the high levels of protection that the directive stipulates regarding the rights of reproduction, communication and distribution of the copyright owner have significantly limited the possibilities of free dissemination.

The directive establishes only one exception to the exclusive rights in a copyright, which affects all the EU 15. The directive, though, does allow member states to provide for further exceptions, such as, for example, reproduction 'for the sole purpose of illustration for teaching or scientific research' (art. 5.3 (a)), if they wish to do so. This might be defined as a sort of 'fûit en avant' from the EU, which envisages only one exception (and in quite restrictive terms), then leaves the member states with the task of choosing among the rest. In other words, states are supposed to scale down the highly protective rights granted by the EU regulation through the optional selection of a pre-established set of caveats for diffusion. However, this creates a difficult dynamic in the decision-making, insofar as the interests at play are most unlikely to be willing to 'lose' at national level the rights already granted by the EU. Only strong counter-lobbying at national level in support of more diffusion might be able to balance that. However, diffusion-oriented lobbyists are highly unlikely to be powerful in member states with low IPR-awareness. Not that the EU impedes, as such, the establishment of a national regulatory system that is more diffusion-oriented than the EU regime, but the scaling down procedure effectively forecloses such a move. The alternative situation – a diffusion-oriented EU regime, where states are left to upgrade the protective realm of rights – would certainly have been better in order to achieve a common EU protective level while ensuring that national regulations are truly adapted to the concomitant informal social practices on this matter. Summing up, this directive will almost certainly result in a 'strong' protection of rights owners, given the few and restrictive exceptions for dissemination, with no real possibility of using the conventional notion of 'fair use'.

Last, but not least, one of the most visible elements showing how strong an

IPR regime is, is contained in the compulsory licensing caveats for patents. In the newly proposed Community patent regulation of 2000, article 21 foresees three different grounds under which the Commission should grant a compulsory licence: if the patent has not been exploited or has been insufficiently exploited; if a national patent granted previously infringes a Community patent granted afterwards; or if there are situations of crisis or emergency. This article also makes specific restrictions regarding semi-conductor technology, and determines that the patent owner should be able to react in good time. With these measures, the Commission seems to have generally followed the relatively narrow scope envisaged by article 31 of TRIPS (Borrás and Ougaard 2001). In real terms, only the first of these grounds, that of insufficient exploitation, seems to go slightly beyond the TRIPS norms. It might still be too early to assess the potential effect of these EU caveats; however, it looks as if the Commission has avoided a more 'generous' listing of grounds for compulsory licensing that would effectively limit the potential abuse of monopolistic power granted in the patent. Another point to be noticed here is that the Commission, and not the member states, is the one who holds this controlling power.

These three examples indicate that the IPR regime emerging in the EU seems to be rather 'strong' in terms of the rights granted to the patent/IPR-owner. Of course, the primary goal of any IPR regime should be to protect rights holders, but this does not need to be at the expense of the wider public interest. Only time will tell to what extent this regime is optimal for stimulating the innovation process, and respects the public interest of diffusing knowledge.

CURRENT PATENT RATIOS IN EUROPE: DIVERSE AND LAGGING BEHIND?

The Commission has repeatedly shown concern about the relative low patenting propensity in Europe, and a subsequent willingness to create an IPR culture. However, there are very diverse opinions in Europe concerning this matter, from the high patenting propensity countries like Sweden and Germany, to the lowest patenting cultures of Spain, Portugal and Greece, and from the large patenting sectors like biotechnology and machinery, to low patenting sectors such as textiles and agro-food. According to the data to be presented in this section, these differences are unlikely to disappear just through efforts to establish EU legal harmonization. Something similar might come from the Central and Eastern European candidate countries which, despite their rapid legal harmonization in accordance with EU requests, will continue to show low patenting ratios.

Intra-EU Diversity

There are large differences in patenting ratios among EU states and regions, and among EU productive sectors. Statistical data about patents provide one of the most clear-cut pictures of the diversity that characterizes the overall EU innovative situation; diversity relating not just to the innovativeness of a region or country, but also to the dominant patenting culture in each territory, which can differ notably. It is easy to anticipate that the EU cohesion countries will score low in terms of patent applications, however, there are still interesting surprises when looking at the Eurostat and OECD annual statistics.

The OECD's 'inventiveness coefficient' is based on the number of resident patent applications per 10 000. This simple coefficient actually indicates the patenting propensity of resident innovators in the national patenting authorities (see Table 3.3).

Surprises in Table 3.3 are the low position of Belgium and the Netherlands in relation to patenting applications at national level. Alternatively, Eurostat data are based on patent applications submitted to the EPO in Munich, which

Table 3.3   Patenting propensity ('inventiveness coefficient'): resident patent applications/10 000 population, EU member states, various years

	1994	1995	1996	1997
Germany	4.6	4.7	5.2	5.5
Sweden	4.6	4.5	4.7	4.7
Finland	4.6	4.1	4.3	4.6
United Kingdom	3.2	3.2	3.1	3.1
Denmark	2.5	2.4	2.5	2.5
Austria	2.5	2.2	2.3	2.3
France	2.1	2.1	2.2	2.2
Ireland	2.3	2.4	2.2	2.2
Luxembourg	1.4	–	2.1	2.1
The Netherlands	1.2	1.4	1.6	1.6
Italy	1.4	–	1.2	–
Belgium	0.8	0.8	0.9	0.9
Spain	0.6	0.5	0.6	0.6
Greece	–	0.4	0.4	–
Portugal	0.1	0.1	0.1	0.1

Source: OECD (2000).

grants patents on a pan-European basis. Using this new ranking, the propensity to patent at international pan-European level scores differently from the one at national level. Belgium and the Netherlands are better positioned here; while the UK innovators seem to be keen on patenting at national level.

Country ranks should not obscure the very clear diversity that exists among productive sectors – Table 3.4 shows patent applications at the EPO on this basis. Sharp differences emerge between the traditional low-tech sectors like paper and textiles and the high patent propensity of sectors such as electricity and electronics or pharmaceuticals and chemistry.

Table 3.4   EU patent applications at EPO by IPC sections from EU-15, 1999* (percentage of total)

Sector	Percentage
Textiles, paper	2.2
Fixed constructions	4.9
Mechanical engineering, lighting, heating, weapons, blasting	10.1
Physics	14.1
Chemistry, metallurgy	14.4
Human necessities	15.2
Electricity	17.7
Performing operations, transporting	21.5

Notes: IPC = International patent classification. * 1999 provisional data.

Source: Eurostat (2001).

As shown in Table 3.5, the less developed economies in the EU show a rapidly growing ratio of patent applications at the EPO, in contrast with some industrialized economies that show more moderate growth patterns. Finland and Sweden are interesting cases here – the recent expansion of the ICT sector in these two countries accounts for most of this significant growth.

Eastern Enlargement and IPRs

The Europe Agreements between the EU and the Eastern European candidate countries impose explicit obligations on the former to provide intellectual, industrial and commercial property protection at a level similar to the one existing in the EU. This obligation means that these countries are required to adopt the *acquis communautaire* in this field and a series of European

*Table 3.5   Average annual growth rates of patent applications at EPO,
             1990-98*

Country	%
Portugal	20.82
Spain	14.49
Finland	13.02
Ireland	12.77
Greece	12.52
Sweden	10.37
Belgium	9.35
Luxembourg	8.02
Denmark	7.21
Austria	5.86
EU-15	5.52
The Netherlands	5.36
Germany	5.03
Italy	4.95
France	3.65
UK	2.96

Source: Eurostat (2001).

multilateral international agreements, as well as ensuring that the legal enforcement of these rights is effective. As Smid has pointed out, the CEECs have made substantial accomplishments in IPR legal developments and in the organizational structure (setting up patent offices, patent agents, technology transfer offices, etc.) (Smid 1998).

Accurate statistical information about patenting ratios is not available for most of the Central and Eastern European EU candidate countries, but some statistical series are found in the OECD main indicators of science and technology (see Table 3.6).

Is the EU Lagging Behind the Triad?

Examining the patenting propensity of applications at country of origin, the EU lies behind Japan and the US. Table 3.7 shows large differences in coefficients between the triad. However, it should be acknowledged that these differences also have to do with the patenting culture. This is most evident in Japan, with a ratio 10 times larger than the overall EU figure.

Table 3.6   *Patenting propensity of selected CEECs ('inventiveness coefficient'), resident patent applications/10 000 population, various years*

	1994	1995	1996	1997
Czech Republic	0.7	0.6	0.6	0.6
Hungary	1.1	1.1	0.8	0.7
Poland	0.7	0.7	0.6	0.6

Source: OECD (2000).

Looking at patent applications abroad in nominal terms, however, the position of the EU does not seem to be as negative vis-à-vis Japan and the US. Table 3.8 shows absolute numbers.

From Table 3.8 Japan seems to be quite a way behind in terms of applying for foreign patents in absolute numbers, whereas the US and the EU are quite close to each other. Another interesting point to note is the fact that the EU's and the US's trends to patent abroad grew spectacularly in the mid-1990s, with the number of applications more than doubling.

The question about whether the EU is behind the Triad in patenting activities depends on whether we look at patenting at national level or patenting abroad, and whether we examine ratios or absolute numbers. In any case, the data manifest differences in the attitudes and cultures towards patenting, which are stronger in the US and Japan than in the EU as a whole. It is interesting to note here that intra-EU disparities are greater than, for example, between the USA and Germany, or the USA and Sweden.

Table 3.7   *Patent propensity ('inventiveness coefficient'), resident patent applications/10 000 population, in Japan, USA and EU-15, various years*

	1994	1995	1996	1997
EU-15	2.5	2.3	2.6	2.5
Japan	25.6	26.6	26.9	27.7
US	4.1	4.7	4.0	4.5

Source: OECD (2000).

Table 3.8   Patent applications abroad, EU-15, Japan and USA, various years

	1994	1995	1996	1997
EU-15	403 366	553 303	682 498	1 033 633
Japan	140 370	154 699	193 451	380 510
US	641 855	852 588	1 175 107	1 583 862

Source: OECD (2000).

CONCLUSIONS

The rapidly evolving EU regulation of intellectual property rights is an important element of the European innovation policy. IPRs regulate the interactions between innovators in the market by setting the limits and permitted use of the objects and subjects of private property, by defining specific market operations (licensing, etc.) and by fostering specific modes of knowledge appropriation/dissemination.

The regulation of IPRs at EU level is the fruit of a sequence of political choices in the late 1990s/early 2000s. The EU has chosen to engage in a vast and ambitious exercise of new norm-setting at EU level through positive integration. Arguably, positive regulation at EU level has been chosen instead of a negative integration solution because it provides a faster and more clear-cut mechanism for dismantling trade barriers and a simplified single instrument for the exercise of these rights, and because it is more transparent and clear than the approximation of national regulations. Today, EU IPR regulation covers almost all legal forms of these rights, and it will incorporate the rest if the Community patent and utility models manage finally to see the light of day. The extensiveness of this IPR regulation combines with the highly integrated EU competition policy, where the EU has exclusive powers to control different forms of unfair competitive behaviour of firms in intra-EU trade. Therefore, IPR regulations and competition policy are the regulatory cornerstone for creating a single market of property rights in the EU. However, this alone might not bring about more innovation in the EU. Most important is how IPRs are regulated; that is, what these rights contain and how they are defined.

One of the premises that EU regulators seem to have followed is that strong and broad regulation of IPRs enhances innovativeness in the EU. Following some commentators, the rights granted in EU copyright, trade marks, design and utility model regulations are strong in terms of awarding exclusive rights to proprietors, but quite restrictive in terms of the free public availability and diffusion of the information/knowledge embodied in these rights. This is at least the situation for the EU regulation on database copyrights of 1996 (David 2000), the directive on harmonization of copyrights in the information society, and the proposed Community patent regulation. In these three cases the EU has emphasized the individual proprietary rights more strongly than the social benefits of free access, with important consequences for specific scientific fields (David 2000) and for wider societal learning and knowledge-generating processes (teaching, etc.). Similarly, the EU seems to be defining quite broadly the object of intellectual property, with the cases of biotechnological patents and software patents being the most salient ones. Beyond the ethical-moral dimension of the first, the relatively generous limits of patentability of both regulations show the political willingness of policy-makers to foster the appropriation of these new issues. The ETAN expert group and many grass-root movements have warned against the extension of exclusive rights into such broad fields by 'privatizing' large parts of key basic knowledge. Moreover, regulators should also take account of the potentially distorting effects of granting excessive market power to the first innovator.

The clear trend towards strong and broad intellectual property rights in EU regulations needs to be reconsidered in light of the role that IPRs have in the innovation process. The outputs of innovation in a country have traditionally been measured in terms of 'patenting ratios', 'inventiveness coefficients' and the 'technological balance of payments'. However, in recent times there has been growing dissatisfaction about the ability of these factors to provide an accurate view of the innovativeness of a system. New forms of innovation-output indicators are currently being developed, which also include productivity and knowledge-generation more widely – the so-called 'innovation indicators' (OECD 2001). EU regulators need to take account of this new approach to innovation results in order to avoid simplified understanding of the innovativeness of a system. Likewise, exploitation of knowledge does not just mean private appropriation of new knowledge, but also social appropriation in the form of competence development and learning abilities (in individual and collective terms) intimately related to the new knowledge.

> An unrealistic reliance on IPRs in the appropriation strategies of firms in many sectors could result in the very outcome that European policy makers are trying to avoid: the failure of European firms to successfully commercialise their innovation. IPR strategies must be placed firmly within the context of an overall appropriation strategy. (Cowan and Paal 2000)

Another important aspect to consider is that the emerging EU IPR regime is still asymmetric, both in a formal and an informal sense. In the formal sense, despite the rapid growth of EU IPR regulation in the 1990s there is still not a universal EU regulation in this field. Whereas in the areas of copyright, designs, plant varieties and trade marks the EU's involvement is quite substantial, patents and utility models are still only at a proposed stage. Furthermore, formal asymmetry also refers to the rapidly transforming levels of international, EU and national regulations. Despite the fact that the ECJ has ruled out the direct effect of the TRIPS agreement, this regulation within the WTO has important consequences for the exercise and protection of these rights in the EU. This chapter has pointed out how the division of authority at different levels becomes increasingly blurred as it opens up for a multi-layered, multi-level form of public and legal authority along the institutionalization of a global polity.

Asymmetry in the informal sense means that the efforts to establish a regulatory uniformity in the EU will not per se uniformize the large diversity in use and social perceptions of IPRs. The high IPR awareness of countries like Germany or Finland contrasts sharply with low rating countries like Portugal or Greece. The same can be said about the diversity between production sectors. This alone indicates the limitations of the understanding that a single regulatory structure will itself foster cross-country and cross-sectoral patenting all through the EU. Informal institutions and practices will persist in the diversified European economic system, particularly with accomplishment of Eastern enlargement. Therefore, it is of crucial importance that decision-makers are aware of this diversity, and take it into consideration when regulating IPRs in the EU.

NOTES

1. This has been so due to the long time-span that public authorities need in order to control the health properties of drugs.
2. Article 295 has been interpreted in a manner that does not interfere with IPRs.
3. A more detailed account of these pitfalls will be developed in a coming section.
4. The ECJ earlier developed the distinction between the existence of these rights (by national regulations) and their exercise (which should not be abused against the free circulation of goods).
5. The list provided in the table is by no means exhaustive. It is the personal appreciation of the author regarding the most relevant pieces of EU regulation in the field of IPR.
6. Regulation (EEC) 2349/84 on the application of article 85(3) of the EC, to certain categories of patent licensing (amended by regulation 2131/95); and regulation (EEC) 556/89 on the application of article 85(3) of the Treaty to certain categories of know-how licensing agreements.
7. Commission regulation (EC) 240/96 of 31 January 1996 on the application of article 85(3) of the Treaty to certain categories of technology transfer agreements OJ L 31, 09/02/1996, p. 0002–0013.
8. This Convention has been in force since 1977, and today has 19 state members: the EU-15 plus Cyprus, Liechtenstein, Monaco and Switzerland.
9. Agreement relating to Community patents settled at Luxemburg on 15 December 1989 (OJ

No L 401, 30 December 1989, p. 1). This agreement never entered into force because only seven member states ratified it.

10. Earlier documents relating more generally to this question are the 'Green Paper on innovation' (Commission 1995); and 'The first action plan on innovation' (Commission 1996).

11. The Green Paper estimates are the following: 'As the average cost of a page of translation is DM 128 and patent specifications run on average to 20 pages, total expenditure on translation would be in the region of DM 25 000, which is clearly a huge cost for firms to bear, particularly SMEs' (Green Paper p. 10).

12. 'Convention for the Protection of Industrial Property', signed in Paris 1883 and amended in Stockholm 1967. The most salient points of this international treaty are 'reciprocal treatment', 'independence of national patents' and 'renewal fees'.

13. The other major 'new trade issue' is trade in services, in the General Agreement on Trade in Services (GATS), concluded in the 1990s also under the GATT–WTO.

14. ECJ Opinion 1/94 of 15 November 1994.

15. Govarere mentions specifically the detailed regulations concerning obligatory minimal standards on IPR forms (part II), and the detailed rules about enforcement (part III), which have no parallel in other international agreements on IPRs (Govarere, 1996: 38). Some articles however, have an open-ended nature, either because they are defined in general terms, or because there were some political intentions to renegotiate them in subsequent WTO Rounds.

16. Decision 16 June 1998; Case no. 53/96, 30 IIC 292 (1999).

17. Case no 181/73, 1974 Haegeman.

18. Cases C-21-24/72, Judgment of 12 December 1972, International Fruit (1972) ECR 1219; and C-28093, Judgment of 5 October 1994, Germany v. Council (1994) ECR I-4973.

19. However, General Advocate Tesauro was of the opinion that the rationale for denying direct applicability of TRIPS is no longer the question of 'unconditionality' of WTO, but rather the question of reciprocity. That is, while the other TRIPS and WTO partners refuse to concede direct applicability to this agreement, the EU is not obliged to do so.

20. Joined cases C-300/98 Parfums Christian Dior vs. Tuk Consultancy, and C-392/98 Assco Grüste vs. Wilhelm Layher; Judgement of the Court 14 December 2000.

21. Opinion of Advocate General Jacobs, delivered on 15 February 2001 about Case C-98/99, also dealing with Article 50 of TRIPS.

22. Particularly article 50(6) stipulates that any provisional measure should follow national law to be determined by a judicial authority, or in the absence of it, should not exceed 20 working days or 31 calendar days.

23. A strongly debated caveat of TRIPS is the 'compulsory licensing' in article 31. The effect of compulsory licensing will however be dealt with in the section about the strong regulatory regime.

24. The European Commission is fully aware of this, since it has recently set up several studies of European SMEs' patenting attitudes, finding out that SMEs do not patent because it is too expensive and complex for them. See for example the report 'Patent protection of computer programs' (Contract no. INNO-99-04) ftp://ftp.ipr-helpdesk.org/softstudy.pdf and ftp://ftp.ipr-helpdesk.org/software.pdf

25. Directive 98/44/EC, OJ L 213, 30/07/1998, pp. 13–21.

26. The European patent convention does not impose any patentability limit on this matter.

27. C-377/98. The Netherlands is supported by Italy and Norway.

28. Opinion of General Advocate Jacobs delivered on 14 June 2001, Case C-377/98.

29. Word stressed by the author (ETAN).

30. Directive 96/9/EC; OJ L 077 27 March 1996 p. 20.

31. Directive 2001/29/EC; OJ L 167 22 June 2001 p. 10.

REFERENCES

Anderman, S.D. (1998), *EC Competition Law and Intellectual Property Rights. The*

110   *The innovation policy of the European Union*

Regulation of Innovation. Oxford, Clarendon Press.

Arundel, A. (2001a), 'Patents in the knowledge-based economy'. *Beleidsstudies Technologie Economie* **37** (Special Issue): 67–88.

Arundel, A. (2001b), 'The relative effectiveness of patents and secrecy for appropriation'. *Research Policy* **30**(4): 611–24.

Arundel, A. and I. Kabla (1998), 'What percentage of innovations are patented? Empirical estimates for European firms'. *Research Policy* **27**: 127–41.

Borrás, S. and M. Ougaard (2001), 'Patentløsninger – Intellektuel ejendomsret, EU og WTO'. *GRUS* **22**(64): 25–42.

Braithwaite, J. and P. Drahos (2000), *Global Business Regulation*. Cambridge, Cambridge University Press.

Cohendet, P. and F. Meyer-Krahmer (2001). 'The theoretical and policy implications of knowledge codification'. *Research Policy* **30**: 1563–91.

Commission, European (1995), 'Green paper on innovation'. Com (1995) 688 final.

Commission, European (1996), *First Action Plan for Innovation*. Luxemburg, Office for Official Publications.

Commission, European (1997), 'Commission's Green Paper on the Community Patent and patent system in Europe: Promoting innovations through patents'. Com (1997) 314. Brussels.

Commission, European (1999a), 'Amended proposal for a European Parliament and Council directive on the harmonisation of certain aspects of copyright and related rights in the Information Society'. Com (1999) 250 final, EU.

Commission, European (1999b), 'The follow-up to the Green Paper on the Community Patent and the patent system in Europe'. Com (1999) 42 final.

Commission, European (2000), 'Proposal for a Council regulation on the Community Patent'. Com (2000) 412 final.

Commission, European (2002), 'Commission Proposal – Com (2002) 092 final on the patentability of computer-implemented inventions'.

Correa, C.M. (2000), *Intellectual Property Rights, the WTO and Developing Countries*. London, Zed Books Ltd.

Cowan, R., P. David and D. Foray (2000), 'The explicit economics of knowledge codification and tacitness'. *Industrial and Corporate Change* **9**(2): 211–53.

Cowan, R. and G. v. d. Paal (2000), *Innovation Policy in a Knowledge-based Economy*. Luxemburg, European Commission.

Cremona, M. (2000), 'EC external commercial policy after Amsterdam: Authority and interpretation within interconnected legal orders'. In *The EU, the WTO and the NAFTA. Towards a Common Law of International Trade?*, J.H.H. Weiler. Oxford, Oxford University Press.

David, P. (2000), 'A tragedy of the public knowledge "commons"? Global science, intellectual property and the digital technology boomerang'. Stanford Institute for Economic Policy Research (SIEPR). SIERP Discussion Paper no. 00-02.

Desmendt, A.G. (1998), 'European Court rules on TRIPS agreement'. *Journal of International Economic Law*: 679–82.

Dijk, T. v. and P. v. Cayseele (1995), 'Economic implications of converging patent breadth in Europe'. In *Technical Change and the World Economy*, J. Hagedoorn. Aldershot, Edward Elgar.

Doern, G.B. (1997), 'The European Patent Office and the political economy of intellectual property policy'. *Journal of European Public Policy* **4**(3): 388-403.

Dörmer, S. (2000), 'Dispute settlement and new developments within the framework of TRIPS – An interim review'. *International Review of Industrial Property and*

Copyright Law **31**(1): 1–36.

EPO (2001), *Facts and Figures 2001*. www.european-patent-office.org.

ETAN (1999), *Strategic Dimensions of Intellectual Property Rights in the Context of Science and Technology Policy*. Brussels, European Commission.

Eurostat (2001), 'Patent activities in the EU'. *In Statistics in Focus - Research and Development*, Theme 9, 4/2001.

Foray, D. (1995), 'The economics of intellectual property rights and systems of innovation: The persistence of national practices versus the new global model of innovation'. In *Technical Change and the World Economy. Convergence and Divergence in Technology Strategies*, J. Hagedoorn. Aldershot, Edward Elgar.

Foray, D. (2001), 'Intellectual property and innovation in the knowledge-based economy'. *Beleidsstudies Technologie Economie. Den Haag: Directoraat-Generaal Innovatie. Ministerie van Economische Zaken* **37** (Special Edition: Industrial property, Innovation and the Knowledge-based Economy).

Ford, R. (1997), 'The morality of biotech patents: Differing legal obligations in Europe?' *European Intellectual Property Review* **6**: 315.

Govarere, I. (1996), *The Use and Abuse of Intellectual Property Rights in EC Law*. London, Sweet & Maxwell.

Granstrand, O. (1999), *The Economics and Management of Intellectual Property*. Cheltenham, Edward Elgar.

Groves, P., A. Martino, C. Miskin and J. Richards (1993), *Intellectual Property and the Internal Market of the European Community*. London, Graham & Trotman.

Jaffe, A.B. (1999), 'The U.S. patent system in transition: policy innovation and the innovation process'. NBER.

Karet, I. (1996), 'Over-broad patent claims: An inventive step by the EPO'. *European Intellectual Property Review* **10**: 561.

Kortum, S. and J. Lerner (1999), 'What is behind the recent surge in patenting?' *Research Policy* **28**: 1–22.

Krieger, A. (1998), 'When will the European Community patent finally arrive?' *IIC* **29**(8): 855–76.

Kyriakou, D. (2000), 'The Seattle WTO impasse'. *IPTS Report* **43**: 2–4.

Lal Das, B. (1999), *The World Trade Organisation. A Guide to the Framework for International Trade*. London, Zed Books.

Lundvall, B.Å. (1999), 'Knowledge production and the knowledge base'. Unpublished, Dept. of Business Studies, Aalborg University.

Maskus, K. (2000a), 'Intellectual property issues for the new round'. In *The WTO after Seattle*, J.J. Schott. Washington DC, Institute for International Economics.

Maskus, K.E. (2000b), *Intellectual Property Rights in the Global Economy*. Washington, DC, Institute for International Economics.

Maursseth, P.B. and B. Verspagen (1999). 'Europe: One or several systems of innovation? An analysis based on patent citations'. In *The Economic Challenge for Europe. Adapting to Innovation Based Growth*, J. Fagerberg, P. Guerrieri and B. Verspagen. Cheltenham, Edward Elgar.

Mazzoleni, R. and R. Nelson (1998), 'The benefits and costs of strong patent protection: A contribution to the current debate'. *Research Policy* **27**: 273–84.

Metcalfe, S. (1995), 'The economic foundations of technology policy: Equilibrium and evolutionary perspectives'. In *Handbook of the Economics of Innovation and Technological Change*, P. Stoneman. Oxford, Blackwell.

Meunier, S. and K. Nicolaïdis (1999). 'Who speaks for Europe? The delegation of trade authority in the EU'. *Journal of Common Market Studies* **37**(3): 477–501.

Mortensen, J.L. (1998), 'The institutional challenges and paradoxes of EU governance in external trade: Coping with the post-hegemonic trading system and the global economy'. In *The Union and the World: The Political Economy of a Common European Foreign Policy*, A. Cafruny and P. Peters. The Hague, Kluwer Law International.

Mortensen, J.L. (2000), 'The institutional requirements of the WTO in an era of globalization: Imperfections in the global economic polity'. *European Law Journal* **6**(2): 176–204.

Mowery, D.C. and A.A. Ziedonis (2000), 'Numbers, quality, and entry: How has the Bayh-Dole Act affected U.S. university patenting and licensing'. In *Innovation Policy and the Economy*, A.B. Jaffe, L. Josh and S. Scott. Cambridge, MA, The MIT Press.

OECD (1997), 'Patents and innovation in the international context'. Paris, OECD: 36.

OECD (2000), *Main Science and Technology Indicators*, no. 2. Paris, OECD.

OECD (2001), *OECD Science, Technology and Industry Scoreboard. Towards a Knowledge-based Economy*. Paris, OECD.

Raasteen, C. and S. Skibsted (2002), 'Direktivforslag indskrænker adgang til patentering af software'. *Computerworld* 5 April: 14.

Ratliff, E. (2000), 'Patent unpending'. *Wired* (June): 208–24.

Sell, S.K. (1999), 'Multinational corporations as agents of change: The globalization of intellectual property rights'. In *Private Authority and International Affairs*, C. Cutler, V. Haufler and T. Porter. Albany, State University of New York Press.

Shapiro, C. (2001), 'Navigating the patent thicket: Cross licenses, patent pools and standard setting'. In *Innovation Policy and the Economy*, A.B. Jaffe, J. Lerner and S. Stern. Cambridge, MA, The MIT Press.

Skjalm, K. (2001), 'Patentret og adgang til billig medicin'. Copenhagen, DUPI. Working paper no. 3/2001.

Smid, S. (1998), 'Intellectual property law uniformity in the CEECs and the EU: Conformity issues and an overview'. In *Intellectual Property Rights in Central and Eastern Europe*, E. Altaver and K. Prunskiene. Amsterdam, IOS press.

Smith, G.W. (1999), 'Intellectual property rights, developing countries and TRIPS'. *Journal of World Intellectual Property* **2**(6): 969–75.

Steen, M. van der (2001), 'An introduction to the theme'. *Beleidsstudies Technologie Economie, Den Haag: Directoraat-Generaal Innovatie. Ministerie van Economische Zaken.* **37** (Special Edition: Industrial Property, Innovation and the Knowledge-based Economy).

Steinmueller, W.E. (1994), 'Basic research and industrial innovation'. In *The Handbook of Industrial Innovation*, M. Dodgson and R. Rothwell. Cheltenham, Edward Elgar.

Tancer, R.S. and S.B. Tancer (1999), 'TRIPS in the Millennium round. Unfinished business'. *The Journal of World Intellectual Property* **2**(6): 889–910.

Vinje, T.C. (1995), 'Harmonising intellectual property laws in the European Union: Past, present and future'. *EIPR* **8**: 361–77.

4. Building the information society

> If information technology is the present-day equivalent of electricity in the industrial era, in our age the Internet could be linked to both the electrical grid and the electric engine because its ability to distribute the power of information throughout the entire realm of human activity.
>
> (Manuel Castells 2001: 1)

INTRODUCTION

Much is being said about the emerging information society and its prospects for the future. Many of these perspectives are already a reality in our daily life, whereas others are supposed to come in the near future. The first discussions about the emerging information society date from the 1970s, mostly in the USA (Bell 1973). They were rather academic, and only involved a few people. Almost three decades later, this notion has become very fashionable, and what initially was a buzzword amid scholars and visionary policy-makers, has now been taken up in wide public debates. The truth is that no other topic matches the ability of the 'information society' to generate popular and imaginative visions of who we are and our collective future.

In addition to these public debates, the information society is also related to a series of governmental actions. They are important because they might enhance or hinder the advent of the expected transformations, and because, at the end of the day, they *do* shape the nature of this future society and economy. Governmental actions relate, primarily, to issues of infrastructure-building, market regulations, and technological development in the ICT sector, but they have also gradually started to include other, more diffuse, types of public actions in the fields of education, health, social policy, or individual rights.

The European Union has been relatively active in the field. The first steps towards EU involvement were taken in the late 1980s, with the liberalization of the telecom sector, following the deregulatory wave of the Single European Market project. Similarly, the mid-1980s saw important EU schemes supporting research and technological development (RTD) in the ICT sector, in particular the well-known ESPRIT programme. Both areas, market liberalization and RTD support, were subsequently repackaged in the mid-1990s under the policy agenda of the information society, which embraced a wider social and economic approach to the use and development of ICTs. Today, the information society constitutes a rather extensive public domain, where a host of de- and re-regulatory exercises are combined with public support schemes, awareness-raising initiatives, and international positioning through negotiations, in the so-called 'e-Europe'.

This chapter deals with public actions launched by the EU under the ever-expanding agenda of the 'information society'. It does so by emphasizing how this agenda is intrinsically related to the innovation policy of the European Union. The rapid development of ICTs has not just generated new opportunities to be addressed and grasped by governments, companies and individuals. Most importantly, it has also generated reconceptualization and reconsideration, in political terms, of what constitutes a good (information) society. The present chapter addresses these issues, examining the path and nature of the EU's strategy to build up an information society, its position in a world-wide context, the concomitant reorganization of public–private spheres, and last but not least, the newly emerging 'digital divide'. The conclusions sum up the findings and point to paradoxes and problems related to the information society and, in turn, their relation to overall innovation policy.

INFORMATION AND THE INNOVATION SYSTEM

To what extent is our society an 'information society'? What are the economic values and effects of information in our contemporary capitalist economies? These questions are at the heart of many social scientists' concerns, not just because ICT industries (including telecommunications, information/computing and broadcasting) are among those which create the most jobs and are most dynamic in the advanced economies, but mainly because the massive use of these technologies is having a pervasive effect on social and industrial organization (and vice versa, obviously). In relation to this book, the most interesting question is what role information has in the overall dynamics of the innovation process. In order to answer it, we first discuss the visions, realities and paradoxes of the 'information society', then the role of information and ICTs in the innovation process. This section ends by tackling the issue of governmental action in building and shaping the information society.

Information Society: Visions, Reality and Paradoxes

In his work on the different theories and visions related to the information society, Frank Webster argues that most social scientists share a common understanding about this issue (Webster 1995). After examining in detail the theories of David Bell, Anthony Giddens, Herbert Schiller, Manuel Castells and Jürgen Habermas, and of the regulation school and post-modernist school, he concludes that most social scientists continue to display, in varying degrees, a technological determinism when dealing with the impact of ICTs in our societies. Yet, the most problematic issue is, in his opinion, that social scientists have focused excessively on the increased quantity of information, rather than on its quality. In addition, too much emphasis has been placed on the 'discontinuous' elements rather than on the 'continuity' that the use and exchange of information has had in historical terms. Webster's fundamental criticism of most social scientists' optimism is his undisguised scepticism about the notion of the 'information society'.

Nevertheless, the extraordinary technological development of ICTs is intrinsically related to some important (actual and expected) transformations in our capitalist economies. Most business practices (especially in the service sector and some advanced productive sectors) have been transformed as a result of the use of ICTs – new products and services have been created, ICTs have also offered new and different ways of organizing the workplace, and a great number of economic transactions have become faster and easier with the use of these new technologies. This is to assert, against Webster's scepticism, that some of the most important transformations in the realm of economic life are related to the advancement of ICTs. This assertion is not necessarily deterministic, as it is compatible with the understanding that the origins and advancement of ICTs are essentially a social phenomenon. The development of ICTs is not the fruit of an autonomous or automatic technological process, it is intrinsically embedded in societal dynamics. Consequently, there is a loop between societal dynamics and ICT developments, and this loop is reflected in the undeniable transformative trends that the advanced capitalist economies have experienced during the last couple of decades.

We will start with the ICT sector itself. The growth of the tele-communications, and information and computer industries over the last two decades has been astonishing. Table 4.1 provides an illustration of this within the EU.

Throughout the 1980s and 1990s, these sectors constantly expanded and grew in terms of production volumes, turnover, employment and job-creation. They created new services and products, and improved old ones by reducing costs and increasing access. It has been argued that this process is primarily supply driven rather than demand driven (Ypsilanti and Gosling 1997: 16), yet consumer interest is so great that this belief needs reconsidering. The data in Table 4.2 are a snapshot of this consumer response.

Tables 4.1 and 4.2 portray an incredibly dynamic set of industrial sectors, matched by consumer interest and demand-side behaviour patterns, yet ICTs have a more pervasive effect on the overall economic system. This stems from their ability

Table 4.1　ICT market by product and its growth ratio, 1999-2000, in the EU

	Overall ICT market per products (%) 2000	Growth ratio (%), 1999–2000
ICT equipment	34	13.7
IT services	16	13.0
Software products	9	13.5
Carrier services	41	12.6
EU total IT sector	100	13.1

Source:　Eurostat (2002).

> to integrate a number of different functions in the production process, to control, monitor and provide information as required in different processes, their role in integrating different economic sectors, and [in] changing existing distribution channels. (Ypsilanti and Gosling 1997: 25)

These features are the ones that define the special character of these technologies. ICTs provide interesting tools for the redefinition of organizational structures in private enterprises and public services, with potentially positive effects on productivity levels and management quality. Admittedly, these features are the reason why economists are increasingly paying attention to the role of ICTs in the economy. However, as we will examine, the promises of a more efficient and productive economy have not always been met.

The IT productivity paradox is an issue that has attracted considerable attention. The paradox is that despite the massive introduction of ICTs into the production process, both in the service and manufacturing sectors, productivity levels do not seem to have increased accordingly. Or in the words of Nobel laureate Robert Solow, 'We see computers everywhere except in the productivity statistics'. This has given rise to a debate among economists as to the causes of this paradox. Two have been suggested, the first concerning the difficulty in obtaining appropriate measurements of ICT-generated productivity (Patterson and Wilson 2000: 79). To this end, the OECD has made efforts to develop more sophisticated measuring instruments (OECD 1998). Other economists have pointed out that there is a time lag between the adoption of ICT and its generation of productivity growth (McGuckin and Stiroh 1998; Lucas 1999). In fact, when dealing with the service sector, new empirical evidence does not sustain the productivity paradox. As Haynes and Thompson have recently shown, 'adopters of embodied IT innovations may enjoy very substantial labour savings by comparison with their non-

Table 4.2   Information society in 2000/01 (in millions)

	EU-15	Japan	USA	World	Source
Number of PCs (Dec. 2000)	108	40	161	449	ITU
– per 100 inhabitants	35	32	59	8	
Internet hosts (July 2001)	12	6	76	120	RIPE, NetSizer
– per 100 inhabitants	3	5	28	2	
Internet users (August 2001)	144	53	174	660	NetSizer
– per 100 inhabitants	38	42	63	11	
Mobile phone subscribers (Dec. 2000)	239	67	109	740	ITU
– per 100 inhabitants	63	53	40	12	

Source: Eurostat (2002).

adopting rivals' (Haynes and Thompson 2000: 94). Although new evidence is becoming available, measuring productivity is still a daunting task, and this is related to the point that Webster underlined at the beginning of this chapter; namely, the inherent difficulty of measuring the new value and role that information has in our economy, beyond the mere depiction of the quantitative accretion in its use. Therefore, we need to move on and consider the role that information and knowledge have in the innovation process.

Information and Knowledge

What is information? How is it related to knowledge? And to what extent have the increase in the use of ICTs and the flow of information influenced the acceleration of the innovation process? In the previous two chapters of this book, we discussed the question of what knowledge is. Particular emphasis was placed on the distinction between tacit and codified knowledge, on the production and appropriation of knowledge, and on the dynamic aspect of learning in social and organizational terms. We now need to tackle the question of information as such. However, this is not easy for, as Lamberton has put it, 'information has been treated as a resource, as a commodity, as perception of pattern, and as a constitutive force in society' (Lamberton 1999). It is not our purpose to review the endless literature about information and knowledge that exists today, nor to provide a historical review of how economists have interpreted this. Happily, good work on the subject already exists (Predergast 1999). Instead, the purpose is to come up with a workable concept of information that relates to the wider process of innovation and the recent trends of our economies. Lundvall has made a useful distinction in the field of economics:

> knowledge and information appear in economic models in two different contexts. The most fundamental assumption of standard microeconomics is that the economic system is based on rational choices made by individual agents. Thus, how much and what kind of information agents have about the world in which they operate and how powerful their ability to process the information are crucial issues. The other major perspective is one in which knowledge is regarded as an asset. Here knowledge may appear both as an input (competence or R&D investments) and output (patent or innovation) in the production process. (Lundvall 1999: 3)

Our focus is not on microeconomics – that is, on how individual agents use (or try to optimize) the (limited or asymmetric) information they have. Instead we have a wider focus on information as an asset within the innovation system.

The incredible advances in information and communication technologies over the past two decades have enhanced the flow of information and its accessibility (both in terms of connectedness and price). However, these technologies have also affected the social and organizational aspects related to the generation, accumulation, processing and usage of information. It has been argued that the ICTs have fostered codification processes, and that the 'stock of information' has grown accordingly. In any case, the important thing is that information has become more easily accessible, transparent, and cheaper, and that this has induced (or has the potential to induce) significant industrial and organizational restructuring. This later point is quite important for the process of innovation – innovation is much more than mere 'technological develop-ment', as it includes substantial organizational and social transformations.

Governing ICTs and the Innovation System

Governing the innovation system is essentially a question of shaping and re-shaping institutions with the view to creating positive dynamics that enhance the innovation process. The role of public authorities in this regard is important either directly or indirectly. Governmental actions deployed in the ICT sector, and later in the information society can be integrated within the range of public actions being undertaken towards the innovation system. This can be argued on the basis of the ubiquitous role that ICTs and information in general have in the functioning of the innovation system. Not only has the ICT sector been a central hi-tech area of substantial technological development in recent times, but the possibilities offered by these technologies in order to get a cheaper flow and better management of information and data have also induced a rapid evolution of the innovation process. Thus what is important from the point of view of innovation policy is that ICTs and the information society do represent a source of innovativeness, both in a social and a scientific–technological way.

The information society is today mostly governed through regulation. This includes not just the de- and re-regulatory waves of the telecoms market, but also issues like privacy, information security, universal service and intellectual property rights. Standardization is perhaps a special case, given its semi-regulatory nature, as we will see in the coming chapter. Public subsidies and financial support are other important instruments focused on research, technological development and the dissemination of results. Other types of actions are 'softer', as they are aimed at communication and campaigning. This last set includes issues like 'awareness raising', helping to establish dialogues between producers and consumers for product development, enhancing access and affordability, and fighting against the emerging 'digital divide'.

There are as many styles of governance of the information society as there are governments. France and Japan were the first to take the lead on this issue in the 1960s. However, in the early 1990s, the US and the EU took interesting and much wider initiatives on infrastructure development. As a fruit of Clinton's presidency campaign pledges, the 'national information infra-structure' was launched in 1993. In terms of content, this initiative was more oriented towards social aspects than the EU Bangemann Report of 1994 (Schneider 1997: 351). The US government focused much more on issues like e-equity, universal service and privacy than the EU was doing at that time. The EU was much more concerned with unleashing market forces through the liberalization of the telecoms sector across Europe.

THE EU INFORMATION SOCIETY: UNBOUNDED AMBITIONS?

This section aims at providing a snapshot of the process of Europeanizing this topic, arguing that the policy agenda of an 'information society' has not only unfolded rapidly with the swift succession of Commission suggestions and action plans but, above all, has expanded in scope, particularly since the late 1990s. At the onset it was concerned with market-oriented matters, with the primary goal of promoting the European ICT sector. As time went by, other aspects were added, mainly from a demand-side perspective. Thus attention moved from the ICT industry to the use of ICTs and their social consequences. That is, from an ICT focus towards a truly information society focus, epitomized by the latest and most ambitious e-Europe initiative. This, it is argued here, has run parallel to an increasing blurring of the powers between the EU and its member states. Consequently, the more the EU has moved away from just constructing a market in the ICT sector, and into building a society, the more complex and multi-layered political interactions between the EU and its member states have become.

The First Steps

The first EU initiatives towards building the information society that developed in the late 1980s/early 1990s, were essentially market oriented and supply driven, with the primary goal of enhancing the competitive position of the ICT sector in Europe. This followed the momentum generated by the single market project, the aim of which was to tear down the many barriers to intra-EU trade and to unleash market forces across national boundaries. Thus the EU strategy was threefold: first, the liberalization of the national telecom monopolies creating a single European market; secondly, common standardization procedures (especially of telecom equipment) in order to support this market-building endeavour, and thirdly, backing EU-wide research networks with specific ICT budget initiatives under the RTD framework programme (see Figure 4.1). Even if they were not formally subsumed within one single line of political action, these three instruments struck a note. The EU decided to address the lack of competitiveness of European industry and grab the chance being offered by the rapid techno-logical development of the sector. The motivation behind these public initiatives was the belief that the ICT sector was the harbinger of the coming new economy, and the fear that the EU would miss out on the opportunities provided by these new technologies.

Beginning with liberalization, it is worth mentioning that the Treaty of Rome did not explicitly include this sector in its vision of a common market. At that time national PTTs (post, telegraph and telephone companies) were providing services, maintaining the networks, and producing equipment on the basis of national monopolies. In the late 1970s, the Commission started to suggest a partial liberalization of these markets.[1] But it was not until the advent of the single European market project that a far-reaching liberalization of this

---

1. The deregulation of the telecoms sector through the single European market project
2. Standardization procedures
3. Financial support for cross-national research networks in ICT

Figure 4.1   The triple track of early EU strategy towards the information society

sector was envisaged, exploiting the possibilities that article 86 (ex. art. 90) provided. The launch of the 1987 Green Paper[2] and the subsequent regulatory programme established by the Council,[3] spearheaded the legislative reforms to come. The focus at this point was on opening up the equipment market,[4] liberalizing telecom services (excluding public voice telephony),[5] and the harmonization of some infrastructure-related provisions (interfaces, usage conditions and tariff principles).[6] This was a first step in the liberalization process, but the prospects for full liberalization of service (including voice telephony) came shortly after.[7] Having broken the national monopolies in equipment and services provision, the Commission now stressed the issue of infrastructure/network. This was finally accomplished in a legislative act in 1996, which laid down 1 January 1998 as the deadline for a fully liberalized telecoms market in the EU.[8]

The second strategy was a series of sustained efforts to establish European standards in ICTs. The thriving technological and market developments of this sector during the 1980s and 1990s made standardization a key issue in both business and politics. It was a key business matter because voluntary standards allow for larger markets and also define the forthcoming technological features of product competition (technological trajectories). It was a key political issue because achieving common standards would help consolidate an EU-wide market for equipment and services. The next chapter of this book is dedicated to the issue of EU standards.

The third and final element of this approach was the financial support given to collaborative research in ICT firms across Europe. As we examined in the chapter about knowledge production (see Chapter 2), the EU framework programme has always had a rather generous budgetary line for ICTs. This was the case for the ESPRIT programme (information technology) in the 1980s, and it still is today. The sixth FP (2002–06) has allocated €3600 million for 'information society technologies', representing almost 30 per cent of all thematic priorities.

The Bangemann Report of 1994 (Commission 1994a) and the subsequent action plan (Commission 1994b) wrapped up these ongoing initiatives within a single strategic document. Most scholars have criticized these early market-oriented initiatives of the EU, and the Bangemann Report in particular, because they reflect a combination of ideological preferences and technological determinism (Miranda and Kristiansen 2001) that disregarded the social dimension of the information society (Soete 1999). Partly as a result of these criticisms and partly because the Commission was cheerfully advised by several groups of experts to move ahead into a more 'social' agenda (Commission 1996a), new initiatives were envisaged in the 1996 Green Paper 'Living and working in the information society: People first' (Commission 1996b), including issues such as regional cohesion, education and training, and the international context of the information society. This broadened substantially the previous agenda of the EU, making it include 'information society' considerations in many other more conventional EU policy areas. For example, awareness of the digital divide among poor and rich regions was addressed through the conventional instruments of regional policy (as we will see later on in this chapter).

Beyond the recurring scholarly criticism, one of the most convincing explanations so far put forward as to why the EU failed in the early 1990s to launch a more 'social agenda' is simply that

> the main actors in each country were essentially (and had been for decades) the public telecommunications operators and, in some cases, related industrial groups providing technological backing. These actors found themselves in totally new circumstances in the mid-1990s as they lost their role in setting public policy and were forced to change their priorities. ... Thus it was only with the dawning of the 21st century that a new set of both private and public actors found themselves in a position to press ahead with policies fostering the Information Society. (Jordana 2002: 11)

Towards an e-Europe

In the late 1990s, EU action expanded to two further issues, which are still under development – a new regulatory wave and the e-Europe initiative. Starting with the regulatory wave, a whole new range of regulations are being issued in the early 2000s. The thrust towards a new EU regulatory framework in this domain was first launched in the Commission's 1997 Green Paper[9] and has broadly been articulated around two main issues: first, the legal matters related to the rapid technical convergence of ICT products; and secondly, the protection of individual and collective rights in the information society (mainly privacy and universal services). Starting with the first, convergence of the telecommunications, computer and information technology sectors, which is being driven by technological developments, is putting increasing pressure on different types of EU regulations. Figure 4.2 is a visual representation of these technological transformations.

As stated by Ypsilanti and Gosling,

> Convergence threatens to overtake communication regulation, which could cause confusion for market players and consumers alike. Anomalies and, more seriously, communication regulatory barriers, which could result from lack of clarity in these areas, risk retarding the development and deployment of new communication services, the creation of job opportunities, and economic growth in the new information industries. (Ypsilanti and Gosling 1997: 35)[10]

With the purpose of addressing these concerns, the Commission recently

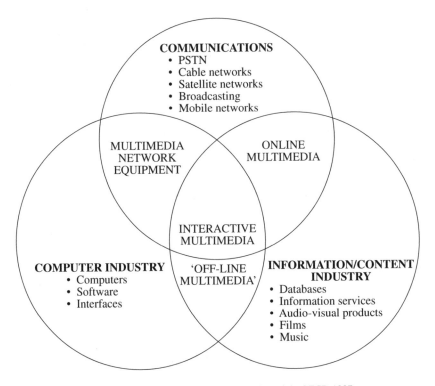

Source: Ypsilanti and Gosling (1997), Figure 2.1, p. 16. Copyright OECD 1997.

Figure 4.2   The process of ICT convergence

released a series of regulatory proposals focusing on access, authorization procedures and other horizontal provisions to enhance competition in the already liberalized market.[11] These are obviously concerned with shaping corporate behaviour and the formal contours of industrial dynamics, yet the new package of regulatory framework also contains two other directives that fall outside this line. These are devoted to granting individual and collective rights – namely, the protection of privacy and universal services coverage, respectively. We will examine them in detail later in this chapter, given their unambiguous implications for the redefinition of the public–private spheres. Suffice it to mention here that both represent the cornerstones of governmental involvement in shaping the information society (and not just the ICT sector).

Last but not least, the ambitious e-Europe initiative reveals a new approach from the EU towards the information society, willing to make the most of ICTs to enhance learning, commerce, health, public administration and many other issues. This initiative was Commissioner Erkki Liikanen's political flagship, attempting to put Europe at the forefront of intelligent and ubiquitous use of ICTs. Launched in December 1999, and subsequently developed in an Action Plan,[12] the initiative had three main objectives: a faster and better internet, people skills, and stimulating the use of the internet (see Table 4.3). From the point of view of this book, the e-Europe initiative has three features worth noting. First, it has quite short-term objectives (most measures/ objectives have to be in place by 2002); secondly, its horizontal nature requires substantial sectoral/functional coordination (i.e. skills with initiatives on training and education); and thirdly, it contemplates the use of the so-called 'open method of coordination' based on 'benchmarking' and 'mainstreaming' of national initiatives. All three make e-Europe a rather ambitious programme. Arguably, the proposals for e-commerce are the most interesting, as they include a bundle of regulations defining copyrights, e-money and financial services; the creation of a dot-EU domain; enhancing consumer confidence on e-commerce; suppressing legal obstacles for electronic procurement; and the compatibility of the EU VAT system with e-commerce.

National and Supranational

The previous account of the historical process of Europeanization has mainly focused on the expanding nature of the policy agenda in the last couple of decades: from the deregulatory trends of the telecoms sector to an information

Table 4.3   Objectives of the e-Europe initiative action plan

A cheaper, faster, secure internet
- Cheaper and faster internet access
- Faster internet for researchers and students
- Secure networks and smart cards

Investing in people and skills
- European youth into the digital age
- Working in the knowledge-based economy
- Participation for all in the knowledge-based economy

Stimulate the use of the internet
- Accelerating e-commerce
- Government online: electronic access to public services
- Health online
- European digital content for global networks
- Intelligent transport systems

Source: Commission (1999b).

society and the e-Europe initiative (Commission 1999a, b). Yet this emphasis on the contents of policy should not overshadow the fact that the dynamics and patterns of policy change as such were anchored in different understandings and interests (sometimes conflicting) among the actors involved, namely the Commission, the member states and private groups (telecom firms and social groups). Several scholars have stressed the policy entrepreneurship role of the Commission (Dang-Nguyen et al. 1993; Fuchs 1994; Sandholtz 1998; Eliassen and Sjøvaag 1999; Jordana 2000). Nevertheless, in the political process of rapidly liberalizing the European telecommunications market, the relationship between the Commission and the member states has not always been smooth. As a matter of fact, some states have challenged the Commission's actions at different stages of this process. The most dramatic events, though, were at the early stages of the liberalizing thrust, when some member states confronted some of the caveats of the regulation on terminal equipment 88/301/EEC and the service directive 90/388-EEC, arguing that the Commisson's role should be limited to supervision. Nevertheless, the disputes were settled when the European Court of Justice ruled in favour of the Commission (Scherer 1995; Sandholtz 1998; Jordana 2002).

Despite the largely liberalized telecommunication market in Europe, and the common EU policy initiatives towards the information society in the early 2000s, there is no unified pattern of political and social dynamics. As for the telecom sector, member states continue to enjoy a significant and central position in legislative and executive matters. First, the EU regulations in ICT have normally been directives, requiring national legislative acts for transposition. This has effectively left a certain degree of latitude to each state, allowing national legislators to define the best way of adopting the EU objectives while respecting national institutional particularities. Secondly, the impact of EU regulations has been very different across countries. Thatcher identifies three types of impact co-existing in different manners in all countries he has examined; the direct (coercive) impact of EU legislation; the indirect impact of EU legislation in terms of other influencing actors' strategies and coalitions; and the legitimizing impact of justifying changes desired for non-EU reasons (Thatcher 2002). The result is a complex and diverse pattern of institutional solutions across the EU, far beyond the initial assumptions that tended to equate liberalization with homogenization.

The same can perhaps be said about the information society. Even if it is still quite early to make a thorough examination of the transformational trends and impact generated by EU initiatives, it is easy to predict large national diversity. This is not just due to the wide spectrum of issues related to the information society, but essentially is because of large differences in the social context where these new technologies are introduced (Ducatel et al. 2000). The current diversity in patterns of ICT use in age/sex cohorts, organizational settings (large/small firms, schools/training centres), geographical areas (poor/rich regions, rural/urban areas) or other specific social groups (digital communities), are likely to persist. This means that open recognition and acknowledgement of the large social and institutional idiosyncrasies of European societies would significantly diminish the risk of misplaced political expectations about a homogeneous, single, European information society.

THE GLOBAL/INTERNATIONAL PERSPECTIVE

Most of the issues related to the development of an information society have a global reach, since one of the most singular features of ICTs is precisely their ability to break down geographical borders. As we saw at the beginning of this chapter, this is far from being a purely 'automatic' socio-technological process: public action has a clear impact on the information society, because it influences the degrees of access and connectivity, and because it intends to address new social problems related to individual and collective rights. This section looks at EU policy towards the global/international level of information society-related issues. It is important to underline that the focus here is on political actions taken by the EU in this topic of external relations, and not so much on the dynamics of an emerging global information society (Currie 2000), or the social and organizational structuration patterns linked to the current global use of ICTs (Castells 1998, 2001). Consequently, we will pay heed to two issues: first, what the EU political strategies towards the international forums governing information society-related matters have been; and secondly, to what extent and how the EU has integrated ICT and information society subjects within its conventional policy for aid to developing countries.

Two Issues Concerning Global Governance

Two topics related to governance of the global information society have recently received much attention in international politics. These are the liberalization of telecommunication services in international trade arrangements and the governance of the internet. In both of them, the EU has worked strategically on the initiatives and has been trying to position itself as a single actor in a global scenario.

The GATS agreement, concluded under the WTO framework, regulates international trade arrangements concerning basic telecommunications.[13] A total of 69 countries agreed to the Protocol on telecommunications, opening up a new era of a liberalized international market.[14] One of the most striking aspects of GATS is the broad reach of liberalization. This was ushered in by two facts: first the broad definition of what constitutes 'basic telecommunications', and secondly, the large scope of what types of transactions fall under the measures. As WTO officials state:

> As a result, market access commitments will cover not only cross-border supply of telecommunications but also services provided through the establishment of foreign firms, or commercial presence, including the ability to own and operate independent telecom network infrastructure.

The two features that make the WTO agreement quite special are the multilateral nature of the agreement vis-à-vis the traditional bilateral dimension of international agreements in this matter, and the saliency of the dispute settlement arrangements, which render the WTO a more effective regime. However, successful implementation of the new liberalized framework depends in great part on how effectively the governments of the signatory parties adapt their national regulations in order to comply with the new obligations. Even though some authors have shown great scepticism about this by assuming an invariable reluctance of national regulatory agencies to effectively open up national markets (Fredebul-Krein and Freytag 1997; Eliassen and Sjøvaag 1999), the truth is that some signatory parties have already started implementation, as can be appreciated in the rising number of official notifications to the WTO.

The EU and its member states were all participants in the negotiations leading to GATS and, given the Solomonic decision of the ECJ, they enjoy shared competences on this matter.[15] In practical terms, it means that the Commission, being the EU negotiator, is obliged to follow very closely the mandate handed out by its member states. At the time the negotiations were opened up in 1994, the EU had not yet accomplished much of the liberalization agenda to come in the second half of the 1990s. Enser maintains that 'this effectively prevented the Community from making any meaningful commitments in the context of GATS' (Enser 1998: 288). However, during the course of the negotiations, which continued until 1997, the EU managed to develop a full range of internal deregulatory measures leading towards full liberalization by 1 January 1998. Enser argues then that the developments of the GATS negotiations put clear pressure on reluctant member states to accept the internal market on telecoms. In other words, external developments at WTO level had a direct impact on the intra-EU political dimension. Furthermore, Enser asserts that despite the ECJ decision in 1994 concerning 'shared competence', the Commission effectively set the EU negotiating agenda as it was able to present an improved offer that was eventually matched by the US and other negotiating partners (Enser 1998: 294). Schneider, however, assigns less leverage capacity to the Commission in both global and European political processes. His alternative understanding is that the

Europeanization of this issue became inserted within a much larger process of policy diffusion that had acquired a global scope.

> A more convincing explanation is to reconstruct the overall reform process as a kind of policy chain reaction which operates in a global context. In such a perspective the major institutional transformations were ultimately triggered by global economic and technical changes being transmitted and reinforced by international organizations and other channels of policy diffusion. (Schneider 2002: 7)

This means a new interpretation of the Europeanization process:

> Europeanization in this context did not create these pressures, but it certainly provided a certain kind of 'catalytic' transmission of these constraints in order to produce favourable conditions for European industry to survive in the context of increased global competition. (Schneider 2002: 18)

In other words, liberalization of the telecom sector in European countries was more a simultaneous response to technical global pressures on their industry than an EU collective action. This is an interesting perspective insofar as it directly links the national political processes to the global pressures of the time (a combination of technical and economic trends). What I do not find convincing in Schneider's argumentation, though, is that he underrates the direct role that the GATS negotiations played in these national political processes, and above all, he disregards the fact that the EU deregulatory shove took place simultaneously, so reinforcing the political pressure on individual member states, which is what Enser argues.

Global governance of the internet is the second interesting issue in international politics where the EU has been playing quite an active role. In 1998, the US government declared its willingness to transfer its managerial powers on the internet to a non-profit organization named ICANN.[16] The years from 1998 until 2000 saw progress in this transition and today ICANN operates under the representation of a wide range of public and private organizations of different nationalities. It has four main functions: IP address space allocation, protocol parameter assignment, domain name system management, and root server system management. The European Commission has followed these institutional developments closely, and has elaborated two communications giving policy suggestions for principles and ideas on the management and governance of the internet.[17] Two matters deserve special attention, one being the attempts by the European Commission to gain more coordinating and negotiating powers in this new area of international politics, which is becoming increasingly important. In this respect, a recent Council resolution has encouraged the Commission to play a coordinating role and to create a European network of experts, but has not granted it autonomous negotiating authority.[18] The second matter is the efforts of the Commission to gain from ICANN the creation of a dot-EU domain. This question is still unresolved at the time of writing, but Commissioner Liikanen has pushed it to the forefront of his political agenda within the e-Europe initiative.[19]

Cooperation for Development

The rapid development of ICTs and their increasing impact on economic development means that they are acquiring paramount importance for developing countries. Most scholars agree on the existence of a divide between the haves and have-nots in ICT. What they do not agree on is whether this divide is likely to be reduced or not, and to what extent ICTs might help these countries' socio-economic development. In other words, what role ICT has and can have in economic development variance (Patterson and Wilson 2000). One of the problems being discussed is to what extent ICT accessibility, in terms of affordability and the skills required, is a key matter for exploiting the equalizing potential of these technologies. In any case, as has been pointed out, there is an overemphasis on what ICTs can do in this respect. After all, what matters is not the technology itself, but the social and economic systems in which it is embedded (Patterson and Wilson 2000: 80).

The attention to ICTs and their ability to enhance development have been reflected in the conventional aid schemes for development policy.[20] A small number of development programmes focused on ICTs are currently being carried out in different regions of the world, all of them with relatively low financial commitments. These regions are primarily Latin America, the Mediterranean, sub-Sahara Africa, Caribbean-South Pacific, and Asia.[21] Recently, EU involvement in this area seems to have been in a transforming phase. The first move came with the Commission's communication on how the EU has to deal with information society matters in development policy.[22] This can be seen as the direct result of a series of discussions on this matter that took place at global level in the second half of the 1990s. Most notorious were the G7 discussions in 1995, and the conference on IT and development organized by President Mandela in 1996. Yet another step was taken recently by the member states, establishing an expert group on the matter in 1999, which produced an interesting report.[23] With its emphasis on the ability of liberalization of telecommunication markets to generate ICT development, the report puts forward a host of suggestions for the information society (IS) that are worth mentioning: IS training, IS awareness and stakeholder involvement, IS and NGOs/human rights, IS and the public sector, and IS and knowledge/south–south, north–south partnerships. This report shows that the focus must be wider than today, and must be organized along the different horizontal lines of development policy already in place.

REDEFINING PUBLIC AND PRIVATE SPHERES

Having examined the Europeanization process and the EU position in the global scenario of the information society, is now time to appraise another matter; namely, how these actions have been shaping the public–private realms. This is intriguing since the increased amount and flow of information available through ICTs, and the enhanced means of communicating between people and institutions, have important implications for the legal rights of individuals and on the organizational structures of public administration and political systems. Looking at the legal rights of individuals, two issues seem to have dominated the political discussions at EU level. These are how to secure privacy in the information society, and how to secure universal service to all users.

Privacy and Individual Rights in the IS

Since the rapid advancement of ICTs, there has been a societal concern about effective ways to protect individuals' fundamental rights. The growing amount of information being stored, transmitted and processed has exacerbated the risk of illegal use of personal data, violating the constitutionally granted human rights. Yet, this need to guarantee fundamental rights and liberties has to be balanced against the public interest of information storage and processing, most notably in relation to the governance of the welfare state, which requires sophisticated and accurate instruments of implementation.

National European governments have, since the early 1970s, regulated these issues. Mayer-Schönberger eloquently argues that it is possible to trace four generations in the history of European national regulations (Mayer-Schönberger 1997). The first one, in the early to mid-1970s, was mostly focused on regulating the emerging large data banks. However, no direct attention was paid to privacy as such. Yet, the introduction of this concern was the hallmark of the second generation of national regulations in the late 1970s and early 1980s, which emphasized the principle of individual consent. Nevertheless, the practical problems associated with effective implementation of individual consent forced a third regulatory generation where mechanisms for individual participation were established. Last, the current fourth generation has advanced the regulatory scope by a range of general laws and complementary sectoral laws about data protection. As we will examine in brief, the EU regulations form part of this generation, enshrining this legal approach for all its member states.

Legal developments at national level have evolved parallel to two highly influential international regulations, namely the OECD Guidelines and the Council of Europe Convention, both deriving from the early 1980s.[24] Even if these two documents have different legally binding nature, they have both had an enduring effect on national, and lately EU, legislation in this area. The internationalization of regulatory measures was a response to the increased cross-border flow of information in the 1980s, and the difficulties that national regulations alone had in ensuring the protection of those individual rights. The EU has been relatively late to regulate this matter, but this is related to how the division of tasks between the EU and its member states was settled politically. The EU regulatory style follows the trends of the fourth generation of Mayer-Schönberger's typology, as it has had a general framework for data protection since 1995,[25] and a sectoral one specifically protecting privacy and personal data.[26] The main aim of the generic directive is to guarantee the free flow of data and information throughout the EU while securing the protection of individual rights. The text of the directive is clearly a political compromise between these two opposing objectives. It is not surprising then that at the time of its adoption, legal experts disagreed to a large extent as to how the balance was struck. For some authors, this directive showed a high level of personal data protection, as it enshrined a number of important principles related to privacy, such as the consent principle in cases of sensitive data, prohibition of processing personal data for purposes of marketing, and monetary compensation in cases of violation (Mayer-Schönberger 1997: 234). For some other experts, though, the directive was problematic. 'There is no doubt that the directive provides protection of personal data, but it is also evident that many provisions permit quite extensive processing' (Blume 1998: 25). The problem for this author is that the legal principles were not specific enough, and that the directive has too large a number of exceptions to create an effective legal basis for individual protection.

Further legal developments took account of these criticisms, and the 1997 sectoral directive provided an extensive and detailed EU-wide regulatory framework for privacy protection. It has been pointed out that 'the specific directive is broader than the general directive in two respects, namely in its coverage of the rights of natural and legal persons, and in its coverage of privacy issues which are not directly linked to data processing' (Commission 1999b: 30). At the time of writing, the Commission has proposed some amendments to this directive in order to take account of rapid technological advancements. Therefore, the new text should extend protection to all forms of electronic communication (especially the internet), and to new types of data such as 'locational data', generated by mobile communication networks, in what seems to be a gradual move towards a more protective stance.

This however, say Pearce and Platten, faces some challenges (Pearce and Platten 1998). The first and most obvious is the nature of the new technologies, and the global dimension of their use. 'Despite the technical efforts to provide Internet users with greater control over the personal information they share, the privacy of the majority of users will continue to be at risk' (p. 545). But, beyond these strict technical matters and their use/abuse, there is a political dimension of privacy and data protection. As these authors assert, 'But perhaps even more fundamental are diverse cultural attitudes to data protection' (p. 545). This is most evident between the EU and the US, and between those two and South East Asian countries. Therefore, more global dialogue on these matters will be central in the near future.

Universal Services and Deregulation in the EU

Another important issue with regard to the redefinition of the private and public spheres is the provision of universal service in the telecoms sector. Before liberalization took off in the 1980s, national PTT monopolies guaranteed universal service nation-wide. Although many differences existed, most EU countries did regulate this provision in one way or another, and it was a shared responsibility of the state and the single national operator. With the advent of full liberalization of services, networks and equipment at EU level, these traditional legal guarantees at national level no longer applied as there was now no monopolist. The political debate was then articulated around the issue of what mechanism was best endowed to secure this objective – market dynamics or regulatory guarantees. The proponents of the first line argued that the market would reallocate resources through fair and free competition, and that, as universal service is essentially linked to affordability and liberalization would invariably put prices down, the market would be able to provide universal service. Opponents of this view argued that the market itself was not able to undertake such a task, and feared that providers would avoid unprofitable customers (most notably those in rural areas or some special social groups). Consequently, a legal guarantee for universal service would be necessary at EU level to limit the risks of social exclusion in the information society, re-establishing political responsibility to accomplish this.

Existing EU regulations on universal service follow this second line of thought, and were the response to rising concerns from some member states and some consumer groups. Hence, the EU legal framework is contained in the Voice Telephony Directive[27] and the Interconnection Directive,[28] with the former defining the mechanisms that states can use for financing the service. It is important to note that universal service applies to the fixed telephony network and service, to public pay phones and to special customers (disabled, etc.). This is an important point, showing that fixed telephony is treated as a utility, and is also related to the role of the welfare state (Skogerbö and Storsul 2000). A key issue is then how to finance the provision of universal service. If in providing universal service to a specific area, the operator's costs are higher than its benefits, the Directive allows some re-balancing mechanisms, either through direct payments or by creating an independent fund for such purposes. The Commission has published guidelines for national regulatory authorities and member states as to how to interpret and enforce these caveats. The complexity of these regulations cannot hide the difficulties of effectively managing the political objective of universal service; and this is the reason why it is still valid to ask whether regulation is the best means of ensuring universal service.

My point of view is that these risks of unequal access and pricing are real in a competitive environment, but that they are currently being substantially reduced by rapid development of wireless technology (making physical access less problematic) and by increased price-related market competition. The rapid technological development of mobile communications might bypass the aims of the EU regulations on universal service, which were envisaged in terms of physical networks. This is so because mobile communications significantly lower the price of network development and maintenance, meaning they are in a position to offer cheaper territorial coverage, and diminishing the previous problem of rural or remote areas' access. Similarly, the rapid convergence of telecom and information technologies, with new products in second and third generation mobile phones, emphasizes the great advancement of mobility versus fixed telecom networks and services. These technological developments are strongly linked with market dynamics. Universal service deals essentially with affordability. Experience shows that liberalization has substantially reduced prices, allowing for greater access in both social and territorial terms. While the political objective of universal service is an important one for achieving a socially and territorially inclusive information society, technological and market developments might simply overtake the regulatory instrument as it is today. Guaranteeing universal service has political and social value, yet not necessarily in the restrictive terms of a fixed telephony network.

DIVERSITY AND DISPARITIES IN THE EU

The advent of the information society is not a uniform phenomenon within the European Union. There is considerable diversity and even notable disparities in the ways in which ICTs are being used and have penetrated the different dimensions of the European citizens' life. We saw in the previous sections that the EU has been moving piecemeal towards introducing a 'social' perspective in its public actions enhancing the information society, beyond the liberalizing efforts. Concerns about disparity came seriously into the political agenda in the mid-1990s. This section examines two aspects of the diversity and disparities in the EU's move to the information society, and the reach of the public actions in this respect. First, the regional/territorial disparities, and the EU measures towards reducing them via regional policy are considered, and secondly, the social disparities, and the EU's limited role in this respect.

Regional/National Disparities

We have seen in previous chapters that the EU economy and society are very diverse. The same is found in relation to the information society. Statistical data show a clear national and regional divide within the European Union. Figure 4.3 illustrates these disparities at national level.[29]

Concerns about the regional divide of the information society have been politically articulated within the functional limits of EU regional policy. The

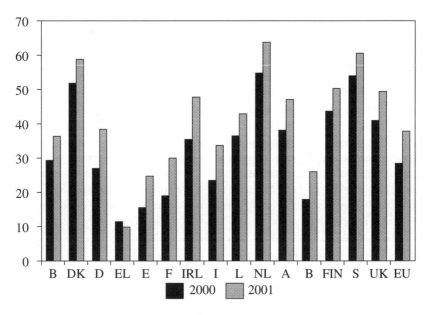

Source: Eurostat (2002).

Figure 4.3   Internet access in EU member states, 2000–01 (percentage of households)

1997 Commission communication on cohesion and the information society provides an overview of the situation.[30] Recognizing the importance of the liberalizing efforts and the role of the 'universal service' concept in accessibility and affordability, the Commission emphasized the fact that policy initiatives should have a bottom-up nature. This has also been largely supported by economic geographers, who have, generally speaking, underpinned the importance of this kind of initiative that emerges from the localities and regions (Gibbs 2001). In this regard, the Commission encouraged member states and the regions to make more use of the instruments of the Community Support Framework (CSF), under the Structural Funds, to respond to the needs of less favoured areas (Alabau 2002). This is an interesting issue since the CSF is the financial and programming instrument that is financed on a 50 per cent basis between the EU and the member state concerned. Apart from this, in 1995–99 the Commission launched a small pilot programme to deal with this issue, through the Regional Information Society Initiative, which financed 31 projects in total (Cornford et al. 2000). After the financial retrenchments for regional policy in the period 2000–06 were agreed in the Berlin Summit, this programme was closed. Since then, all initiatives on cohesion and information society have been subsumed under the CSF programming schedules.

The Social Divide

The gap produced between ICT haves and have-nots, does not have only a territorial/regional dimension; a social divide is also emerging within the same country, area and city. A recent OECD report stressed the social dimension of PC penetration and internet use. Cross-country data are still scarce, but the OECD comparative analysis of five countries has found that household income is a crucial factor. In France, for example, the highest income bracket had 74 per cent PC penetration in 2000 and the lowest income bracket only 11 per cent (OECD 2001: 18). Another finding is that educational attainment also explains differences, as those with tertiary education have the highest PC penetration ratio. Family structure also makes a difference – families with children under 18 years old are more likely to have a PC and internet access than other types. Sex and ethnic origin are also significant variables in this regard.

Since the mid-1990s, there has been general political and social awareness of this situation in most European countries. Whereas some states have launched national initiatives trying to address this problem, the EU is only doing so in a very limited manner. The social divide in the information society is a domain of political action where the EU has generated a great gap between words and deeds. Despite endless remarks about the need to create an information society that is socially inclusive (in numerous of reports and statements) the EU, as a level of governmental action by itself, does not have instruments to address such a problem. This has to do primarily with the division of tasks between member states and the Union. Bridging the social divide is essentially a goal under the domain of social policy, an area where the EU has restricted competences.

The political spur generated by the liberalization of the telecoms sector gave rise to the expectation that market forces could enhance industrial competitiveness and technological development, reduce consumer prices and improve telecoms services. Even if some of these expectations were partly accomplished, the social divide would not just vanish by itself. The information society does not bring a perfect society, where current political and social problems have a technical solution through the use of ICTs. Despite the general acknowledgement of this, most of the political discussions since the Bangemann Report were focused on a few specific issues, like the need to guarantee universal service, or the importance of young people's access to ICTs within the educational system. Nevertheless, the e-Europe initiative in the early 2000s has brought a wider view of the digital divide, focusing most notably on disabled people. Still, some issues have been left aside, like for example job-creation, elderly people, integration of immigrants in the labour market, or other general social policy objectives. The OECD seems to have been much more explicit on these matters. First in relation to ICTs and job-creation (OECD 1998), and secondly, in its efforts to provide analysis of the limited statistical data available (OECD 2001).

CONCLUSIONS

From the point of view of the innovation process, the massive advance in the use of ICTs has had two important effects. First, ICTs enhance the availability of codified knowledge, which is important with regard to a wide range of innovation related activities such as scientific research, education and training, industrial organization and business practices. Secondly, they help to enhance connectivity between innovators. Different innovation-related social communities such as researchers, consumers, manufacturers, and service producers, can develop their own communication and discussion channels, cutting across conventional organizational boundaries. All in all, the greater availability of codified knowledge and the enhanced connectivity might promote the creation of content-information products, and network and service solutions specifically shaped for EU consumers' needs, with the overall effect of fostering innovation in services and industrial production.

The EU has made a substantial effort in terms of liberalizing the telecoms market, supporting the development of technological competencies in the information-computer sector and in terms of awareness raising – pointing out the importance of ICTs in European life. In this sense, we can also trace a transition from essentially a market-building concern, towards a more social concern. The recent e-Europe puts substantial emphasis on crucial aspects of the digital economy, and some social aspects of ICTs. However, and despite scholarly criticisms, the EU should refrain from expanding the social agenda of the information society; the reason being that social policy falls generally within the competences of national governments, and a division of tasks assigning the EU deregulatory and reregulatory powers fits in best with the subsidiarity principle that guides EU politics.

In relation to the global position of the EU as a single actor in this domain, we have seen that the EU is making an effort to take part in the rapid institutionalization of governance structures of the internet and in the negotiations/implementation of the telecoms regulatory framework within the WTO regime. But we have also seen that more challenges are emerging at global level. The increased protective stances for personal data that the EU has recently passed need to be correlated with similar public actions in the US and Asia. However, large cultural differences regarding privacy, combined with rapid technological transformations, both with a global reach, might effectively water down the political expectations enshrined in the new directives. In other words, the global dimension might be inevitable in some issues, like privacy. In any case, the 'European model' of the information society has been addressing other matters, like for example universal service. Here the EU has made an effort to avoid deregulation leading to social exclusion. Defining fixed telephony as a 'basic service', the EU has obliged telecom operators to provide service in a universal manner. This chapter argued that whereas the political goal of social inclusion is laudable, the actual implementation of these new rights might be complex, requiring perhaps more flexible and adaptable solutions to specific national–regional circumstances. Last but not least, this chapter examined the situation regarding the diversity and disparities in the use of ICTs across the EU. Geographical disparities seem to be as large as social disparities, and although the EU has envisaged a number of policy initiatives, particularly for regional disparities, the field of social divide will probably remain under the scope of national public action.

Summing up, the rapid development of the information society political agenda does not just reflect the growing saliency of ICTs in socio-economic dynamics, it also represents the widening of the EU's innovation policy content, bringing in issues about the social embeddedness of ICT use. This topic will come to the surface again in the chapter about risk and social (dis)trust in science, directly associated with biotechnology (see Chapter 6).

NOTES

1. The 'Information Technologies Task Force' submitted a paper to the Commission in 1979, suggesting the creation of a European market for telecommunications equipment and services.
2. Green Paper on the development of the common market for telecommunications services and equipment COM (90) 490.
3. Council resolution on the development of the common market for telecommunications services and equipment up to 1992 88/C 257/01; OJ C27/1, 04 October 1988.
4. Commission directive on terminal equipment 88/301/EEC; OJ L131/73, 27 May 1988.
5. Commission directive on telecommunications services 90/388/EEC; OJL 192/10, 24 July 1990.
6. Council directive on open network provisions 90/387/EEC; OJ L192/1, 24 July 1990.
7. This came with the Council Resolution in 1993 (93/C 213/01, OJ C213/1, 06 August 1993).
8. Commission directive regarding the implementation of full competition in telecommunications markets (96/19/EC, OJ L74/13 22 March 1996).
9. The 'Green Paper on the convergence of the telecommunications, media and information technology sectors, and the implications for regulation towards an Information Society approach' COM (1997) 623.
10. An example of these uncertainties is whether TV set-top boxes (digital decoders) are a broadcasting or a telecommunication concern.
11. At the time of writing these proposals have not yet been approved. Detailed information about them can be found at http://europa.eu.int/ISPO/infosoc/telecompolicy/review99/Welcome.html.
12. 'e-Europe: An Information Society for All' COM (1999) 687 final. The Action Plan was launched in June 2000, coinciding with European Council in Santa Maria da Feira, under the Portuguese Presidency.
13. GATS (General Agreement on Trade in Services) considers basic services: voice telephony, data transmission, telex, telegraph, fax, and leased lines services.
14. The agreement has been implemented since February 1998, when only 12 countries were still pending acceptance. Today 65 of the signatory countries have formally accepted, and only five are still pending.
15. See Chapter 3 on intellectual property rights and the ECJ ruling in this topic.
16. The full text of this document can be found at http://www.icann.org/general/white-paper-05jun98.htm.
17. The first one was 'Communication on the Internet Governance' COM (1998) 476, final, 29 July 1998; and the second was: 'Communication on the organisation and management of the internet. International and European Policy Issues 1998–2000' COM (2000) 202 final, 11 April 2000.
18. Council Resolution on the organisation and management of the Internet, 11318/00, Brussels, 28 September 2000.
19. The exchange of letters between Liikanen and Roberts (from ICANN) can, naturally, be found on the net: http://europa.eu.int/ISPO/eif/InternetPoliciesSite/DotEU/LetterLiikanenRoberts.html; and http://www.icann.org/correspondence/roberts-letter-to-liikanen-10aug00.html.
20. See the initiatives of the UN in this respect, especially for Africa: http://www.un.org/Depts/eca/divis/disd/index.htm.
21. Detailed accounts of these actions can be found at http://europa.eu.int/ISPO/intcoop/i_int.html.
22. Communication from the Commission: 'The Information Society and Development: the Role of the European Union'. COM/97/0351 final of 15 July 1997.
23. EC/member states Expert Group on the Information Society and development. Issue Paper on the information society and development: Towards a European Union Response.
24. The OECD Privacy Guidelines, adopted as a Recommendation on 23 September, 1980; and the Council of Europe Convention for the protection of individuals with regard to automatic

processing of personal data, signed on 28 January 1981, and entered into force in 1985.
25. Directive 95/46/EC OJ L281, 23 November 1995, p. 31, on the protection of individuals with regard to the processing of personal data and on the free movement of such data.
26. Directive 97/66/EC, on the processing of personal data and protection of privacy in the telecommunications sector. Soon to be replaced by the proposed directive on the same topic COM(2000) 385 final.
27. Directive on the application of open network provision to voice telephony and on universal service for telecommunications in a competitive environment 98/10/EC, OJ L 101/41, 01 April 1998.
28. Directive on the interconnection in telecommunications with regard to ensuring universal service and interoperability through application of the principles of open network provision 97/33/EC, amended by Directive 98/61/EC.
29. Regional data is not so easy to find in this regard. Eurostat has some important regionalized data, but not on the use of information or communication technologies.
30. Communication on cohesion and the information society COM (97)7 final.

REFERENCES

Alabau, A. (2002), 'The European regions and information society policy instruments'. In *Governing Telecommunications and the New Information Society in Europe*, J. Jordana. Cheltenham, Edward Elgar.

Bell, D. (1973), *The Coming of Post-industrial Society: A Venture in Social Forecasting*. New York, Basic Books.

Blume, P. (1998), 'New technologies and human rights: Data protection, privacy and the information society'. Copenhagen, Retsvidenskabeligt Institut B – University of Copenhagen. Study no. 67.

Castells, M. (1998), *End of Millennium*. Malden, MA, Blackwell Publishers.

Castells, M. (2001), *The Internet Galaxy: Reflections on Internet, Business, and Society*. Oxford, Oxford University Press.

Commission, European (1994a), *Europe and the Global Information society: Recommendations to the European Council* (The Bangemann Report). Brussels, European Commission.

Commission, European (1994b), 'Europe's way to the information society: An action plan'. Com (94) 347 final.

Commission, European (1996a), *Building the European Information Society for Us All: First Reflections of the High Level Group of Experts*. Brussels, European Commission.

Commission, European (1996b), 'Green Paper – living and working in the information society: People first'. COM(96)389.

Commission, European (1999a), 'Commission staff working document: Europe's liberalised telecommunications market – a guide to the rules of the game'. Unpublished document, available on the internet.

Commission, European (1999b), 'e-Europe 2002: An information society for all'. Action plan. COM (1999) 687 final.

Cornford, J., A. Gillespie and R. Richardson (2000), 'Regional development in the information society'. In *The Information Society in Europe*, K. Ducatel, J. Webster and W. Herrmann. Boston, Rowan & Littlefield Publishers Inc.

Currie, W. (2000), *The Global Information Society*. Chichester, John Wiley & Sons.

Dang-Nguyen, G., V. Schneider and R. Werle (1993), 'Networks in European policy-making: Europeification of telecommunications policy'. In *Making Policy in*

Europe: The Europeification of National Policy-making, S. Andersen and K.A. Eliassen. London, Sage.

Ducatel, K., J. Webster and W. Hermann (2000), 'Information infrastructures or societies?' In *The Information Society in Europe. Work and Life in an Age of Globalization*, K. Ducatel, J. Webster and W. Hermann. Boston, Rowan & Littlefield Publishers, Inc.

Eliassen, K.A. and M. Sjövaag (1999), 'Introduction'. In *European Telecommunications Liberation*, K.A. Eliassen and M. Sjövaag. London, Routledge.

Enser, J. (1998), 'EU telecommunications policy and the WTO'. In *The Union and the World. The Political Economy of a Common European Foreign Policy*, A. Cafruny and P. Peters. The Hague, Kluwer Law International.

Eurostat (2002), 'Information society statistics'. *Statistics in Focus - Industry, Trade and Services* **8**(Theme 4).

Fredebul-Krein, M. and A. Freytag (1997), 'Telecommunications and WTO discipline. An assessment of the WTO agreement on telecommunication services'. *Telecommunications Policy* **21**(6): 477–91.

Fuchs, G. (1994), 'Policy-making in a system of multi-level governance. The Commission of the European Community and the restructuring of the telecommunications sector'. *Journal of European Public Policy* **1**(2): 177–95.

Gibbs, D. (2001), 'Harnessing the information society? European Union policy and information and communication technologies'. *European Urban and Regional Studies* **8**(1): 73–84.

Haynes, M. and S. Thompson (2000), 'Productivity, employment and the IT paradox: Evidence from financial services'. In *Productivity, Innovation and Economic Performance*, R. Barrell, G. Mason and M. O'Mahony. Cambridge, Cambridge University Press.

Jordana, J. (2000), 'La política de telecomunicaciones. Una integración negativa?' In *Políticas Públicas en la Unión Europea*, F. Morata. Barcelona, Ariel.

Jordana, J. (2002), 'Regulating telecommunications and enforcing the information society in Europe'. In *Governing Telecommunications and the New Information Society in Europe*, J. Jordana. Cheltenham, Edward Elgar.

Lamberton, D. (1999), 'Information: Pieces, Batches or Flows?' In *Economic Organisation and Economic Knowledge*, S.C. Dow and P.E. Earl. Cheltenham, Edward Elgar.

Lucas, H.C.J. (1999), *Information Technology and the Productivity Paradox*. New York, Oxford University Press.

Lundvall, B.-Å. (1999), 'Knowledge production and the knowledge base'. Unpublished, Dept. of Business Studies, Aalborg University.

McGuckin, R.H. and K.J. Stiroh (1998), 'Computers can accelerate productivity growth'. *Issues in Science and Technology* **14**(Summer): 41–8.

Mayer-Schönberger, V. (1997), 'Generational development of data protection in Europe'. In *Technology and Privacy: The New Landscape*, P.E. Agre and M. Rotenberg. Cambridge, MA, The MIT Press.

Miranda, A.D. and M. Kristiansen (2001), 'Technological determinism and ideology: The European Union and the information society'. Unpublished paper.

OECD (1998), *Technology, Productivity and Job Creation. Best Policy Practices*. Paris, OECD.

OECD (2001), *Understanding the Digital Divide*. Paris, OECD.

Patterson, R. and E.J. Wilson (2000), 'New IT and social inequality: Resetting the research and policy agenda'. *The Information Society* **16**: 77–86.

Pearce, G. and N. Platten (1998), 'Achieving personal data protection in the European Union'. *Journal of Common Market Studies* **36**(4): 529–47.

Predergast, R. (1999), 'Knowledge and information in classical economics'. In *Economic Organization and Economic Knowledge*, S.C. Dow and P.E. Earl. Cheltenham, Edward Elgar.

Sandholtz, W. (1998), 'The emergence of a supranational telecommunications regime'. In *European Integration and Supranational Integration*, W. Sandholtz and A. Stone Sweet. Oxford, Oxford University Press.

Scherer, J. (ed.) (1995), *Telecommunications Laws in Europe*. London, Baker and McKenzie.

Schneider, V. (1997), 'Different roads to the information society? Comparing US and European approaches from a public policy perspective'. In *The Social Shaping of Information Superhighways - European and American Roads to the Information Society*, H. Kubicek, W. Dutton and R. Williams. Frankfurt/New York, Campus Verlag.

Schneider, V. (2002), 'The institutional transformation of telecommunications between Europeanization and globalization'. In *Governing Telecommunications and the New Information Society in Europe*, J. Jordana. Cheltenham, Edward Elgar.

Skogerbø, E. and T. Storsul (2000), 'Prospects for expanded universal service in Europe: The case of Denmark, the Netherlands and Norway'. *The Information Society* **16**: 135–46.

Soete, L. (1999), 'Europe and the emerging information society: The need for policy innovation'. In *Governing the Information Society. Collective Action and European Interest*, B. Lasserre. Paris, Hermes.

Thatcher, M. (2002), 'The relationship between national and European regulation of telecommunications'. In *Governing Telecommunications and the New Information Society*, J. Jordana. Cheltenham, Edward Elgar.

Webster, F. (1995), *Theories of the Information Society*. London, Routledge.

Ypsilanti, D. and L. Gosling (1997), *Towards a Global Information Society. Global Information Infrastructure, Global Information Society: Policy Requirements*. Paris, OECD.

5. The world of standards

Por eso afirman que la conservación de este mundo es una perpetua creación y que los verbos *conservar y crear*, tan enemistados aquí, son sinónimos en el Cielo.
[It is stated that the preservation of this world is a perpetual creation and that the verbs 'preserve' and 'create', so opposed to each other here, are synonymous in Heaven]

(Jorge Luis Borges, *Historia de la eternidad*, 1957: 35)

INTRODUCTION

Standards play a crucial role in defining the market share of entire industrial sectors (and not just high-tech ones), shaping the technological advances of technological systems, and defining the overall performance of these. Standards can be formal agreements or regulations, or can be de facto standards defined strictly by market dynamics. Yet, common to them all is that they are essential elements in the innovation process, with notorious path dependency effects. Defining the technical specifications of a product or a production process does not just affect the level of interconnectivity and interchangeability of that element within the technological system it is embedded in, it also affects the patterns on which the product and the overall technological system are likely to evolve in the future. In other words, by defining current technical specifications, we narrow significantly the options for the technological developments to come, since alternatives are ruled out by a combination of technological and market choice. Social actors make the choice in different contexts, depending on how the standards were achieved and what type of standard is being referred to. 'Choice' here implies the collective selection of technical specifications. All this refers to what the economists of innovation have called the 'path dependency of the innovation process'.

This chapter addresses some general aspects of standardization and the innovation process, and how they relate to the EU's innovation policy. Following the pattern of previous chapters, it starts by exploring the economic and social considerations of standards and the innovation process, in particular questions concerning public action. Secondly, it analyses the Europeanization process of standard-setting. This is an interesting issue since it has been linked so strongly with one of the core political projects of the Union – the establishment of a single market. The chapter then moves on to devote attention to the changing patterns of the global and international structures of standardization and the role that the EU plays in this. Last, as usual, this chapter will argue that there is also a clear shift in the nature of the public–private partnership at EU level, and that this raises new questions regarding the accountability and responsibility of regulatory delegation, the efficient results of the EU efforts on standardization, and the question of 'who controls the market'.

STANDARDIZATION AND INNOVATION

The process of standardization is intrinsically related to the creation, industrial application and usage of technology, and hence to the innovation process as such. There have been standards throughout modern history, with examples such as electricity, steam engine models, and national railway systems (Barry 2001). Standards have increasingly gained a central position in advanced economies which are characterized by both high levels of internationalization and the role that knowledge plays in the development of new products and processes. Most experts point at the unprecedented proliferation of standardization in the last two decades. More important than the numbers, though, is the nature of these standards and their direct effects on industrial dynamics and innovation processes. But how do standards exercise this influence in industrial dynamics? Why do they seem so central, particularly for some industrial sectors and not for others? How are the 'standard battles' won, and what are their effects? What are standards, and why should innovation policy be concerned about them?

Standards, What Standards?

There are a wide variety of definitions of standards, both broad and narrow. Ironically, this variation reflects the lack of standardization when talking about standards. In any case, and in order to avoid confusion, any author must begin with a conceptual clarification of his or her understanding of the term. One of the broadest definitions has been provided by Brunsson and Jacobsson (2000), for whom a standard is any rule that has a voluntary nature, no matter how or by which body it was produced. In other words, standardization is a form of regulation, namely non-mandatory regulation. It is not surprising that they present a vast range of examples, including the rules on how handball should be played (defined by the corresponding international association), textbooks defining how firms or public administrations should be managed, recommendations of international organizations like the UN or the OECD (the so-called soft law), and technical specifications for products defined by national standardization bodies. Their comprehensive definition of standards serves the purpose of their book, which is to bring to the fore the pervasiveness of rule-making and its central position in modern society. However, their definition is too broad for the purposes and subject matter of this book. This requires a narrower conceptualization of standards, which looks at only the technical specifications of products and processes in which technological development is embedded. In other words, a concept of standards more directly applicable to the world of industrial dynamics.

Therefore, the concept proposed by Paul David seems to be more workable: 'A "standard" is to be understood as a set of technical specifications adhered to by a producer, either tacitly or as a result of a formal agreement' (David 1995: 16). The benefits of this definition are that it applies directly to the world of industrial dynamics and it looks at the real processes of standardization. David's focal point is the producer's adoption of a technical specification. Therefore, the type of specification (tacit or explicit), and the way in which it has been established (by adherence, agreement or simple adoption of a compulsory regulation) shape the taxonomy of standards available. Table 5.1 summarizes David's four types of technical standards.

The first two types (unsponsored and sponsored) are 'de facto' standards

Table 5.1   Taxonomy of standards

Type of standard	Characteristics
Unsponsored standards	Sets of well-documented specifications that exist in the public domain, but in the absence of any identified originator with proprietary interests, or any sponsoring agency
Sponsored standards	Agencies and firms hold proprietary interests, and induce others to adopt particular sets of technical specifications
Standard agreements	Those technical specifications agreed under the auspices of voluntary standard-writing institutions
Mandated standards (harmonized standards)	Those technical specifications promulgated by governmental agencies with some regulatory authority

Source: Elaborated from David (1995: 17).

because 'they emerge from market-mediated processes' (David 1995: 17). The other two are 'de jure' standards, voluntary and mandatory in nature, respectively.

This chapter mainly focuses on the third and fourth types of standard; namely, standard agreements and mandatory standards. Since the end of the 1980s, the distinction between them has become blurred in the context of EU politics, in a manner that we will examine in detail. Yet, the point to underline here is that these two types are the most interesting from a policy point of view, as they are formalized through an institution. Hence, policy is able to shape ex ante the conditions for effective and relevant standards and become one aspect of the public governance of the economy. For the other two standard types mentioned earlier – unsponsored and sponsored standards – there is only ex post policy action, as public authorities might control the potentially harmful effects of the standard and the corresponding illegal behaviour of firms under the rules of competition policy. It is essentially this ex ante policy action that is in focus here.

So far our attention has been on the upstream standardization process; that is, the processes by which public–private interactions or strictly public regulatory processes set and define common industrial standards. But common for all de jure standards ('standard agreements' and 'regulation') is that the downstream standardization process becomes very relevant for achieving the expected goals. Downstream standardization refers to the process of certification, testing and measurement to which industrial products might be subject for sale in a specific market. This is based on a public system of legal/semi-legal accreditation carried out by laboratories enjoying such abilities. Public action is central here, since public authorities shape this accreditation system and grant laboratories the rights to perform such tasks. Although downstream standardization has tended to receive relatively little attention from economists of innovation, it is an essential step for individual firms' entry into a market. High barriers to entry, either due to costs of certification or complex and time-consuming procedures, have a tremendous impact on market structure and on technological development, in ways that have been described as one of the most pervasive 'technical barriers to trade'. This chapter will also address this matter within the EU context.

The Costs and Benefits of Standards

Standards are economic institutions that shape the path of technological development. Either in their formalized or non-formalized manner, they have two potentially positive effects. First, standards significantly reduce transaction costs involved in the development and application of a technology by firms and consumers, since they reduce variation; secondly, standards generate positive network externalities, since they operate in economies of scale. This is especially relevant for standards that seek interoperability and connectivity, because they are elements within large technological systems, which have very high establishment costs. Positive network externalities emerge because the value of using a particular technology increases with the number of other agents who are also using it, in the way that if one user adopts the technology it will benefit all other users in the market who have adopted the same technology. Following this line of argument, economists point to the fact that standardization is likely to take place because there are global increasing returns in network economies (Arthur 1989). The controller of the standard captures increasing returns to scale because it gets market dominance as the initial market penetrator, generating rapid market growth. Network externalities are also related to the fact that agents communicate and share information about how to use a technology, so a learning-by-using process shapes future technological decisions in both global and spatially circumscribed manners (Cowan and Miller 1998).

However, standards might also have negative effects, which are the other side of the coin of the benefits we have just examined. One of the most obvious is that the choice embodied in the standard might be a *sub-optimal technical solution* vis-à-vis other choices that never became the dominant standard. This is a 'static' negative effect, since at a given point in time the hegemonic technical solution is inferior to already available technologies that are alternatives to the standard. An often quoted example of this is the market for videocassette recorders in the 1980s. Sony's Betamax had a clearly superior picture quality to the VHS product developed by JVC. However, VHS became the industry's standard by the end of that decade due to JVC's active encouragement of other manufacturers to adopt it by sharing future product development. The business strategy rather than the inherent technical superiority of the product was what eventually tipped the balance in favour of the VHS standard (Besen and Farrell 1994).

A second negative effect is that the level of standardization is so high that it results in a *lock-in situation* where dynamic variation is effectively hindered. In contrast with the previous form of negative effect, 'lock-in' refers to a dynamic process, not a static situation. A frequently mentioned example of lock-in was provided by David's study of the 'QWERTY' keyboard design (David 1985). QWERTY has continuously managed to win out over rival keyboard designs that were obviously better, becoming a platform for the current keyboard standard. The conclusions that David reaches at the end of the case study about path dependence have been contested by neo-classical economists, in a theoretical debate that still continues today (Liagouras 2002).

A third negative effect of standardization is 'the reduction of costs of entry to production of standardized products, thereby intensifying price competition to the point that the developers of the successful system are unable to recoup the fixed costs of its logical improvements' (David 1995: 26). In other words, the first mover is unable to appropriate the benefits of its own investments, resulting in a disincentive to the initial innovation. This negative effect is directly related to the appropriation problem that we examined in Chapter 3. The result might be that innovators would prefer to obtain property rights rather than engage in the definition of collective standards, in a situation where capital investments have already been made.

The fourth negative effect refers to 'the stranding or "orphaning" of a substantial body of users who had adopted network products that failed to become industry standards, and consequently ceased to be supported and further improved' (David 1995: 2). This might have a parallel to the biological evolutionary metaphor. Those standards that fail to become hegemonic in the market run the risk of being left behind as a result of the mainstreaming effect generated by the dynamics of the economies of scale, independently of their technological superiority. The result is invariably a decrease in the learning-by-using process of the orphan users, and subsequently, of the learning-by-doing process of the producers, which reduces overall innovative performance of the economy.

What we can see from this is that standards have to be understood dynamically. The overall performance of standards in a market depends on whether the benefits of variation reduction, economies of scale and network positive externalities are greater than the costs related to sub-optimal technical solutions, dynamic locks-in, disincentives to invest and/or orphan users. In other words, a market structure where standardization shows signs of openness and flexibility, so that the innovation process is guaranteed by creativity and renewal. It can therefore be argued that the tension and dialectics between order and variation in standards contribute to innovation and economic development.

Standardization and Innovation Policy: Some Open Questions

According to historians of science, standardization was a concomitant element of the industrial revolution and of the state-building practices in the 19th century. As Wise puts it:

> Rapidly expanding national and international commerce, carried especially on those new media of long-distance uniformity, the railroad and the telegraph, had made standards a necessity of life for engineers, manufacturers, and traders alike. ... The so-called 'second industrial revolution' of science-based industries, especially chemical and electrical industries, was under way. (Wise 1995: 222)

This is especially true for the US, France, Germany and Britain, where the first national standardization bodies were already in existence in the late 19th century, most of them focusing on issues of measurement and precision. This was perceived to be a necessity not only to improve industrial production and its reliability, but as Barry suggests 'measurement and quantification were viewed increasingly as a critical instrument for government' (Barry 2001: 62).

With the advent of the knowledge-based economy at the dawn of the 21st century, standards have regained a central position as primary elements of industrial dynamics and the innovation process. Tassey suggests several reasons for this: first, the fact that, today, many new technologies are developed as overall technical systems results in more economies of scale producing good incentives for standardization. Secondly, there is higher user demand for particular product characteristics, which also stimulates standardization. Consumers' increased preferences for reliability, safety, quality and interoperability have certainly fostered standardization. Thirdly, technology life-cycles have shortened considerably, particularly in some high-tech sectors like consumer electronics or IT, which also increases pressure for standardization, so competition can take place within a standardized platform of product development (Tassey 2000).

To my mind, this third feature of the contemporary economy is the most important in terms of relating standardization to the innovation process. The life-cycle of most manufacturing products has shortened spectacularly over the last couple of decades. This refers as much to high-tech products as to medium and low-tech ones, where patterns of change have also accelerated tremendously. But why do time patterns imply transforming economic institutions? The ability to compete no longer just depends on embodying the knowledge stock that the firm has into a product, it also depends on the firm's organizational ability to develop successful strategies for standard-setting or standard-following products, a solid service-support network, and a consumer interface for mutual information and learning. Price competition continues to be pivotal, but no longer in an exclusive manner, since technological and organizational advantages in the market have to be exploited quickly if the firm is to succeed in profiling its product in a rapidly changing market.

There are different traditions concerning public action and how to approach the issue of standard-setting. In the US, the overall philosophy has been to leave the process of defining industrial standards to the market, 'Because the US domestic market is large with considerable internal competition in most industries, American economic philosophy has allowed the competitive dynamics of the marketplace to set product-element standards' (Tassey 2000: 600). The collective preference in the US has therefore been 'de facto' standards, with relatively few 'de jure' standards, particularly standard agreements that have a quasi-legal status (Warshaw and Saunders 1995). This preference is combined with strong ex post control mechanisms through the active enforcement of anti-trust law when there is evidence that standards are used in an unfair manner. A good example of this is the anti-trust case against Microsoft which was brought because the firm's business strategies were linked to its de facto standard. In contrast with the US, the EU has been actively involved in the field of de jure standards since the late 1980s. This is true for both market-making objectives through common harmonized standards, and occasionally in anticipatory industrial standards of a voluntary nature (standard agreements, in David's typology). The transfer of competences from national to EU level, and the partial delegation of power from the EU to the standards-bodies characterizes the 'EU model'. Yet the question remains as to why the issue of standards was linked to the market-making political initiatives of that decade. And if there are any lessons to learn from the successes and failures of mandatory and voluntary standards set in Europe.

EUROPEANIZATION

The EU's involvement in the field of industrial standards is related to the political objective of constructing a common market. This objective has been the leitmotif of European integration since the 1950s. Nevertheless, it received a decisive push in the 1980s through a series of political initiatives among which standardization had a prominent place. This section will argue that the transfer of power from national level to the EU on standardization is far from being the 'only possible' step. To establish EU-wide standardization procedures and bodies in the way they were conceived in the mid- to late 1980s was not teleologically pre-determined in the 1950s, nor in the 1980s thrust to a single market. The move towards generating common industrial standards in the EU responds to specific political decisions about what is appropriate and optimal at a given point in time, and these decisions are based on world-views and ideas that give meaning to policy-makers. Needless to say, though, these decisions have substantially affected European industrial dynamics. As everywhere, there are success stories and fiascos, and interesting lessons might be learnt on this basis. In their relative short life, EU standardization procedures have experienced some interesting adaptations. It is worth arguing that a more decisive linkage with innovation policy could also be desirable. We shall now turn to these issues.

The Single European Market Project and Standardization

The creation of a single European market for goods is a centerpiece of the functional path for the European integration process. Despite the diverse mechanisms found in the EEC treaty for that purpose,[1] real intra-EU trade barriers have always existed. One reason for this has been the rapid, and somehow unexpected, growth of the so-called technical barriers to trade since the 1960s. When reading the original Treaties, much emphasis was placed on quantitative restrictions like import quotas and tariffs. However, the development of substantial national legislation on human health and environmental safety, and other technical regulations defining products' technical specifications were directly affecting trade flows and having the same effect as protectionist barriers. The nature of these regulations rendered the reconciliation of two central legal and political elements in Europe quite difficult; namely, the national sovereignty of member states to define such technical regulations and the goals of a single market for goods as foreseen in the Treaties.

This tension became increasingly obvious in the 1970s, when a growing number of cases were piling up on the desk of the European Court of Justice, waiting for a judgment on whether some specific national regulations were against the spirit of the Treaties. In this context, the Court defined the legal principle of 'mutual recognition' in its path-breaking 'Cassis de Dijon' case in 1979.[2] The mutual recognition principle means that products produced legally in one EU member state should also be admitted for sale in another state. Restrictions to this principle are rather limited; namely, to questions of health, environmental and consumer protection. The effects of this new legal principle were devastating to the previous technical barriers between EU members, since it automatically generated an open market for a wide spectrum of products.[3]

With this new principle, the EU enjoyed powerful 'negative integration' instruments for market-making objectives by the end of the 1970s. Negative integration refers to the creation of an EU single market by breaking trade barriers between member states (Scharpf 1999). The distribution of tasks between member states and the EU was rather clear at this point: member states kept their right to produce national regulations on technical specifications, whereas the EU allowed the free flow of goods between member states by determining that the principle of mutual recognition must be respected. However, this distribution of tasks brought to the fore an entirely new political situation: the risk that mutual recognition would generate regulatory competition between EU states, lowering the overall levels of safety requirements. This was perceived as a very real danger, particularly in the mid-1980s, when issues of health, environmental and consumer protection were gaining in political visibility among European citizens. This, together with other factors, successfully triggered the move from strictly negative integration solutions towards 'positive integration' solutions entailing common decisions.

It is in this context that the project of the single market emerged. Several authors have pointed out the pro-active role of the Delors Commission in advancing an eminently liberal political view, seeking 'more market', anchored in the political repercussions of the Cassis de Dijon case (Armstrong and Bulmer 1998). As Egan puts it:

> The Commission took advantage of the trend among member states to champion the liberalization of markets, renew efforts to stem the rise of protectionist barriers to trade, and enhance international competitiveness through market integration, so that regulatory reform found a receptive audience during a timely window of opportunity. (Egan 2001: 111)

And Nicolaïdis and Egan commented that:

> The emergence of this new paradigm can be explained through the interplay of change in the incentives faced by politicians – for whom the failure of delivering on the core EU promise came at an increasingly high price – and changes in prevailing ideas about trade liberalization in regulated sectors. On this last count, both mutual recognition and delegation of standardization tasks to private bodies resonated with the ethos of the 1980s and the new emphasis on diversity in Europe along with growing skepticism over centralization and 'common policies'. (2001: 460-61)

The new (de)regulatory strategy for market integration worked on three fronts: (1) to actively prevent new technical barriers to trade from arising, (2) to harmonize regulatory differences through the promotion of European standards, and (3) to provide market surveillance mechanisms (Egan 2001: 115). From this strategy we can see that the creation of common European standards has been a centerpiece in the overall strategy of the single market project. Before 1985, the procedure was such that member states regulated their own technical specifications and implemented their own conformity controls for manufactured products. EU legislation setting common standards was possible, but rather exceptional, and few common standards ever saw the light of day. Besides, EU legislation followed a 'maximilistic' harmonization approach, setting out in exhaustive detail the performance objectives and design specifications on a product-by-product basis. This 'old approach' to EU standardization generated a number of problems, as Farr has put it:

> it was a very time-consuming procedure, required unanimity as it was based on art. 95 (ex. Art. 100), the maximilistic approach was very inflexible and uniform, there was an entire separation with the work carried out by the volunteer standardization-bodies at European level, it was not able to prevent the proliferation of new national regulation, despite common EU regulation member states continued to proceed with national certification, third countries were excluded in the process of technical regulations, and there was a high ratio of non-compliance from member states. (Farr 1996)

The renewed attention to standards in the mid-1980s required a significant reform of the standard-setting process. This was called the 'new approach to technical harmonization and standards', which is still operative. The new approach was laid out in a number of official documents,[4] and is based on the following principles: EU directives specify only the essential requirements for health, environmental and consumer protection. This meant abandoning the previous approach based on maximalistic and detailed EU regulation. Directives are no longer on a product-by-product basis, but deal with relatively large families of products, like for example low voltage products or medical devices. The Commission and the member states define a clear political mandate to the European standardization bodies. Apart from specifying the legal framework – the essential requirements just mentioned – this mandate includes clear guidelines on the type of work to be pursued, and the territorial reach of the standard (EFTA or only EU). The resulting harmonized standards are voluntary, since manufacturers may choose either to apply them directly or to demonstrate that their products comply with the mandatory essential requirements by means of conformity assessment (testing and certification). Testing and certification are carried out by independent bodies that are designated by member states and are within their jurisdictions (typically privately/publicly owned laboratories). The directives define the conformity assessment procedures and manufacturers are legally responsible for ensuring that their products comply with the essential requirements of the directives. Moreover, it is the member states that carry out market surveillance, so non-conforming products are withdrawn from the market and, if necessary, legal action is undertaken against infringing firms. Summing up, the new system is based on EU technical regulations setting 'essential requirements', voluntary standards that define these further, and conformity assessment procedures for the control of products in the market.

The standard-setting bodies are the showpiece of the new approach. There are mainly three: CEN,[5] CENELEC[6] and ETSI.[7] They are independent from the EU, and have distributed their tasks between themselves according to the principle of functional differentiation of industrial sectors. The oldest is CEN, which was established in 1961 as a nonprofit-making international association. It covers a wide spectrum of fields, such as for example mechanical engineering, health technology, and the environment, but it openly excludes electro-technical products and telecommunications, which fall respectively under the sphere of CENELEC and ETSI. CENELEC was established in 1973, closely following the structure and objectives of CEN. Both these organizations are based on national membership, with 20 members each.[8] In contrast, ETSI, a much newer organization set up in 1988, has 874 members, because it consists of a system of individual membership for companies operating in the telecommunications field (including national telecommunication administrations). CEN and CENELEC have a decision-making process based strictly on national representation, which is why Hawkins argues that this standard-setting process is in reality 'technological diplomacy' based on international negotiations (Hawkins 1995). ETSI, however, enjoys a slightly more flexible decision-making mechanism where other stakeholders are directly involved, yet national representatives hold important voting powers. This is represented in Figure 5.1.

Figure 5.1 only applies to the procedure for setting harmonized standards, where the Commission and/or the EFTA secretariat send a mandate to the European standards bodies based on a specific EU Directive. Yet, these bodies are also in charge of developing 'standard agreements', based on a more 'bottom-up' procedure, where individual firms, associations or national standards bodies engage in the definition of technical specifications, typically in an anticipatory manner, in order to develop the compatibility and interconnectivity of specific products.

As Egan points out, in recent years the bulk of activity has tended to be dominated by specific mandates from the European Commission under the New Approach (Egan 1998: 493). This corresponds well with the comments that several experts have made about the fact that the delegation of semi-

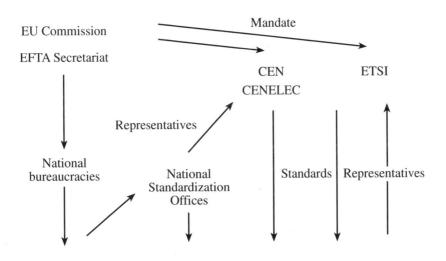

Source: Goerke and Holler (1998: 98).

Figure 5.1   The standardization process under the new approach

regulatory activity from the EU to these independent bodies has put significant pressure and workload on them (Farr 1996). Nevertheless, the specific dynamics of the industrial sectors where these three bodies operate has also played a role (particularly in electro-technical and telecommunication products). As Tables 5.2 and 5.3 show, CEN has a relatively high ratio of harmonized standards in relation to the total standards produced.

One point deserves further attention at this stage, namely the nature of European standards. Following the rules of the new approach, the harmonized standards produced under the auspices of the three bodies are voluntary. That is, individual firms have two options: either they choose to follow the

Table 5.2   Indicative figures of the standards made at CEN, 1997-2001

Year	Harmonized standards[a]	Total standards[b]
1997	450	3912
1998	570	4720
1999	650	5566
2000	800	6398
2001	840	7455

Notes:
[a] Not including amendments. Officials at CEN indicate that obtaining the precise figure is a complex issue due to the question of the nature of the amendments, particularly in construction products. The problem is that if amendments are excluded then the figure is underestimated, because the amendments make the previous standards 'harmonized'.
[b] This figure includes amendments.

Source: CEN indicative figures.

Table 5.3   Indicative figures of the standards made at CENELEC and ETSI, 2001

	Total standards	Harmonized standards
CENELEC*	4004	820
ETSI**	2318	560

Notes: *   Figures corresponding to all standards active by 31 December 2001.
            **   Figures corresponding to all standards published from January to December 2001.

Source: The CENELEC online Info Service and the ETSI standards are available from http://pda.etsi.org./pda/ and http://www.etsi.org/eds/.

standards, or they comply with the obligatory 'essential requirements' stipulated in the corresponding Directive. Hence, manufacturers are allowed not to follow the standard, but then they have in any case to conform to certain compulsory minimum specifications. This means that there is an onus on producers who decide not to follow the European standard, since the procedure to get products certified under the essential requirements seems to be longer and more expensive than the standard solution. This, together with the fact that it is very difficult to change a European standard once it has been decided, means that in reality the European standards produced by the standard-setting bodies are not entirely voluntary, but are quasi-mandatory standards (Bundgaard-Pedersen 1997). This is the reason why, in the present work, we consider the harmonized standards as part of the 'mandatory' category, following David's typology (1995), even if we might agree that the division is not so clear-cut.

More than 15 years have passed since the new approach was agreed, and questions about its effectiveness and overall results are now emerging. In the mid-1990s, Sebastian Farr mentioned two weaknesses that time has tended to confirm.

> In the first place, the essential requirements enumerated in the directives are often stated in very general terms, and the European standards organizations do not have clear directions to carry out the technical task of drawing up the standards themselves. (Farr 1996: 32)

This results in important delays, even if it leaves wider scope for decision-making among the partners involved in the standard-setting negotiations. 'Secondly, the European standard bodies are now obliged to draw up thousands of high quality standards, and this in turn has placed a tremendous strain upon the resources of these organizations' (p. 32). The administrative structure of these organizations has been under pressure since the early 1990s. The two weaknesses have been partly confirmed and voices clamouring for a more rapid and effective system were raised in the second half of the 1990s. As Egan argues: 'The regulatory strategy which had appeared to solve the Commission's problems by delegating negotiations onto other institutions proved to be just as prone to endless bargaining and inaction as the harmonization process it replaced' (Egan 2001: 167).

European Success and Failure Stories: Any Possible Lessons?

The history of European standardization, although short, is full of significant stories of both failure and success. As we will see in this sub-section, it is not that easy to draw lessons that can serve as overall guiding posts in the future. Each European standard is intrinsically related to a set of specific industrial, technological, business-strategic and political factors, and is therefore deeply context-bounded. Nothing daunted though, the four cases examined here are interesting in their own right since they were important hints to the contemporary history of industrial politics in the EU and Europe at large. They might, thus, provide useful insights as to the processes involved in the complex issue that is a successful European standard. With this purpose in mind, we have chosen two cases, one successful and the other a failure, relating to each type of standard. The first two cases to be presented, namely GSM and HDTV, fall under the category of 'standard agreements'; that is, industrial standards that are fully voluntary. GSM has been successful, whereas HDTV was a failure. After that, we present the cases of standards for toy safety, a success, and for construction products, a failure. These two come under the 'harmonized standards' or 'mandatory standards' type, where a EU directive stipulates the 'essential requirements' for health, environmental and consumer protection, and a series of product-family standardization mandates have been issued from the EU to the corresponding European standardization body (see Table 5.4).

Starting with the first, the GSM standard for mobile telephony that today is operative in the EU and EFTA countries has been one of the most highly acclaimed successes of European standard-setting. The story starts in the early 1980s. The first movers in Europe were Scandinavian firms, who had already established the common Scandinavian NTM-450 standard in 1981. This early success showed how a cooperative strategy could help to increase market size and advance competitive positions based on high-tech developments (Funk and Methe 2001). In 1983, initial Franco-German cooperation on GSM (Groupe Spécial Mobile) gave way to several proposals (narrow band, wide band and hybrid band), which were discussed among the largest European PTT operators in the mid-1980s. At that time, the Commission had already started considering the GSM standard as a truly strategic project and in 1985 it produced two reports that foresaw a real market need for mobile telephony and the benefits that could be derived from a common open European standard (Pelkmans 2001). Later, the EU was involved at two crucial points of the

Table 5.4   The four cases of European standardization presented in this section

	Standard agreements	Harmonized standards
Successful	GSM	Toy safety
Failure/less successful	HDTV (MAC)	Construction products

cooperative agreement on GSM – namely, the 1987 Directive binding states to reserve and free frequencies in the 900 MHz band (thus generating the necessary 'space' to develop GSM); and the Council recommendation the same year for a cooperative development of GSM, which paved the way for the essential 'Memorandum of Understanding' to be written and subscribed to by 15 telecoms operators. However, and despite the active political brokerage of the EU in this regard, GSM was an industrial standard developed essentially by the corresponding firms. In the late 1980s and early 1990s, when the fate of GSM was decided, all European telecom operators were without exception national monopolies. What was the incentive that made them move towards the cooperative solution, leaving the standard 'open', rather than towards a competition strategy based on proprietary rights of key technological elements, as in the US? Pelkmans argues that the following factors were important: the monopolistic nature of the European telecom operators, the lessons of the Scandinavian success, the fact that none of the firms had invested massively in the technology, the almost vertical integration of equipment suppliers, and the prospects of a large market beyond national frontiers. Even if the list is long, 'when a network compatibility standard is open, however, the non-proprietary nature and measured form of private/ public co-operation to create investor confidence are surely among the crucial elements' (Pelkmans 2001: 451). Other authors, however, posit that the structure of IPR (intellectual property rights) ownership was determinant. In particular, they point to the fact that most of the dominant firms in the GSM alliance had essential IPRs, and that their relative position in the network depended on those (Bekker et al. 2002). Therefore the cross-licensing agreements on which the GSM standard was made possible were dominated by Motorola, the firm with the largest essential IPR portfolio. We can conclude then, that proprietary matters were more important than Pelkmans assumed. However, collective action was possible because all the factors he enumerated were in place, together with the fact that none of the firms involved had the technological elements sufficient to launch a successful market standard by itself. Ten years after its launch, the GSM standard has expanded to other parts of the world, becoming the most successful standard within second generation mobile telephony.[9] The use of the standard is managed by the GSM Association, which represents the interests of 384 GSM satellite and network operators, regulators, administrations and GSM manufacturers/suppliers from all over the world. In 1996, ETSI launched GSM phase 2+, which incorporated some third generation features but still on a second generation platform.[10]

The second case to be presented here is far from being a success. On the contrary, the attempt to develop a common EU standard for high definition television (HDTV) in the late 1980s and early 1990s has repeatedly been proclaimed to be a clear failure (Peterson and Sharp 1998; Curwen 1994; Cawson 1995). In the early 1980s, the Japanese company Sony developed the HiVision standard for high definition television. This was a proprietary standard which had the potential to give Sony considerable scope for gaining a significant share of the world market. European producers reacted strongly to this, mainly because the Japanese were enjoying a growing world market share of consumer electronic products. Yet, as Austin and Milner argue

> European preferences were dictated not only by the Japanese threat, but also by the fact that by the mid-1980s both Philips and Thomson had a significant investment stake in the US market ... An international standard, based on Japanese technology, would only give the Japanese greater access to Europe and the US. (Austin and Milner 2001: 422)

The European response was to launch the generously funded EUREKA project in 1986 to develop a new-generation TV system based on a technical standard developed in Europe. Philips and Thomson (respectively Dutch and French TV manufacturers) became deeply involved in the research and negotiation efforts for the MAC standard (Multiplexed Analogue Components), which was based on analogue technology. In 1986, the Commission issued a proposal for an HDTV directive, which would promote the use of the MAC standard for satellite broadcasting in the EU.[11] However, strong disagreement between national governments on this issue arose shortly afterwards. The Netherlands and France insisted on a 'hard line' regulation, forcing all satellite broadcasters in the EU to use the MAC standard. Yet, the UK was opposed to this, since the successful British Sky TV satellite broadcaster already used a non-MAC standard. This later opinion was shared by other satellite broadcasters in Europe, as they had little confidence in the technological viability of the MAC standard (Peterson and Sharp 1998: 168–9). Amid these strong political reactions, the Commission tried to launch an 'HDTV Action Plan' in the early 1990s, only for it to be rejected by the UK at the Edinburgh Summit of 1992, and to become technologically obsolete shortly afterwards with the unexpected development of a fully digital system for TV in 1993 (Austin and Milner 2001). What is the situation today? In 1996, the first digital commercial television was launched in France, and things have moved rapidly since then. In 1997, ETSI approved the DVB standard (Digital Video Broadcasting) endorsed today by most of the European TV producers and broadcasters. DVB is interoperable and is based on the MPEG-2 common coding system, which enables it to be used in high definition televisions or in conventional PAL/NTSC and SECAM televisions.[12] Of particular interest is the DVB-MHP (Multimedia Home Platform) group, a spin-off from the DVB standard, which at the beginning of 2000 was established to exploit the potential that DVB offers in the convergence of broadcasting, consumer electronics and computers in the home.

Moving now to our two cases of mandatory standards, the development of a series of European standards on toy safety stemming from the Toy Safety Directive of 1988[13] has traditionally been perceived as a successful story of EU harmonized standardization. Toy safety was one of the first directives to be passed under the new approach, and its significance is not just politically symbolic, as proof of the well functioning of the new procedure, but, most importantly, for the complex and broad issue it addressed.[14] In his excellent recounting of this case Michelle Egan points at the unsuccessful attempts in the mid-1970s to establish uniform toy safety standards in the EU. The proposal submitted by the Commission to the Council in 1980 was extremely complex, with 80 pages of technical annexes, and it encountered fierce opposition from trade associations, toy producers and the working group of technical barriers to trade (under the Council). All of this resulted in several years of deadlock, until in 1986 Lord Cockfield, the new Commissioner for the Internal Market announced the intention to submit this case to the new approach procedure. The political debates that surrounded the decision of the current EU directive were, however, not that straightforward. The European Parliament pushed for amendments to ensure maximum uniformity, whereas the Danish government wanted to retain its own stricter safety rules. Once the directive was approved, the Commission gave a mandate to CEN on six different toy standards.[15] Negotiating these specific standards under the auspices of CEN was not an easy task either, and on several occasions they were on the verge of complete breakdown. Nevertheless, final decisions were reached by the mid-1990s, and toy producers can therefore obtain the CE mark by complying with the European standards. Despite the undeniable success of the new approach procedure in EU toy safety, Egan argues that there are still important difficulties in relation to mutual recognition of testing and certification (Egan 2001: 177–8); that is, in downward standardization. It is still not unusual for retailers to demand additional tests of other EU products, to be performed by their own national testing and certifying bodies, and there have been repeated complaints by consumer organizations that there continue to be illegal toys on the market (those that do not conform to the EU requirements).

The set of harmonized standards developed under the Construction Product Directive[16] is our fourth and final case. Until very recently, this was a case that was obviously less successful than the toys safety standards mentioned above, mainly because, as the Commission itself put it, the Construction Product Directive had, for a long time, difficulty in creating sufficiently strong incentives to elaborate on European harmonized standards (Commission 1998a: 3). However, we might argue, along with Michelle Egan, that the reason for this is due to a combination of several factors. First, the industry has never been particularly interested in setting common standards, and ambiguous positions were held among different firms in the sector. Secondly, this area includes a vast number of products, which has rendered the whole process of setting common standards a daunting task. Furthermore, some firms have complained that the essential requirements of the Directive go beyond safety and protection. Last but not least, the member states' different traditions on safety and health protection have not helped in this direction, rendering the political and technical negotiations for individual standards within CEN a slow process. To be implemented in a proper manner, further interpretative legal documents to the Directive were necessary, and these were passed in 1994. This delay significantly hampered the implementation of the Directive, and introduced an important element of legal and technical complexity. The relevant EU mandates to the standard-setting bodies have also generated considerable problems. The Commission's working group on construction products was very delayed, probably overwhelmed by the production of 40 mandates for families of products falling into the 'construction product' category. However, the mandate process has also been complicated by member states' disagreement as to how the interpretative documents have to be translated into specific standard mandates, and how to introduce detailed regulatory requirements into the mandates. The result of all this has been a considerable delay in the standardization process in this area, and far too detailed content in the mandates and standards. As Egan argues, this might indicate that the Directive on construction products has been actually creeping back towards the 'old approach' method. However, despite all this, in 2001 the process accelerated significantly, and more than 45 standards were decided, to be applied within one year. Twelve years after the enforcement of the Directive, the first fruits are being harvested.

Are there any possible lessons to be drawn from these four cases? The answer is positive, yet relatively different depending on whether there are standard agreements, as with GSM and HDTV, or harmonized standards, as with toy safety and construction products. Starting with the first two, there seem to be at least three lessons to be drawn. The first is that to be useful and effective, standards have to be based on technical advancements rather than on current technical solutions with a relative short life-cycle. This is the obvious case of the HDTV failure, based on the analogue technology of the MAC standard, which was developed at a time when digital technology was rendering it completely obsolete. The lesson is that technological stubbornness does not pay off in the current economy with its short technology life-cycles and accelerated innovation process. A second lesson for standard agreements, particularly stemming from the GSM case, is that even if public intervention does not necessarily bring the best possible standard, it might occasionally turn out to be decisive for forcing common solutions. There will always be problems of collective action in international standardization processes. Public action might work in reassuring the partners involved, by guaranteeing the enforcement of mutually-binding decisions. In these cases, public action serves the purpose of establishing basic conditions for the generation of trust. Naturally, it is another story when private interests have captured the public actor and are instrumental in pushing for decisions that are technologically and industrially unsustainable, as the disastrous HDTV case poignantly illustrates. Last but not least, a third lesson might be drawn here: IPRs might not a priori be positive or negative for the process of standardization as such, since it depends on the nature and distribution of the IPRs among actors, and on the combined standard-market strategy envisaged by each relevant actor towards the emerging market. This suggests cooperative solutions are more likely to appear in a situation with a relative distribution of IPR ownership (not too many firms), with IPRs that are by nature mutually complementary (because the knowledge competences are relatively evenly distributed), and with emerging technological markets (that anticipate new rather than already existing technologies). The lesson is then that IPRs are not per se opposed to open standards. However, their interaction in the real world is very complex, and further research is needed in order to make a better assessment of the circumstances in which overall positive innovative dynamics are generated, and in which bottle-necks and lock-in situations dominate.

As for mandatory standards, one single lesson might be identified. Independently of the old or new approach procedures, implementing new and collective standards for safety might turn out to be extremely difficult in those cases where the industry is openly reticent to such dynamics. Deadlocks and/or significant delays in the negotiations of European standards would invariably appear, potentially rendering the overall standardization exercise costly and pointless. Perhaps, in such complex situations, the EU strategy could be that of defining the compulsory 'essential requirements' in the corresponding Directives, but leaving open its actual enforcement by industry, with no mandates to the three standard bodies. With such a political strategy no European standards are defined, but considerably more attention should be paid to the actual enforcement of the 'mutual recognition' principle in certification and testing – the real 'Achilles' heel' when trying to create a truly single European market for goods.

Standardization and EU Innovation Policy

Since the very inception of the Research and Technological Development (RDT) policy in the mid-1980s, the EU has pursued the strategy of integrating research with standard-making. This is especially true for the ESPRIT and

RACE programmes, in the information and telecom sectors respectively, where a large share of projects addressed standards like the OSI (Open Systems Interconnect) initiative (Peterson and Sharp 1998: 72–3). As time has gone by, the different Framework Programmes have subsequently increased the budgetary line supporting horizontal activities of this type, making more explicit efforts to link research with European standards. In 1995, the Green Paper on Innovation mentioned the importance of standards for improving competitiveness and innovativeness in the context of the single market. However it did not foresee any new policy directions in this regard other than the steps towards a new approach already taken in the mid- to late 1980s and the continuous inclusion of this objective into the FP design (Commission 1995). More explicit than the Green Paper though, was a working document from the Commission dealing directly with the issue linking collaborative research with standardization activities (Commission 1998b). Some of the points expressed were that performance standards are preferable to product standards, intellectual property rights have to be protected in the process of standardization, and the Joint Research Centre (JRC) needs to open a dialogue with CEN to improve the utilization of its research through standardization.

However, these questions are too general, and the EU needs a more attentive strategy to position standardization within the overall innovation policy of the EU, particularly in relation to its emerging EU IPR regime. In the context of the rapid construction of a single EU-wide intellectual property rights regime and the willingness to generate a dynamic innovative economy in the EU, this matter acquires increasing relevance. As we mentioned earlier, the relationship between IPRs and standardization processes is rather complex and still relatively unexplored, at least from the point of view of policy implications. Scholars cast a different light over this matter. On the one hand, some authors argue that intellectual property rights are a major reason for disagreement over successful standardization (Egan 2001: 168). If that is true, there is an apparent dilemma in the EU, since the rise of the IPR regime might eventually prevent firms from engaging in collective standard agreement strategies. But is it so simple? Alternatively, in their concluding remarks on the potential policy impact of the new approach to standardization, Goerke and Holler stress the need to link further proprietary issues into the European standardization process as a mechanism for overcoming problems of incentives for firms. As they put it:

> It is well known that markets can only induce welfare maximizing outcomes if property rights and also costs are precisely assigned. European standardization as outlined under the New Approach partly lacks this feature. The EC Commission still has fairly high influence on standards and norms by defining 'essential requirements'. Moreover, financial arrangements for European standardization bodies are rather vague. ... If companies, their representatives, research institutions,

consumer organizations, trade unions and other relevant bodies are to take a long-term interest in standardization policy in Europe and if they are to share the financial burden involved in doing so, they must be sure of their exact duties, responsibilities and influence in the standardization process and hence of possible gains resulting from involvement. (Goerke and Holler 1998: 109)

The problem with this suggestive paragraph is how to enforce it. Linking proprietary rights to standardization poses two immediate problems: one is the question of wider participation in the decision-making for mandatory standards. The participation of environmental, consumer groups and trade unions, which with all probability lack such proprietary issues to negotiate, will invariably be problematic. And secondly, the lessons earlier did not show that IPRs were a problem for mandatory standards, but they potentially were for standard agreements. In other words, Goerke and Holler's proposals are not so easy to implement, nor do they represent a solution to an identified problem.

In any case, the complex relationship of IPRs and standardization calls for a balanced innovation policy where the individual firm's interest in appropriating the rewards of its investments does not hinder the long-term collective interest of a dynamic competitive market with positive network externalities. It is necessary to articulate a clear vision of the EU's innovation policy strategy for achieving this, particularly because the relatively strong IPR regime that is currently emerging in the EU runs the risk of not combining well with the goal of reinforcing the standardization dynamics in the European economy.

THE GLOBAL DIMENSION

Intrinsic to the market-making ability of setting common standards is the question of what level and what actor(s) are to set them. This is not banal, since it shapes the entire structure and effects of these fundamental economic institutions. Traditionally, international standards were defined by national standards bodies in neat diplomatic negotiation processes based on consensus. With the rapid growth of international trade and the rapid acceleration of technological development (mainly in the heavily standards-based ICTs), this structure has become untenable. What we have seen in recent decades is the emergence of new modes of setting international standards, a fantastic growth in the number of these technical specifications, a higher political willingness to tackle the barrier effects that these pose to free trade, and the emergence of new types of non-governmental standard-setting consortia as new actors in the international scene. This section addresses two issues. The first is how we can characterize the recent dynamics of international standardization, both as regulatory standards and standard agreements. And secondly, what the role of the EU standardization process is within this general context.

The Recent Dynamics of International Standardization

The practice of setting standards internationally under the auspices of international organizations with national representation is rather old. This is as much true for mandatory standards, where states regulate technical specifications of products, as for the truly voluntary standard agreements where producers and consumers jointly define the common industrial standard that is to be used internationally in large technological systems. Today there is an endless list of international standard-setting bodies with very different technical and geographical scope, nature and membership,[17] where virtually any international organization is named a 'standardization body'. For the sake of clarity, it is worth recalling that this chapter deals with the standardization of products and trade goods. This has a resolute analytical effect, as we will not address international regulatory standard setting in areas such as working conditions (set by ILO: International Labour Organization), or shipping safety (set by IMO: International Maritime Organization).

Traditionally, the three most important international standard bodies have been the ISO (International Standards Organization), the ITU (International Telecommunications Union), and the IEC (International Electrotechnical Commission). These bodies have several things in common. First, they are international organizations and the fruit of corresponding international Treaties, either under the UN system (ITU) or fully independent (ISO and IEC). Their membership is essentially national. Yet, whereas ISO[18] and IEC[19] membership only includes national standardization bodies, the ITU follows the ETSI model of combined membership with 'member states' and 'sector members' – firms or industrial associations.[20] This leads us to the next common point of these three organizations, which is the public–private partnership in standard–setting. Opposed to the flexible and open membership of this latter organization, the ISO and the IEC seem to be more hierarchically organized in their decision-making procedures. For these two organizations, it is solely national members that are taking decisions, since they are supposed to represent both their national producers and consumers simultaneously. Private partners are not allowed to participate formally in these decisions, but they are allowed to be informed about content and progress.[21]

These formal standardizing bodies have been experiencing two important impulses since the late 1990s, the first being the recent link established between international standards and free trade arrangements – most importantly the WTO. The Technical Barriers to Trade (TBT) agreement was signed in 1994, and is also commonly known as the 'Standards Code' under the WTO. Its aim is to ensure that national regulations, standards, testing and certification procedures do not create unnecessary obstacles to international trade. For this reason, the TBT explicitly encourages member states to make use of international standardization, and to comply with a 'code of conduct' for national standardization and certification procedures.[22] This code of conduct has to be applied by all public and private authorities undertaking standardization activities within the signatory member state. Among other issues, the code of conduct stipulates that national standardization bodies have to follow and participate closely in the development of international standards, and have to apply these international standards in full or in part when developing their own national standards. The implementation of these regulations has taken place through cooperation between the ISO, IEC and ITU with the WTO,[23] in such a way that standards now form part of the expanding international trade regime.

A second recent impulse of these three organizations is the envisaged formalized cooperation between the ISO, ITU and IEC in the ICT sector, under the name 'World Standards Cooperation in ICTs'. This initiative was launched officially in spring 2002 and aims at achieving a more stable framework for cooperation and communication between these organizations in this specific industrial field. Arguably, this initiative is the direct response to what we identified in Chapter 4 as the convergence of computer, information and broadcasting technologies. The new technologies and businesses emerging at the crossroads of two or even the three of them are challenging the previous division of tasks between international standard bodies. The new standards solutions that are needed can hardly be encapsulated within one or the other sector. Formalized cooperation between the three bodies is the attempt to make them, collectively, the relevant forum for businesses negotiating anticipatory standards in this vast and rapidly changing industrial sector. The question is, nevertheless, whether this strategy is already too late.

Parallel to these developments and impulses of the formal standardization bodies, new players had been stepping into the field of international standard-setting throughout the 1990s. This is not just a matter of new arrangements or new actors, but it essentially indicates new dynamics about by whom and how standards are defined globally. As Werle puts it:

> Most dramatic, however, has been the growth of private consortiums and forums. Thus 'official' standard setting is confronted with an 'informal sector', the evolution of which indicates some discontent with the traditional organizations and entails an inherent potential of jurisdictional conflict. (Werle 2001: 392)

There are at least two different types of new arrangements, both of them of a non-governmental or 'informal' nature. The first type is consortia formed by a wide variety of actors, generally firms and business associations, which develop common standards within very specific functional areas. We might call them *functional consortia*. One example is the World Wide Web Consortium (W3C), which has recently developed a host of standards in the form of common protocols that ensure interoperability on the Web. This Consortium was created in 1994 and is today a highly consolidated forum on the Web, with more than 500 members. One of the most acclaimed standards it adopted was XML (extensible markup language) in 1998. This standard is becoming the new 'lingua franca' of the Web, and will with all probability become the successor to the current HTML standard (hypertext markup language). The story of this standard started when a group of experts led by Sun Microsystems[24] met with the objective of shaping a new language on the basis of the already operative SGML (standard generalized markup language), a formal ISO standard (Bosak 1998). XML is another success story and multiple products are being developed with this language. What interests us here is the fact that the forum within which the standard was defined and collectively agreed was not the ISO, as one might have expected from the SGML standard. Instead, the developers of XML choose W3C as the relevant forum for the promotion of this new technology as a common technical standard. The question is here, why was W3C preferred to ISO as a forum for standard-setting? Even if there might not be a simple answer, the choice of W3C might indicate new dynamics in the governance structure of international standards. We will examine this below, after having looked at the second type of new player in the standardization arena.

The second type of non-governmental/informal standardization consortia is associations of specific firms which have strategically come together in order to develop a new standard based on a radically new technology. We might call them *strategic consortia*. Their difference from the 'functional consortia' mentioned above, is that 'strategic consortia' come together exclusively to promote one single new standard, and therefore have an ad hoc nature, while 'functional consortia' are more stable fora with a wider scope of action. One brilliant and recent example of strategic consortia is the DVD consortium within the multimedia business. DVD (digital versatile disc) is a new type of CD (compact disc) used in the computer and multimedia industry.[25] The story started in the early 1990s, when two different groups of firms developed alternative first trials of this new generation CD. Toshiba/Warner developed the super density disc and Sony/Philips/Pioneer developed the multimedia compact disc. Both groups got together under the DVD consortium in 1995, and in the same year a set of common DVD standards was developed. Arguably, two factors underpin this collective strategy. First, there were lessons from the past. The dire straits that most partners were in during the competition between VHS and Betamax video systems in the 1980s were still vivid and fresh in the memory of all. Secondly, the new disc had to satisfy the needs of both the computer and the movie industries, and this required a large collaborative effort. The first DVDs reached the markets in 1997, and by the end of 1998 a total of 250 Hollywood film titles were available in Europe (Oosterveld 1997). Part of the success is to be found in the common licensing programme of the patents held by the partnering firms. Without doubt, the DVD consortium provided an understanding platform for such critical decisions, enhancing the chances of successful collective action.[26]

All this indicates some transitory trends in the patterns of governance of voluntary industrial standard-setting at international level. One of the areas where this has been most obvious is in the ICT and multimedia industries. This is hardly surprising given the extraordinary dynamism of this sector over the past three decades, and the large network economy of these complex technological systems. Arguably, this has put pressure on the structure of international standardization bodies in two interrelated ways. On the one hand, the industry has searched for diversified modes of setting common standards through non-governmental instruments, most typically by 'functional consortia' and 'strategic consortia'. This responds in part to the needs of industry for greater flexibility and rapidity in the standardization process, something that the three official bodies could not fully offer. These needs have been recently recognized in a EU working document concerning international standardization (Commission 2001: 8). On the other hand, this situation has put pressure on these three official bodies in a way that has forced them to improve their working procedures by opening up decision-making power to non-national representatives (most notably ITU), looking at new areas of activity (such as ISO, with its ISO 9000 and ISO 14000 business management standards), working more strategically (as with the IMT-2000 standard for 3rd generation mobile telephony, of ITU), and forging closer ties between these three governmental organizations (such as their partnership with the WTO in the enforcement of the TBT agreement).

The question of whether it is best to have national or international standards, or to have public or private arrangements is not easy to answer. In his recent article Werle's points out that:

> the analysis of the SOs' landscape (standardizing organizations of all kinds) has shown that coordination and co-existence is the prevailing structural pattern. This appears to be inconsistent with reports on spectacular 'standard wars' including the ongoing conflict related to the Third Generation Wireless Telecommunications Standards which gives the impression that hostility, antagonism and mistrust are the rules of the game. Many participants in standardization recall such conflicts. However, most conflicts occurred within standards committees during the process of negotiations on standards. ... Conflicts between SOs over their claims of competence or their involvement in overlapping areas of standardization have been rare. (Werle 2001: 403)

Firms seem to choose public or private solutions depending on the circumstances:

> If the diffusion and implementation of a standard is regarded as the central problem, firms prefer to submit a proposal to one of the official organizations; they are recognized by governments, and their products enjoy high legitimacy. If the companies expect difficulties in achieving consensus, they prefer approaching a more exclusive arena with a small circle of participants, often one of the new specialized private consortiums and forums. (Werle 2001: 408)

More clearly in favour of formal international standards, though, Abbott and Snidal mention at least two benefits: formal international standards bodies like the ISO or IEC can discipline national governance without replacing it; and secondly, they can improve overall representativeness in decision-making when compared with the private consortia (Abbott and Snidal 2001: 365). However, they conclude that there is no single solution since problems have an increasingly trans-national character, and hence a combination of public/ private, and national/regional/international approaches is necessary.

European Standardization in the Global Context

Given the recent growth of international standardization it is relevant to ask when regional or global solutions are preferable, and how regional and global structures hang together. Here it is again necessary to distinguish between mandatory standards and industrial standard agreements. Seen from an international and yet global perspective, the harmonized European standards have some effects beyond the strict EU frontiers. The thrust of the EU mutual recognition and standardization arrangements in the late 1980s had some implications for the EU's trade partners at different levels, namely, pan-European, transatlantic and global. Different international arrangements have addressed the potential adverse position of third country products' accessibility to the EU market, along with reciprocal agreements of different types. We start with the pan-European dimension of harmonized standardization: the European Economic Area (EEA) and accession countries.

Under the EEA agreement, Norway, Liechtenstein and Iceland participate in the EU's single market, and hence follow the principle of mutual recognition. This tight cooperation also extends to the question of harmonized standards. All EFTA countries are members of the three European standardization bodies, and participate on equal terms in the decision-making process concerning the harmonization of European standards. The relationship with the CEECs is not so close, however. Apart from ETSI (which has an open membership policy), these countries are still not members of the European standardization bodies,[27] despite their commitment to conform with EU regulations regarding product and food safety under the European agreements. This obviously shows a degree of asymmetry in the relationship, which will be overcome with the full EU membership of the accession countries.

Less institutionalized are the transatlantic relations, which have proved more difficult and were only developed at the end of the 1990s. The 1998 Mutual Recognition Agreement (MRA) between the EU and US contained some legal specifications about the mutual recognition of products and services, and there are currently cooperative efforts on regulatory matters relating to these issues. However, as Nicolaïdis and Egan point out, the implementation of these agreements has encountered many hurdles, showing that the institutional foundations for improving free market relations between both partners has to be improved in the future (2001: 467). Arguably, the different 'cultures' regarding economic governance, and values and norms concerning the protection of consumers that have been echoed in the 'trade wars' over beef hormones and GMOs, are behind these diplomatic hitches.

Last, the role of EU standardization at global level can be examined in terms of the increased cooperation between European standardization bodies and their corresponding global counterparts. This is true for ISO/CEN and IEC/CENELEC, which follow similar patterns of collaboration between both levels, whereas ITU-T/ETSI collaboration is more fluid. Taking the example of IEC and CENELEC, both institutions signed an agreement in 1996 stipulating that work starting at CENELEC might be promoted to IEC level. This procedure ensures a direct and strong European influence at international level. It is worth pointing out that the relationship between ETSI and ITU-T is somehow different given the strong standard agreements nature of both institutions. Collaboration here is not as clearly bilateral or vertical as in IEC/CEN, but more multilateral, framed in the Global Standards Collaboration agreement between the most important telecom standardizing bodies. Arguably, this responds more to the challenges posed by the increased number of functional consortia solutions in the realm of ICT standardization than to a wish from the European body to directly influence standards at a higher level.

Underpinning the multilateral and bilateral dimensions of European standards at international level, the Commission has recently proclaimed some European policy principles on international standardization (Commission 2001). This document is nothing more than the mere adoption of the TBT principles (transparency, openness, impartiality and consensus, effectiveness and relevance, and development dimension), reflecting the specific European view on these issues – most notably the need to improve efficiency and the participation of stakeholders in the procedures of formal standard-setting at international level.

Another story is, however, the dynamics of industrial standards agreements. When examining the international scope of European standardization from this point of view, the question to be asked is when do European firms prefer global or regional standards? And under what conditions do individual firms pursue one strategy or the other? Austin and Milner have recently argued that firms' preferences depend on the technological position of the standard in question. These authors have established a direct correlation between the firms' technological capabilities and their strategies regarding the choice of type and level of standardization. Their argument runs that technological leaders prefer global standards of an informal nature (i.e. a market-based solution, which we defined earlier as de facto, sponsored standards), whereas technological followers prefer regional standards of a formal nature (i.e. an institutional-based solution, which we defined as 'standards agreements' under standardization body procedures). They analyse this in the EU context, but unfortunately, base their empirical analysis on just two case studies, from the 1960s and early 1980s. Therefore, we can cast some doubts about how representative their cases are, and how relevant their empirical results are nowadays. Much has happened since then in the realm of standards, among other things being the extraordinary development of ICT, a heavily standardizing industrial sector, which shows, we will argue, different patterns of preferences from those Austin and Milner have identified.

Why do ICT firms in Europe still find it valid to settle their common standards with regional scope? When are regional solutions preferred to global ones? The answers must be found in a set of factors (rather than in one single dimension like technology follower/technology leader, as Austin and Milner boldly put it). One of the issues that might have a clear effect on the preferability of regional standardization is the decision-making procedure. The formal standards bodies generally follow decision-making procedures based on consensus. This requires a broad range of agreement between partners, which might be difficult the larger the forum is. From this viewpoint, regional standards might then be preferable to global standards simply because there are fewer actors involved. A second factor that tips the balance in favour of regional standards is related to the strategic options of firms. Regional scale agreements give an opportunity to 'test' market reaction before launching a product on the larger international market. This might be underpinned by the solid cooperation between the functional global and regional standards bodies, such as ITU and ETSI, providing a good institutional basis for undertaking this 'first regional then global' approach. Last but not least, specific technologies might still be geographically relevant. In the telecoms sector, for example, geography still matters, meaning that there are clear market incentives to cooperate regionally, following market dynamics.

ISSUES OF PUBLIC-PRIVATE GOVERNANCE

The distribution of power between public and private actors in the field of standardization is an issue that has attracted some attention among social scientists. It is generally argued that the transfer of competences from the strictly public realm to private hands has resulted in the blurring of clear division lines between one and the other. Formal standardization procedures, where governmental actors and stakeholders take an active part, have been portrayed as one of most salient examples of the growth of a 'grey area' of politics, neither entirely private nor entirely public. This is particularly evident at EU level, with the objective of constructing a common market.

> The process of harmonization (standardization) does not create a huge centralized European state, but relies on a much more dispersed set of governmental institutions which exist as much within the so-called 'private' as the 'public' sector and take the form of laboratories, expert committees and testing stations as much as conventional administrative offices. In effect, the logic of harmonization cuts across the distinction between the 'state' and the 'market', and between 'science and technology' and 'administration'. (Barry 2001: 72)

This situation suggests a series of relevant questions about the forms of modern governance of technology and the economy at large; who is accountable and responsible in the (semi)regulatory delegation at EU level, and how is it possible to ensure efficient procedures and results?

Accountability and Responsibility for Regulatory Delegation

The new approach to standardization introduced an important institutional novelty: essential requirements were obligatory whereas the definition of standards was voluntary. If producers could not reach an agreement or were not interested in it, they would still be on the right side of the law if they just complied with the essential requirements. The voluntary nature of European standards was an atypical feature of the previous governance structure at national level, especially considering that those standards refer to the safety of products. Not all experts were equally enthusiastic about the idea. In fact, some reflected deep concern about this 'privatization' of public interest in critical areas such as health, environmental and consumer protection. Indeed, the aspect of the new approach that has raised most academic awareness has been the delegation of powers from the European Union to the European standardizing bodies (CEN, CENELEC and ETSI). That is, regulatory delegation insofar as those three bodies are to define in detail and bring to life the essential requirements stipulated in the corresponding EU directive. As we saw earlier in this chapter, the Commission issues a 'mandate' to the corresponding body, giving clear content and deadlines for the process of standardization. In principle, if the body fails to comply, either in terms of the technical content of the final standards or in terms of the deadlines, the Commission can do very little to reverse the situation. The standardizing body is then fully in charge of shaping the content of the standard. Therefore, as Egan suggests, the relation between the Commission and these three bodies is best portrayed in terms of principal–agent (Egan 1998).

Regulatory delegation is a complex matter for several reasons: first, because legitimacy and responsibility might not be easily allocated to the principal or the agent. This is the most difficult factor, since the principal represents the general interest, and the agent an aggregation of private interests; secondly, and more fundamentally, because it challenges the conventional bureaucratic principles of public administration as an impersonal and detached decision-making body where general rules transcending personal narrow interests are applied equally and universally in expression of the public interest (Ladeur 1999: 154–5). Even if the participation of private interests in public decisions has always existed, it has never assumed this dimension – challenging the core of the conventional mode of public administration that used to be hierarchically organized. This trend is the most problematic since it is taking place at a supra-national level where there is more heterogeneity of industrial/technological and social interests than in the national domain (Ladeur 1999).

The legitimacy problem in the mode of European harmonized standard-setting is derived from the fact that industrial interests, particularly large companies, are over-represented in the work leading to the standards. Despite the significant subvention of the Commission, environmental, consumer and other groups have been largely under-represented (Egan 1998). This asymmetric participation means that there might be a large gap between the aggregation of private interests and the public interest defined by the conventional legislative process. In other words, the outputs of this delegation to the private realm would invariably be different from the outputs of detailed legislative and administrative action. Given the constraints on turning back to the hierarchical, solely public mode, the solution to this legitimacy gap is obviously to engage a wider spectrum of participants – particularly non-industrial groups. In this regard, the Commission has pushed CEN and CENELEC to adopt the ETSI model, where membership is open to non-governmental actors (Egan 1998). Different industrial forums complement this open membership, giving full access to participants in the decision-making process. Traditionally, the ILO has also adopted tripartite negotiating bodies in the decision-making process that ensure legitimate back-up from labour and industrial representatives in issues (labour standards) that matter to them most directly.

The allocation of responsibility is a second conventional problem of regulatory delegation. This is again particularly difficult in a supra-national context. One of the central topics related to the delegation of regulatory power under the new approach deals with how specific the political mandates from the EU have to be. Some member states wish for mandates that are much more precise, arguing that this would improve efficiency and speed up the standardization process, while keeping a high element of democracy by national representation at EU level. However, this would significantly affect the latitude of manoeuvre of the European standards bodies, and consistently question one of the principles of the new approach – namely, the active definition of standards by stakeholders. In other words, implementing such a suggestion would undermine the relationship that has existed between principal and agent, as the principal regains power by reducing appreciably the agent's capacity for action. This debate started in relation to the problems of implementing the construction products directive. Some member states adduced that the problem was not to do with the nature of the industrial products themselves (seeking European standards in a sector dominated heavily by local market dynamics), but with the unclear and open nature of the mandates issued by the EU to the standards bodies. The argument has been that there is a negative correlation between efficiency and open mandates, the more of the one, the less of the other. Despite these arguments, the Commission has stuck to the initial purpose of rather open mandates. It has argued that 'If in the course of standardization work a need arises for more precise indications regarding the terms of the related mandates, the European standards organizations should raise that question with the Commission, who ... will clarify the mandate' (Commission 1998a: 11). It is another story, however, when interested parties cannot agree on a standard. Here the blame is not to be placed on the nature of the mandate, but on the vested interests of participants: 'When interested parties cannot agree on technical specifications, the Commission should not be considered as a "court of appeal" to make technological choices' (Commission 1998a: 11).

Problems of Efficiency

The three European standard-setting bodies have been under constant pressure to improve their procedures and their overall efficiency. Considerable delays result from excessive bureaucratization such that, as Egan has suggested, there is virtually no difference between the old approach to standardization and the new approach that replaced it (Egan 2001). Only a few years after the new approach was operative, the Commission published its Green Book on standards in which it was already suggesting some reforms, especially of the CEN and CENELEC modes of operation (Commission 1990). One of the most controversial issues was the idea of radically changing their national voting system, hence disrupting the hierarchical representation of national standards bodies, and opening them up for a wide form of membership, such as ETSI has. Not surprisingly, this suggestion was strongly opposed by the national standards bodies, and so it has remained the way it was. Nevertheless, the topic of efficiency has continuously been on the agenda, especially for the Commission, as it is frustrated to see such little improvement in terms of time delays and an unsatisfactory number of harmonized standards. This triggered a second round of discussions that started in the second half of the 1990s with two documents – one from the Commission (1996) and one from the Danish Agency for Trade and Industry (1997), both pointing to the delays and the need to reform the European standardization bodies. A more straightforward report was submitted in 1998, which again underlined the Commission's willingness to see these three standard-setting bodies producing standards in a faster and more participatory way. The concrete suggestions were:

- use of qualified majority voting in decision-making rather than the traditional consensus practices based on the absence of sustained objection by most partners;
- improvement of internal organizational procedures by using ICT;
- open participation, improving legitimacy among stakeholders;
- the merger of CEN and CENELEC is not necessary if important reorganizational thrust and enhanced cooperation between them is put in place.

Although the three standards bodies have significantly improved the speed of their procedures, and some long-awaited families of standards have been issued (such as construction products), some of the suggestions of the Commission have not seen the light of day. This is because of open participation in CEN and CENELEC, which continue to be dominated by national standards bodies and the informal influence of large industrial firms.

In spite of all this, experts indicate that the real problem with the efficiency of European standardization does not lie so much with the 'upstream' standardization process and its delays, but most fundamentally with the bottle-necks that continue to exist in 'downstream' standardization, namely certification and testing (Nicolaïdis and Egan 2001). The 'global approach to testing and certification' adopted in 1990 provided common rules for mutual recognition among the diverse certification bodies operating in Europe at national level. The European Organization for Testing and Certification (EOTC) was created with the purpose of implementing and controlling such processes. However, as these authors state:

The EU's sponsorship of the EOTC has failed to produce significant results, as member states have used safeguard clauses to restrict the circulation of products, disregarding EOTC approved stamps conformity with 'essential requirements' issued in the home countries. National variation in certification practices, coupled with continuing implementation problems, administrative delays, and difficulties in agreeing to testing and certification requirements for innovative products and services, have all contributed. (Nicolaïdis and Egan 2001: 463)

CONCLUSIONS

The political thrust towards European standardization since the late 1980s has been a mechanism for creating a single market in the EU. The rationale is that common standards prevent tariff barriers to intra-EU trade, already overflowing with national standards defining the technical specifications of products. Apart from the increased political attention that has perceived common standards as a viable solution to this problem, the new approach introduced a novel way of defining the standard-setting procedures, resulting in delegation of power from the public realm to the semi-public realm of the three European standards bodies (ETSI, CEN and CENELEC). While examining the rationale and dynamics of this transfer of power, the current chapter stressed that downstream standardization processes, namely testing and certification, are still problematic in Europe, representing serious barriers to trade. This is also true for the entire EEA where EFTA countries take part (with the exception of Switzerland). These countries have an active role in the construction of a single market in Europe, and are fully-fledged members of the three standardization bodies.

Parallel to this rapid Europeanization of standard-setting, more and more standards have been defined at international/global level. The traditional standard-setting bodies at international level like the ISO, ITU and IEC have experienced rapid growth in their production of standards. This has however been closely followed by the emergence of private consortia that define important standards in the field of ICT. In any case, increasing collaborative efforts in this field are noticeable. In geographical terms the EU is developing mutual recognition agreements with its trading partners, and in functional terms, the European regional standards bodies have now stable frameworks of cooperation with their global counterparts operating in the same field, such as ETSI and ITU. But why do regional standards continue to be perceived as relevant in this increasingly globalized economy? The reason is complex but the existence of clear regionalized market dynamics, and firms' strategy of 'first regional then global', might be among the possible responses.

In the section dedicated to the interactions between private and public actors it was argued that there are important changes in patterns of governance in this respect, which refers as much to the delegation of power under the new approach as to the increasing preferences of firms to reach standard agreements through private consortia. Problems relating to the responsibility and accountability of regulatory delegation, and of efficiency in terms of the optimal time-scales for production of standards, are still visible in the EU context.

How does standardization affect innovative processes and how does it relate to innovation policy? Also, what are the challenges posed by the dynamics described earlier to the governance of the innovation policy of the EU? As to the challenges for EU innovation policy, answers are not clear cut. Perhaps two issues deserve attention in this regard. First, the need for policy-makers to be aware that standardization has to keep the inherent tension between variation and unity. If standardization is to comply with its objectives of lowering transaction costs, increasing market accessibility and competition, and enhancing innovation through positive network externalities, it has to do it while avoiding falling into too much technological streamlining that might result in lock-in situations. Therefore, standardization should not tip the balance in favour of unity at the expenses of variation. The endemic difficulties of reaching collective agreements on a voluntary basis between producers are unlikely to disappear. Thus the role of public action in this regard is to provide the mechanisms and incentives for collective action to reach common standards, but not to impose their content coercively, nor standardization itself. In this respect, the EU should pay increasing attention to the real problems of downstream standardization, and launch a more decisive action towards full implementation of the mutual recognition principle in the field of certification and testing. The second issue for the coming governance of standards in the EU is how to combine it better with the efforts towards creating a single regime of intellectual property rights. The endeavours to reduce the costs and legal uncertainty related to IPR protection in the EU might result in a significant pro-patent attitude of European firms. This might have a reverse effect on the efforts towards developing common standard agreements in the EU (yet not necessarily in all circumstances). These should be balanced against each other for the sake of the common market and innovativeness of the European economy.

NOTES

1. These are the articles 28-31 (ex. Art. 30-37) prohibiting quantitative restrictions; and the articles 81-85 (ex. 85-94) establishing the competition policy.
2. Case 102/78 Rewe Zentrale v. Bundesmonopolverwaltung für Branntwein, ECR 649.
3. Some social scientists argue that the Treaty basis for development of this revolutionary principle of law is relatively weak, since it stems from a rather generous interpretation of the

spirit of article 28 (ex. Art. 30) (Poiares Maduro 1998).

4. The most important of these documents were the Information Procedure Directive (83/189/EEC), the Council Resolution of 7 May 1985 (OJ 1985 C 136/1), the Green Paper on standardization in 1990 (Commission 1990), and the 'Global Approach to Certification and Testing' Council Decision 22 July 1993.

5. CEN: Comité Européen de Normalisation.

6. CENELEC: Comité Européen de Normalisation Electrotechnique.

7. ETSI: European Telecommunications Standards Institute.

8. CEN and CENELEC members are the national standards bodies of the EU and EFTA countries, the Czech Republic and Malta (20 in total).

9. Other 2nd generation cellular standards are D-AMPS (Digital AMPS), CDMA (Code Division Multiple Access, and PDC (Personal Digital Communication).

10. Third generation mobile phones are already on the market, supported by the IMT-2000 family standard, created under the auspices of ITU. Nevertheless, the undeniable success of setting a global standard with wide agreement among leading firms does not necessarily preclude commercial success. As a matter of fact, in early 2002, experts were already sceptical about the third generation's commercial future.

11. Internal EC memo, 34/86 'Support for a European world standard for high-definition television', 1986.

12. The US is pursuing its own technical solutions to digital television under the ATSC standard, and the Japanese under their ISDB-T standard.

13. Directive 88/378/EU OJ L 187, 16 July 1988.

14. By 1980 it was estimated that the toy industry marketed approximately 60000 toys.

15. Those were: Mechanical and Physical Properties, Flammability, Migration of Certain Elements, Experimental Sets for Chemistry and Related Activities; Chemical Toys; Graphical Symbols for Age Warning Labels.

16. Directive 89/106/EEC.

17. For a comprehensive list of international standardization bodies of all possible types see the following web page: http://www.wssn.net/WSSN/.

18. ISO has 140 members, which are national standardization bodies.

19. IEC members are 60 national standardization bodies, who represent their respective national producer and consumer interests.

20. ITU has in all 664 members, including both state members and sector members.

21. Some successful cases of international standards generated by these bodies include banking card standards, freight containers in transport, and ISO 9000–ISO 14000 standards (by ISO), and the security protocols for commercial transactions on the internet and of IMT-2000 for mobile telephony (by ITU).

22. This is the 'Code of good practice for the preparation, adoption and application of standards', stipulated as Annex 3 to the TBT Agreement, and which is also known as the WTO Code of Good Practice.

23. This implementation is carried out by the Information Centre located at the ISO Central Secretariat in Geneva, which collects notifications of acceptance to this code of conduct by all standardization bodies of the signatory countries.

24. Bosak mentions that these experts came from other large companies (Sun, Hewlett-Packard, Netscape, Adobe, and Fuji Xerox), key SGML vendors and systems integrators (ArborText, Inso, SoftQuad, Grif, Texcel, and Isogen), representatives of the academic community (NCSA and the Text Encoding Initiative), early adopters (Data Channel and Vignette), and one of the world's leading SGML experts, James Clark.

25. DVD storage capacity (17 Gbyte) is much higher than CD-ROM (600 Mbyte).

26. Partly as a spin-off of this consortium, the newer DVD+RW Alliance, created for the development of the DVD+RW format, the optical storage technology based on DVD. One step ahead of competitors, Philips launched in summer 2001 the DVD recorder, which allows for full recording processes.

27. In January 2002 Malta and the Czech Republic were the only accession countries to be members of CEN and CENELEC.

REFERENCES

Abbott, K.W. and D. Snidal (2001), 'International standards and international governance'. *Journal of European Public Policy* **8**(3): 345–70.

Armstrong, K.A. and S.J. Bulmer (1998), *The Governance of the Single European Market*. Manchester, Manchester University Press.

Arthur, B. (1989), 'Competing technologies, increasing returns and lock-in by historical events'. *Economic Journal* **99**: 116–31.

Austin, M. and H. Milner (2001), 'Strategies of European standardization'. *Journal of European Public Policy* **8**(3): 411–31.

Barry, A. (2001), *Political Machines. Governing a Technological Society*. London, The Athlone Press.

Bekker, R., G. Duysters and B. Verspagen (2002), 'Intellectual property rights, strategic technology agreements and market structure. The case of GSM'. *Research Policy* **31**(7): 1141–61.

Besen, S. and J. Farrell (1994), 'Choosing how to compete: strategies and tactics in standardization'. *Journal of Economic Perspectives* **8**(2): 117–31.

Bosak, J. (1998), 'Four myths about XML'. *IEEE Computer* **31**(10): 120–2.

Brunsson, N. and B. Jacobsson (2000), *A World of Standards*. Oxford, Oxford University Press.

Bundgaard-Pedersen, T. (1997), 'States and EU technical standardization: Denmark, the Netherlands and Norway managing polycentric policy-making 1985–95'. *Journal of European Public Policy* **4**(2): 206–24.

Cawson, A. (1995), 'High-definition television in Europe'. *Political Quarterly* **66**(2): 157–73.

Commission, European (1990), 'Green Paper on the development of European standardization: Action for further technological integration in Europe'. COM (90) 456 final.

Commission, European (1995), 'Green Paper on innovation'. Com 95 (688) final.

Commission, European (1996), 'Action plan for the single market'. COM (96) 520 final, 30 October 1996.

Commission, European (1998a), 'Report from the Commission to the Council and the European Parliament: Efficiency and accountability in European standardisation under the new approach'. COM (1998) 291 final.

Commission, European (1998b), 'Research and standardization. Greater consideration of the prenormative dimension in Community research programs'. Working document. COM (1998) 31 final. Brussels.

Commission, European (2001), 'European policy principles on international standardization'. *Staff Working Paper SEC 1296 of 2001-07-26*. Brussels, European Commission.

Cowan, R. and J.-H. Miller (1998), 'Technological standards with local externalities and decentralized behaviour'. *Journal of Evolutionary Economics* **8**(3): 285–96.

Curwen, P. (1994), 'High-definition television: A case study of industrial policy versus the market'. *European Business Review* **94**(1): 17–23.

Danish Agency for Trade and Industry (1997), *The European Standardization work: Analysis and Recommendations for Efficiency Initiatives*. Copenhagen, Danish Agency for Trade and Industry.

David, P. (1985), 'Clio and the economics of QWERTY'. *American Economic Review* **75**(2).

David, P. (1995), 'Standardization policies for network technologies: The flux between freedom and order revisited'. In *Standards, Innovation and Competitiveness. The Politics and Economics of Standards in Natural and Technical Environments*, R. Hawkins, R. Mansell and J. Skea. Aldershot, Edward Elgar.

Egan, M. (1998), 'Regulatory strategies, delegation and European market integration'. *Journal of European Public Policy* **5**(3): 485–506.

Egan, M. (2001), *Constructing a European Market. Standards, Regulation, and Governance*. Oxford, Oxford University Press.

Farr, S. (1996), *Harmonisation of Technical Standards in the EC*. Chichester, John Wiley & Sons.

Funk, J. and D. Methe (2001), 'Market- and committee-based mechanisms in the creation and diffusion of global industry standards: The case of mobile communication'. *Research Policy* **30**(4): 589–610.

Goerke, L. and M.J. Holler (1998), 'Strategic standardization in Europe: a public choice perspective'. *European Journal of Law and Economics* **6**(2): 95–112.

Hawkins, R. (1995). 'Standards-making as technological diplomacy: Assessing objectives and methodologies in standard institutions'. In *Standards, Innovation and Competitiveness: The Politics and Economics of Standards in Natural and Technical Environments*, R. Hawkins, R. Mansell and J. Skea. Aldershot, Edward Elgar.

Ladeur, K.-H. (1999), 'Towards a legal concept of the network in European standard-setting. In *EU Committees: Social Regulation, Law and Politics,* C. Joerges and E. Vos. Oxford, Hart Publishing.

Liagouras, G. (2002), 'Are there limits to the use of the path dependence principle?' Unpublished paper submitted to the workshop: Cognitive processes, values and institutional change, 11–12 January 2002, Skodsbord, Denmark.

Nicolaïdis, K. and M. Egan (2001), 'Transnational market governance and regional policy externality: Why recognize foreign standards?' *Journal of European Public Policy* **8**(3): 454–73.

Oosterveld, J. (1997), 'DVD – at the brink of a successful European launch'.

Pelkmans, J. (2001), 'The GMS standard: explaining a success story'. *Journal of European Public Policy* **8**(3): 432–54.

Peterson, J. and M. Sharp (1998), *Technology Policy in the European Union*. London, Macmillan Press.

Poiares Maduro, M. (1998), *We, the Court: the European Court of Justice and the European Economic Constitution: A critical reading of Article 30 of the EC Treaty*. Oxford, Hart Publishing.

Scharpf, F.W. (1999), *Governing in Europe: Effective and Democratic?* Oxford, Oxford University Press.

Tassey, G. (2000), 'Standardization in technology-based markets'. *Research Policy* **29**: 587–602.

Warshaw, S. and M. Saunders (1995), 'International challenges in defining the public and private interests in standards'. In *Standards, Innovation and Competitiveness. The Politics and Economics of Standards in Natural and Technical Environments,* R. Hawkins, R. Mansell and J. Skea. Aldershot, Edward Elgar.

Werle, R. (2001), 'Institutional aspects of standardization – jurisdictional conflicts and the choice of standardization organizations'. *Journal of European Public Policy* **8**(3): 392–410.

Wise, N. (1995), 'Precision: Agent of unity and product of agreement'. In *The Values of Precision*, N. Wise. Princeton, Princeton University Press.

6. Risk and the social sustainability of innovation

> You would say I have lost my faith in science, and progress...
> (Sting: 'If I Ever Lose My Faith in You')

INTRODUCTION

Since the second half of the 20th century, there has been increasing criticism of scientific and technological advances. Some examples of this are the popular opposition and concerns related to nuclear energy, environmental pollution's effect on health, human reproductive technologies, and genetically modified organisms (GMOs). These reactions differ a great deal from country to country (as in the case of environmental pollution awareness), from one period of time to another (anti-nuclear energy groups were particularly strong in the late 1970s), and from issue to issue (human cloning has been universally rejected, whereas opinions about abortion vary considerably). Scientific and technological advances that take place in our industrialized economies constantly pose new social and political questions about the limits to scientific activity and how our society should deal with itself. Answering these questions is a matter of political decision anticipating risks and solving new ethical dilemmas, in what is essentially a matter of collective values and choices. This chapter deals with the former issue, that of risk, as it has been a hot topic of political debate in the EU, and represents in many ways the 'tip of the iceberg' of a much wider political and social concern about the 'governance of science' in the European Union.

What has this to do with innovation policy? The EU's technology policy of the 1980s was hardly touched by popular dissatisfaction. Most of the popular concerns and oppositions to scientific and technological-related applications were about issues that were not Europeanized at that time. Those that were Europeanized, such as environmental and consumer protection issues, were dealt with in a way that was detached from technology policy. This scenario has changed dramatically since the dawning of the new century. The BSE crises, GMOs and biotechnology patents have swept aside the hitherto technocratic attitude of the EU regarding science and technology. These cases received much popular attention throughout the EU, generating dissatisfaction and distrust of the political and scientific elite who manage the situation. These political disputes are still raging, while the EU is trying to provide satisfactory solutions with some organizational, regulatory, and media campaign measures. Above all, these crises indicate that the innovation process includes a self-reflection of the risks and ethics involved in techno-economic development, and this self-reflection has become a core social dynamic in this century. The wider agenda of the innovation policy of the EU should be impelled to include questions of risk and the social sustainability of innovation as central topics.

This chapter addresses the transition to a 'risk society' and the new social dynamics that are related to risk, and social trust in science, with special reference to EU politics. The second section examines the political process of Europeanizing some public controversies and their solutions in times of scientific and political uncertainty, particularly the storm surrounding the release of GMOs in the EU. This has also had a global dimension, and the chapter will analyse the role of the EU in this wider context, mainly related to trade issues. The focus is particularly on the role of the EU in the context of the WTO. The changing relationships between public and private spheres deserve careful analysis as they are central to the new forms of governing science and innovation at EU level. Here, the recent initiatives launched by the Commission are critically analysed. The chapter finishes with some remarks about the growing importance of social sustainability of innovation for the overall governance of innovation policy in the EU, and the constitutive and legitimacy aspects related to it.

INNOVATION, SCIENCE AND SOCIETY

The complex relationship between science, innovation and society in our contemporary lives is the fruit of a historical process. The innovation process is deeply embedded in the social and economic context from which it has emerged. In our post-modern, or late modern societies, risk has acquired a key position in the interaction between society and science. Ulrich Beck's theory of the 'risk society' is directly relevant for us if we wish to understand and study the recent scares about science and technology at EU level. The question to be addressed is whether we can define these events as signalling the emergence of a post-national risk society in the EU.

Risk Society as Reflexive Modernity

Ulrich Beck's conception of the risk society is one of contemporary sociology's most discussed theses. Briefly, it states that we are in a transformation from a society essentially focused on 'wealth production', to a society focused on 'risk aversion' (Beck 1992). This 'risk society' is mainly emerging in industrialized countries and is related to growing popular awareness of the risks involved in mass production and applications of technology. Another central topic in Beck's arguments is that the risk society is a second modernity, which is characterized by its reflexive attitude towards science, technology and progress in general. Hence, he uses the notions of 'new modernity', 'second modernity' and 'reflexive modernity' almost interchangeably throughout his work. Beck's understanding of 'reflexivity' is essentially that the new popular perceptions of risk put an important perspective on the unspoken and implicit values embedded in the socio-political objective of 'progress'. The new social perception of risk is not just one among other features of our contemporary societies; it is 'the' defining element of a society that becomes more independent from previous knowledge structures based on scienticism and naturism, as it becomes more distrustful and self-reflecting about the values and ethics of the first modernity.

> We are therefore concerned no longer exclusively with making nature useful, or with releasing mankind from traditional constraints, but also and essentially with problems resulting from techno-economic development itself. Modernization is becoming reflexive; it is becoming its own theme. (Beck 1992: 20)

What is risk? When giving examples, Beck almost invariably refers to ecological and environmental hazards. He repeatedly mentions radioactive accidents and chemical disasters, or more generally the effects of pollution. Nevertheless, he obviously defines risk at a more abstract level, and this is the level at which it matters most, since we will try to expand it to other types of hazards, not necessarily related to the environment. The definition of risk is arrived at by contrasting it with the definition of wealth. Wealth deals with consumer goods, incomes, educational opportunities, property, and so on, and these are 'desirable items in scarcity', characterized by 'the positive logic of acquisition' (Beck 1992: 26). In contrast with this, 'risks are an incidental problem of modernization in undesirable abundance. These must be either eliminated or denied and reinterpreted' (p. 26). Therefore they pursue a 'negative logic of disposition, avoidance, denial, and reinterpretation' (p. 26). But risk and wealth are not contrary to each other: although they follow opposite logics, they are different sides of the same coin.

Risk is distributed in a different way from wealth. In early modernity, wealth was distributed according to the rules of class and social structure. However, risk is distributed in a more complex manner. The geographical aspect (given the environmental nature of risk) is important, but risk is essentially a fruit of a social and political construction where different causal elements are identified and responsibility placed. 'In modernization risk, then, things which are substantively-objectively, spatially and temporally disparate are drawn together causally and thus brought into a social and legal context of responsibility' (Beck 1992: 28). Causality, responsibility and risk are deeply inter-related.[1]

This is an important aspect of the emerging risk society. On the one hand, the growing environmental impact of industrial production means that environmental hazard is becoming a transnational phenomenon that does not respect the political borders of states; the new territoriality of risk is increasingly borderless. The high degree and speed of the current transnational interdependence means that in reflexive modernity risk is no longer confined to national borders, but is increasingly assuming a transnational, global dimension (Beck 1999). In his latest book Beck's emphasis on the global dimension forces him to consider risk in a wider sense: not just in environmental terms, but also in socio-economic ones. The cosmopolitan manifesto of the world risk society points to a new dialectic of global and local questions, which do not fit into national politics. On the other hand, the essential elements of causality and responsibility in risk make it a direct product of each given society at a given time, typically in a given national context. Risk is socially defined, depending on the social values of a given society. This means that risk is a subjective matter rooted in collective and individual perceptions. 'Behind all the objectifications (of science), sooner or later the question of acceptance arises and with it anew the old question: *how do we wish to live?*' (Beck 1992: 28). And this is essentially constructed within the borders of the strongest political system so far: the state.

The rapid development of biotechnology and life sciences in the past two decades has accentuated the questions of choice and social values, opening up a Pandora's box of collective definitions of what risks are emerging and what political action is required.[2] Consequently, the next section examines the social dimension of the innovation process.

The Social Sustainability of Innovation in the Risk Society

How does the thesis of the risk society relate to our view of innovation? Turning back to our initial discussions in Chapters 1 and 2 about the nature of the innovation process, we saw how the transition from a 'technology policy' to a broader 'innovation policy' relies on a new theoretical conception of the innovation process. This new conception is the notion that innovation is not a linear process starting with a scientific discovery and ending in its industrial application, but is a more complex and recurrent process that involves social learning and organizational change. This new approach to the nature of the innovation process places its emphasis on social and organizational aspects, rather than on the nature of knowledge itself. This social dimension in turn means that the specific path of a given innovation is related to the 'success' that a new knowledge had in a given social context, and its continuous usage. Innovations are so because they are socially relevant.

Several philosophers and social scientists have explored the constitutive effect of knowledge in society. Foucault, for example, defined language and knowledge as the exercise of power, in what was to be a highly influential post-modern philosophical school of thought in the late 20th century (Foucault 2000). Susan Strange, on the other hand, included 'knowledge' among the elements that define power structure in the international political economy, and by knowledge she mainly meant technology (Strange 1988). Most relevant for us here are the scholars interested in the so-called 'social shaping of technology' (SST). This is a truly interdisciplinary line of research that has gained momentum since the 1980s.

> SST stands in contrast to post-Enlightenment traditions which did not problematize technological change, but limited the scope of enquiry to monitoring the social adjustments it saw as being required by technological progress. SST emerged through a critique of such technological determinism. SST studies show that technology does not develop according to an inner technical logic but is instead a social product, patterned by the conditions of its creation and use. (Williams and Edge 1996: 866)

Therefore, one of the most important propositions of this school is that in the design of individual artefacts, and in the trajectories of innovation, there are implicit and explicit social choices. This is rather central, since it directly contests the assumption that technological change produces social and organizational change. Quite the opposite, social dynamics are those shaping and defining technical change.

If innovation is so deeply embedded in social organization and its transformation, then the growing popular distrust in science, and the risk-aversion attitude associated with it, might constitute a social limit to the innovation process. One thing is clear, citizens and consumers have been increasingly denying and rejecting the acquisition or use of specific technologies they dislike. This is not a mere hypothetical possibility, it is an actual choice being made in the market arena (by consumers refusing to buy specific products), in the political arena (by specific regulatory decisions on, for example, the obligation to label products containing GMOs), and in the realm of private life (by individuals partly reshaping previous social actions in order to avoid specific scientific and technological-related practices). This 'reactive' attitude of consumers, citizens and individuals in these three realms of social life, points at a growing self-consciousness that fits Beck's idea of a transition towards a risk society.

In this emerging late modernity, characterized by the reflective attitude of individuals about the pros and cons of wealth production, the question of risk and trust in science acquires a central position. Progress is essentially social progress, and innovation is essentially social and organizational innovation. All this stresses the fact that beyond the economic and technical rationale implicit in all technical and knowledge advancements, innovation cannot take place without a certain degree of social support, and this social support and choice is what we might define here as the social sustainability of innovation. The next section examines how these questions are increasingly transcending the conventional borders of states, and how some of them have recently been 'Europeanized'.

EUROPEANIZING RISK AND (DIS)TRUST IN SCIENCE

Recent studies point out that diminishing public trust in science was a remarkable trend throughout Europe during the last decade (Jensen 2000). These statistical results are not surprising; they confirm quantitatively the theoretical postulates of Beck's risk society, and more generally a growing critical attitude to science and its impact on human life. What is interesting for this book, though, is that this public change of attitude correlates to a Europeanization of the latest food safety crises, particularly the BSE and GMO cases. It is interesting because the context where such crises have been taking place is no longer within the confines of the state, but is in a heavily internationalized and Europeanized situation where the scientific, technical and political decisions are placed in a multi-level political system. Admittedly, the complexity (and occasional obscurity) of this multi-level political system has done little to encourage public trust in times of uncertainty. Above all, people's strong reaction to new scientific uncertainties and health risks has pushed to the limits the previous mechanisms of risk assessment and management, placed the issue of consumer protection in the headlines of the EU political agenda, and underlined the social sustainability of innovation.

In the following section we focus on the case of GMOs at EU level. The primary objective is to explore the process and the tensions that the Europeanization of this case have generated, with the intention of identifying the characteristics and impacts of the social distrust associated with them. Subsequently, the political solutions offered in order to provide a more accountable and focused policy-making process are analysed in the light of their possibilities for re-establishing social trust and consumer confidence by means of new principles and modes of action that pick up generalized social values.

The GMO Case: Europeanizing Distrust

Genetically modified organisms are those that have received a selective transfer of genes from another organism (even from a different natural species). In the mid-1980s, these organisms were released into the environment in a limited way for research purposes with the eventual intention of developing agricultural products, but in the 1990s many countries increasingly made use of them beyond the goals of scientific trial, into conventional crops/production and consumable goods, with the US in the lead.

In Europe, GMOs are a highly sensitive issue, and not by chance. They became a political issue in the mid-1990s, almost simultaneously with the BSE crisis (Bovine Spongiform Encephalopathy, 'mad cow disease') (Gonçalves 2000), and both cases came under the topic of 'food safety' in the EU, which in recent years has been under media scrutiny. To a much larger extent than BSE, strong popular scepticism about GMOs has led to the end of their use in Europe. In 1998 several member countries obtained a de facto moratorium on the release of GMOs into the environment and the market, until new stricter rules for risk assessment are in place at EU level. At the time of writing this book the moratorium is still effective.

The political reaction in this matter relies on the profound disagreement and sensitivity regarding the potential effects of GMOs. Far from over, the arguments in favour and against are still raging. Detractors suggest three possible types of risk: first, the environmental/ecological hazard generated by an undesired and uncontrolled spread of these organisms into other species; secondly, the potential risk to human health by the transfer of allergens or carcinogens; and thirdly, the unknown effects of GMOs on antibiotic resistance in humans and animals (Runge and Jackson 2000). On the other hand, supporters of GMOs downplay these concerns, putting forward two counter-arguments. The first is that so far 'there is no scientific evidence that the use of the technology is itself inherently unsafe' (Commission 2001: 2). GMO supporters argue that there is no significant difference between organisms modified by these new advanced techniques of genetic manipulation, and those modified by traditional methods. Furthermore, the intense screening which GMOs are subject to makes them safer than those produced by traditional methods, because of the intense control procedures they follow. And secondly, GMOs have some interesting benefits for the environment and human health, as they might enable a reduction in the use of pesticides in agriculture, and generate products in a more selective manner (*The Economist* 1999). Indeed, contrasting the arguments in favour and against GMOs is insufficient if we wish to understand the essential nature of the disputes. Eike has argued that the root of the dispute is to be found in two elements. First, the scientific 'facts' point in different directions, and depend very much on the specific scientific background from which each perspective comes. Secondly, the potential impact of GM food on human health and the environment is a complex issue over which there is a great deal of uncertainty that science is unable to solve, because there are no straightforward answers (Eike 2000).

It is worth pointing out the fact that opponents of GMOs have shown some concern about the proprietary nature of those products and their effect in the global and local markets of seeds, feed and food, in agricultural and industrial production. A recent economic study of the GM food industry shows that there are evident signs of industrial concentration in this new industry, in terms of both IPR ownership and approved products (Harhoff et al. 2001). Interestingly, these authors conclude, among other things, that a new dilemma for policy-making might be emerging between food safety policy (with time-consuming approval mechanisms) and competition policy (wanting to avoid too much market dominance by a few actors): 'The approval process may create a policy dilemma for policy makers: while it provides the benefit of ensuring food safety, it comes at the cost of further industrial concentration' (Harhoff et al. 2001: 288).

The 1998 moratorium imposed a temporary halt on the rows over GMOs in the EU, but the question of how far and in what circumstances they would be introduced into the market are still open, as European consumers continue to be sceptical about the idea. But above all, the GMOs case brings to the fore how scientific uncertainty is able to plunge the EU into a political crisis that involves different stakeholders and different perceptions of risk. Indeed, it exposed to the public the inadequacy of the decision-making procedures to deal effectively with unexpected events and public unease, and the disregard that the scientific and political establishment had shown for popular legitimacy and trust in scientifically based decision-making. One thing that the GMOs case will almost certainly be remembered for is that social trust in science will never again be shrugged off as unimportant by political and administrative elites. This, as we will see, might *perhaps* mean that the technocratic approach to the governance of science at EU level is on the wane.

Struggling to Find Satisfactory Solutions

Even though the GMO case dates from the late 1990s, the EU has still not shaped a definitive compromise and political and administrative solution to deal with these matters. It looks as if the upheaval that followed the food scandals has not yet fully settled down. The Commission speedily produced the 1997 communication on a new approach to food safety,[3] but the reforms it proposed failed to gain wide support. The European Parliament (EP), the Council and most stakeholders saw it as an insufficient, piecemeal transformation that did not come to grips with the real problems about food safety in the EU (Vos 2000: 243). Besides, the Commission was itself under fire, and it became quite clear that the Council wanted wider political action, rather than the mere adaptation of Commission rules (ibid.).

The need to find common EU solutions to the food safety problems was an inescapable political question, due to the diplomatic and legitimacy dimension that conveyed those crises. The effective mobilization of consumer groups at EU level, the political leadership of the Parliament, and the highly sensitive inter-state relations in this matter, all contributed to crystallizing the understanding that there should be a common EU political response to the food safety crisis, and that part of this response involves reshaping the governance of science at EU level. Hence, the White Paper on food safety was issued in January 2000 and seems so far to be a first real step in the direction of more substantial policy reform in this realm.[4] The paper establishes the principles guiding the new food safety policy, and defines lines of action in the regulatory field, controlling mechanisms, international dimension, and the European Food Safety Authority. As we will see, the concretization of these lines of action is forging ahead with astonishing rapidity. We will concentrate on what, in my view, represents the three core elements of the political solution that has so far been put forward, namely, the nitty-gritty of food regulations, the 'precautionary principle', and the European Food Safety Authority.

Starting with the first, GMO regulations in the EU today can be described as patchwork (Héritier 1996). The rapid succession of regulatory initiatives in this area, together with the incomprehensible co-existence of vertical regulations (food–feed–seed law) and horizontal regulations (specifically on GMOs), renders the picture rather confusing. Moreover, there are clear signs of overlap between them, as there is no clear political guideline about which of the two dimensions, vertical or horizontal, will predominate. Figure 6.1 represents these vertical and horizontal regulations.

During the first half of the 1990s, the EU accepted the release of 18 different GMOs into the environment or on to the market, following the procedures of risk assessment stipulated in Directive 90/220/EEC. However, at the onset of the GMOs crisis in 1996–97, this directive came under fierce attack by environmental and consumer groups for what was perceived to be a far too lenient risk assessment procedure. Fears were aired that many GMOs were to be released without exhaustive evaluation because of a narrow understanding of risk. These groups' activism was followed by the flourishing of different understandings between member states (Levidow et al. 1997). Some countries, led by Greece, wanted stricter assessment rules. The unease that this provoked ended in 1998 with the political compromise of a de facto 'GMO moratorium' until new rules were adopted. The moratorium has

	GM food – novel food Reg. 258/97	GM feed (not regulated)	GM seeds – Dir. 98/95
Authorization to market release Dir. 90/220/EEC, new: 2001/18/EC			
Labelling – proposed regulation: Com (2001) 425			

Figure 6.1   EU vertical and horizontal regulations on GMOs, by 2002

provided a thinking and negotiating period for stakeholders, but in the view of the general public, it has only postponed the issue, in what is still a matter that attracts much scepticism among consumers.

New rules have recently arrived. The new directive 2001/18/EC introduced stricter risk assessment and risk management procedures, and entered into force in October 2002. Striking a bargain on this has not been an easy process; the EP showed a strong attitude in favour of consumer protection, and the final decision was taken in the conciliation committee between the Council of Ministers and EP representatives.[5] Likewise, the question of labelling and traceability of GMOs will soon have a new horizontal regulation which will cover GM food and feed. Today, labelling is regulated by two vertical regulations on novel food and seeds, though no requirements for labelling animal feed are so far in place. Apart from covering animal feed, the coming regulation (proposal Com (2001) 425) will extend the existing labelling requirements for food to a much wider range of food products and ingredients, such as, for example, highly refined soya oil produced from GM-soya, which is a very common ingredient in pastry. Labelling is an important issue because it empowers consumers by giving them information and options to choose.

Following the 1998 political agreement, it is expected that the GMO moratorium will be lifted when full labelling and risk assessment directives are in force (CORDIS 2001: 8). Does this mean that there is light at the end of the tunnel for GMO troubles in the EU? It all depends on what one expects from this. On the one hand, the new directive on risk assessment and the proposed one for labelling traceability are a 'victory' for GMO-sensitive countries and groups by forcing more control and information for the benefit of consumers and the environment. On the other hand, the new directive 2001 strengthens the principle of risk assessment on a one-to-one basis, something that can be seen as the 'victory' of those countries and groups that are positive about GMOs, and that blocked any attempt to ban GMOs altogether. Hence, there seems to be a win–win situation for most of the stakeholders, but not for the most radical ones, who are likely to take up the issue at the time when the moratorium is lifted. In any case, we should not forget that the new directive is the fruit of negotiations between representatives, both national democratic representatives and NGO representatives. It is still unclear what kind of popular reaction there will be when the moratorium is lifted. Several authors point out that the social unease about GMOs is essentially a question of trust, which will not be alleviated by more technical information or administrative control, but by a political acceptance of consumers' concerns (Teknologirådet 2001).

Less contentious is the question of the precautionary principle, the second core issue of the new EU food safety policy. Still rather unknown to the general public, this legal principle has become highly politicized, in both EU and international trade matters. This principle is not new at all – the EU has long applied it within the context of environmental protection, as enshrined in article 174 TEU. What is new is its extension to the area of food safety.

> Although the precautionary principle is not explicitly mentioned in the Treaty except in the environmental field, its scope is far wider and covers those specific circumstances where scientific evidence is insufficient, inconclusive or uncertain and there are indications through preliminary objective scientific evaluation that there are reasonable grounds for concern that the potentially dangerous effects on the environment, human, animal or plant health may be inconsistent with the chosen level of protection. (Commission 2000: 10)

The main aim of this communication from the Commission has been to clarify the conditions and the procedures under which this principle will be invoked in its administrative competences with respect to risk management. This clarification is most welcome in light of the significant imprecision of this principle in international law (Shepherd 2000: 14). Moreover, this document has been used strategically for diplomatic purposes. The EU sought to advance the acceptance of this legal principle at international level, particularly in connection with the WTO, but without much success as we will see later in this chapter (Skogstad 2001). Following the communication, the five elements that will guide the enforcement of this principle are: proportionality, nondiscrimination, consistency, demonstrated benefit and monitoring. Most recently, this principle has been enshrined into the acquis communautaire in article 7 of the regulation on food safety.[6] In September 2002, the Court of First Instance extended the precautionary principle to the issues of human and animal health, in the judgment of cases T-13/99 and T-70/99, also known as the Pfizer case. The court decision sets out the conditions for the application of this principle in EU law beyond environmental issues, and follows to a large extent the Commission's Communication of 2000. Consumer protection agencies have almost unanimously hailed the decision, seeing it as a turning point for improving food safety in the EU.

Last but not least, the European Food Safety Authority (EFSA) is the third, and probably the most highly visible political initiative of the new EU food safety politics. The expectations are high, in the belief that this new agency will provide the much-desired transparency required for this policy area, but its effects remain to be seen. The main function will be to provide independent scientific advice, to have a role in the 'rapid alert system', and to collect and analyse data. It is worth noting that the EFSA will not have independent regulatory powers, but has just been endowed with advisory prerogatives. We will see later in this chapter how the new agency is part of an important makeover of scientific advice and of the overall institutional role of the Commission.

A New Post-national Risk Society?

Solutions to the problem of food safety have been rapidly 'Europeanized' since the second half of the 1990s, and the EU is well on its way to gaining further competences and powers in this matter. Could it have been otherwise? There was a great deal of dissatisfaction with the Commision's management of the GMO case, and with the risk assessment procedure at EU level. This could easily have resulted in the reverse transfer of competences from EU to national level. As national regulations on food safety have a longer legal tradition and respond to specific national societal requirements, the 'national solution' was in fact not far from being enforced, so why was the supra-national level chosen?

The argument here is that both technical and market factors and societal factors tipped the balance in the EU's favour. In terms of the former, the idea of maintaining a well-functioning single market put substantial pressure on member states to avoid 'national solutions'. National bans on other EU members' food products on the basis of national food safety regulations/considerations (which were enforced in the BSE case) would not only have generated considerable diplomatic tensions, but also a lot of work for the ECJ since the principle of 'mutual recognition' would invariably have been invoked. Yet, amid scientific uncertainty and consumers' extreme sensitivity, the solution of 'mutual recognition' would have proved to be both socially and politically untenable. It would have been socially untenable because consumers would have considered it an illegitimate mechanism employed to introduce GMOs into member countries, and politically untenable because in such circumstances 'mutual recognition' could very probably generate a spiral of ever weaker regulatory laws as members sought to gain competitive advantage. In other words, a negative integration solution based on national regulation and mutual recognition would have increased problems rather than solved them. Therefore, a positive integration solution through direct EU action and regulation with a homogeneous effect all through the EU appeared to be less costly.

Nevertheless, the societal factor was central to the EU's regulatory solution. The overwhelming public reaction to these matters was extremely negative throughout the Union. The unequivocal and widespread reaction of consumers and civil societies surprised all the national and European elites. The fragility of consumers' confidence in the food industry and public authorities' capacity to make food safe was not easy to restore, mainly because it was based on value attitudes rather than just bad information (Frewer et al. 1997; Davison et al. 1997). This was evident in the immediate aftermath of the BSE and GMOs crises. The Commission's 'new approach' in 1997 proved to be a quick but clumsy political response, mainly because it was seen as a mode of undertaking 'business as usual' with only minor changes. The popular demands for a much wider and deeper transformation of risk assessment and management, pushed by consumer groups aligned with the EP, and by some member states, succeeded in establishing the de facto 'GMO moratorium'. The BSE and GMO cases were the 'tip of the iceberg' of a severe legitimacy crisis about the hitherto cosy relationship between science and politics, at national as well as EU level (ESRC 1999).

Beck's theory about risk and the social perceptions of it were validated by both the BSE and GMO cases only a few years later. Are we seeing the emergence of a post-national risk society in Europe? The recent Euro-barometer survey on European science and technology of December 2001 shows interesting data about European attitudes towards GMOs and science in general (see Tables 6.1 and 6.2).

One of the survey's most interesting findings is that the higher the level of scientific knowledge of respondents, the more critical is their attitude towards the idea that science can solve every problem. This is also the group that demands the highest accountability and social control of scientific activity and its usage. Although in some issues statistical differences exist between sex, age and country of origin, other issues show an astonishingly similar response throughout the EU such as, for example, the wish to have the possibility of

Table 6.1   Europeans' opinion about GMOs, in percentages for the EU-15, 2001

Questions	Agree	Disagree	Do not know
I want to have the right to choose	94.6	2.5	2.8
I want to know more about this kind of food before eating it	85.9	9.3	4.8
They should only be introduced if it is scientifically proven that they are harmless	85.8	8.0	6.1
I do not want this type of food	70.9	16.9	12.2
They could have negative effects on the environment	59.4	11.9	28.7
The dangers have been exaggerated by the media	33.1	44.3	22.6
This kind of food does not present any particular danger	14.6	54.8	30.6

Source: Eurobarometer (2001).

rejecting products containing GMOs (Table 6.1) or the 84.4 per cent agreement that 'a discovery in itself is neither good nor bad, what is important is the use which is made of it' (Eurobarometer 2001: 36). Nevertheless, as we will see in the next section, all these matters, and particularly the GMO issue, are intrinsically related to international dynamics that are beyond the strict limits of the EU.

THE INTERNATIONAL DIMENSION

Nowhere but in the international regime of biotechnology is it so blatantly clear that there are deep differences in the understanding of risk and trust in science existing today at global level. This is not just a matter of north–south divisions between developed and developing countries in the gap between have and have-nots of knowledge, but as we will see, also between developed countries that have a solid industrial and scientific knowledge basis. This section addresses first the rapid, yet weak, articulation of the current international regime of biotechnology. This will serve as a basis for understanding the issues at stake in the international scenario, and the way in which it has run parallel to the developments of the EU policy examined earlier. After that, the section looks in detail at the upsurge of US–EU controversies in this area, specifically on the GMO issue. Last but not least, it considers the role of the EU as an international actor in this domain, and the negotiating strategy of the European Commission in this regard.

Table 6.2　　*Answers to the question 'GMOs could have negative effects on the environment', by level of knowledge cohorts in percentages for the EU-15, 2001*

Level of knowledge	Agree	Disagree	Do not know
0 to 4	47.7	9.3	43.0
5 to 6	57.1	11.9	31.0
7 to 8	60.3	11.6	28.1
9 to 10	61.1	13.2	25.6
11 to 13	66.0	11.9	22.1
Total	59.4	11.9	28.7

Note:　The levels of knowledge have been defined by the answers given to a range of scientific questions in the same questionnaire.

Source:　Eurobarometer (2001).

The International Regime of Biotechnology and Food Safety

The international conventions and agreements that today constitute the biotechnology and food safety regime have evolved at breakneck speed since the early 1990s. The definition of this regime is a complex matter for two reasons. First, because of its fluid functional boundaries: under the terms biotechnology and biosafety there are issues involving environmental protection, consumer protection, food safety, fair trade, and industrial and technological development. Secondly, because the international regulations that constitute this regime have unclear and rapidly changing interactions between them, rendering extremely difficult the question of 'how things hang together'. Nothing daunted, though, it can be asserted that two important events in the formation of the regime were the Cartagena Protocol (signed in 2000), and the SPS agreement under the WTO (signed in 1995), both of binding nature, and both covering the field of GMOs in food and seed.[7]

Turning to the specific issue of GMOs, their regulation at international level has followed two parallel developments, the first being related to the consequences that GMOs could have for biosafety. 'Biosafety' is here understood in rather broad terms, comprising mainly environmental protection, but also human health protection, as the Cartagena Protocol stipulates. The second development in the international regulation of GMOs is related to free trade. Since they have increasingly become objects of international trade, they have become an issue within the phytosanitary measures of trade arrangements, first within the GATT, and since the mid-

1990s within the WTO. These two approaches to regulation mean that the constitution of the international regime of biotechnology and food safety is complex and contains many unresolved matters, especially about GMOs.

Questions of biosafety related to GMOs were raised at international level at the end of the 1980s during the United Nations Conference on Environment and Development (UNCED). Concerns about the ecological impact of GMO releases into the environment and their impact on human health were present at the negotiation of the Convention on Biological Diversity, and eventually became enshrined into this non-binding Convention in 1992. In 1997 further diplomatic efforts to produce a binding international agreement managed to launch a new negotiating round that ended with the Cartagena Protocol in 2000.[8] The argument was the regulatory gap at international level 'that had emerged in the early 1990s with regard to the rapid expansion of GM technologies (genetic modification) in commercial agriculture' (Falkner 2000b: 303). Although negotiations were several times on the verge of collapse, negotiating parties buckled down over three years until the final agreement in January 2000. The Cartagena Protocol on Biosafety is, today, the cornerstone of the international regime on these matters, with binding effects on signatory members.

Three issues were at stake. First was the matter of what scope the Protocol should have. Against the will of the so-called Miami group (the five leading GMOs exporter countries[9]) the Protocol agreed on a rather wide range of products with the only exception being pharmaceutical products. Secondly, there were the so-called AIA procedures,[10] which define the terms that exporter and importer countries have to follow, and that strengthened the regulatory powers of the latter. And thirdly, even if the precautionary principle was not defined explicitly in the text, it was implicitly accepted in the wording of article 10.6. All in all, the Protocol is a significant step in the institutionalization of procedures at international level, and in the reinforcement of national mechanisms for biosafety control. It succeeded in avoiding the splintering of the world's political map on this matter, by cobbling together a bunch of basic notions and procedures. However, its wording is occasionally unclear and contradictory in a manner that might present problems for legal interpretation.

Nevertheless, the role of the Protocol in relation to other international arrangements is still an open question, most notably its relation with the WTO. The Sanitary and Phytosanitary (SPS) measures were agreed in the mid-1990s along with the Marrakesh Agreements that created the WTO. SPS defines precisely the conditions under which national countries might use these measures, while respecting the overall objective of free trade. The newly created SPS agreement was the means to achieve the requirement that food safety measures be based on scientific evidence (Skogstad 2001). The trade-oriented character of the WTO makes it a more attractive international framework for GMO exporting countries than the protection-oriented spirit of the Cartagena Protocol. Above all, the SPS provides another legal basis for striking the balance between free trade and consumer protection, which has been contested. On the one hand, article 5.7 introduces a precautionary approach[11] even if it is partial and implicit (Pardo-Quintillán 1999: 155). On the other hand, however, by sticking strictly to scientific evidence, the SPS agreement does not include other criteria like 'genuine consumer concerns' as the EU would have wished (Skogstad 2001: 490–91). This indicates that the real reach of SPS depends to a large extent on the interpretation and implementation of these caveats, which will be subject to international negotiations and practices. Interesting in this regard is the role that the Codex Alimentarius Commission (Codex) is acquiring in spite of its voluntary nature. Created in 1962 to facilitate fair trade in food the Codex has been systematically used in the context of WTO dispute settlement.

Having briefly examined the international arrangements that deal with food safety and biotechnology, it is easy to conclude that the regime has been structured with astonishing speed during the last decade, but that it is still unfinished. First, despite the strong thrust towards institutionalization that the Cartagena Protocol on Biosafety and the SPS agreement under WTO represent, there are still many open questions about how to implement these regulations. The occasionally unclear wording of both is the fruit of political compromises that have left the hard task of interpretation to international dispute procedures, unlikely to bridge the gap of national sensitivities in these matters. Secondly, the relationship between both international regulations is still quite unclear, and the potential conflict between them stems from their very different approaches and paradigms (Skogstad 2001; Phillips and Kerr 2000). Whereas the Cartagena Protocol endorses the precautionary principle and allows socio-economic criteria other than strict scientific evidence, the SPS only has superficial acceptance of the precautionary approach, and denies any criteria other than 'sound science'. Some authors claim that the dispute settlement authorities under WTO have tended to get closer to the spirit of the Cartagena Protocol and EU legal reasoning (Miller and Conko 2000), while others see the opposite trend, with no evident bridging between the paradigms (Pardo-Quintillán 1999).

The EU–US Disagreements

The US is the largest exporter of GMOs in the world. By 1996 it had extensively commercialized genetically modified corn (maize), cotton and soybeans and by 1998, 500 GM plant varieties were available on the US market. This situation contrasts sharply with the caution with which the EU has addressed this issue, where only 18 GM crops were authorized before the de facto moratorium – provisionally – stopped that. The reason for such large differences is to be found in a combination of regulatory factors (the procedures and scope of risk assessment) and social factors (mainly consumer concerns). As to the first, the strengthening of risk assessment procedures in the aftermath of the food safety scandals in Europe rendered the process significantly longer and stricter for each GMO. For its part, no pre-market evaluation was specifically required for GM foods in the US until very recently.[12] Nevertheless, the most important factor explaining the EU and US differences is a social one. As we saw earlier in this chapter, a series of food scandals in the 1990s (BSE, Dioxine, Salmonella and Foot and Mouth Disease) made European consumers sensitive to food safety issues. The uncertainties still related to GMOs, especially to their environmental impact, have made Europeans unwilling to accept the political and scientific elites' reassuring messages. This sensitivity is not shared on the other side of the Atlantic. Here Europeans are portrayed as 'anti-technological' and 'hysterical activists' (Miller and Conko 2000) and it looks as though Europeans have not understood science. Nevertheless, despite the clear US–EU tensions and differences on this topic, the US has so far refrained from raising a case against EU policy on GMOs in the WTO disputes settlement procedure. However, its potential to start a new trade war, similar to the never-ending squabbles over hormones in beef, should not be underestimated.

The issue of beef fed with hormones has been a test case for the SPS arrangements under the WTO, and for the diplomatic relationship between both trade partners. The EU ban on US beef is still in place at the time of writing, and the EU Commission refuses to comply with the WTO dispute decisions of 1997 and 1998,[13] arguing that its own measures are non-discriminatory and coherent with its internal EU regulations in this field. In other words, the EU claims that the ban is a legitimate measure. Without entering into a detailed discussion about this long and complex dispute, it is worth noting that labelling might provide a solution for both beef and GMOs (Runge and Jackson 2000). Labelling provides consumers with the possibility of informed choice, while allowing for free trade. However, this is not without problems, especially with regard to segregation procedures for GMOs and non-GMOs, and labelling of processed food.[14]

The EU–US dispute over GMOs is at the centre of the international politics of biotechnology and food safety (Falkner 2000a: 143). In the late 1990s, voices calling for transatlantic dialogue on these matters had a certain impact (Laget and Cantley 2001), with diplomatic efforts at the highest level leading to the creation of the EU–US forum on biotechnology in May 2000, composed of independent experts from both sides. Its final report contains a series of recommendations, among the most interesting being the 'role of precaution': 'When substantive uncertainties prevent accurate risk assessment, governments should act protectively on the side of safety (recommendation 12)'. Even if the report has obviously not solved the ongoing differences between the US and the EU in biotechnology, it has certainly helped to smooth their relationship on this thorny question.

Speaking with One Voice?

The US–EU diplomatic efforts of the last few years have not deterred the European Commission from forging steadily ahead in its efforts to ensure that the precautionary principle becomes a basis for international law, and to gain acceptance at world level for its high protection standards. Concerning the precautionary principle, the Commission recently raised this issue at the SPS Committee meeting in March 2000. It wanted to make the case for that principle at a time when the Committee was discussing new guidelines for interpreting 'consistency' within the scope of the SPS agreement. The Committee declared that this principle is already contained in article 5.7 of SPS, and expressed its concern that it might weaken WTO rules giving leeway to trade protectionism. In an attempt to gain international support the EU also raised this issue in the context of the recent considerations about GMOs by the Codex Alimentarius (under the FAO–WHO realm), and in the context of the OECD biotechnology talks. This is not surprising given the growing centrality of these two non-binding agreements in the consolidation of the international regime (particularly the Codex). Another dimension of these diplomatic efforts is the EU's attempts to defend its high standards of protection. EU civil servants and legal experts are extensively arguing that scientific evidence need not be the ultimate or sole requisite for forbidding products to enter the market, but that genuine consumer concerns should also be considered (Noiville 2000; Brom 2000), provided that the measures are coherent and non-discriminatory (Pardo-Quintillán 1999).

When looking at the international role of the EU in this matter, it is worth pointing out the apparent unanimity between EU member states (Skogstad 2001: 493), when compared with negotiation of the TRIPS agreement. Member states seem to agree more widely with each other on the precautionary principle and on the position of EU negotiators in international fora. This is not just related to the fact that GMOs and food safety fall under the 'old' issues of trade policy, where the Commission has relatively large room for manoeuvre, but has to do mainly with the commonly shared attitude among member states on these matters. The BSE crisis generated major intra-EU trade squabbles, but the GMOs dispute with the US gained general support from European capitals. This has to do perhaps with the 'importance of being

European' that some states showed in the turbulent waters of food safety (Gonçalves 2000).

In the run up to the Doha meeting (November 2001), that opened the next WTO negotiation round, the European Commission expressed in its official preparatory document that 'consumer protection' is a key issue for Europeans, and that further clarification of the WTO rules in this area is needed. As the document says: 'There is no reason to believe that measures based on the precautionary principle are incompatible with WTO measures'.[15] Furthermore, the EU wants to clarify WTO rules about compulsory labelling.

PUBLIC AND PRIVATE INTERACTIONS: THE NEW GOVERNANCE OF SCIENCE

The public rows about food safety in the EU have brought to the fore with unexpected virulence questions over the democratic dimension of technical decision-making, and the interplay between science and politics. In this section the new interactions between public and private interests are examined.

Science and Politics in Times of Uncertainty

The relationship between science and politics is a topic that has received much attention during the last decades, and still manages to raise controversy. Some authors argue that science and politics are two separate realms of social action, which follow distinct logics (the scientific method and political logic) and ethos (the advancement of scientific knowledge, and the welfare of the population, respectively). This means that the problematic relationship between them is based in these inherently different logics and ethos, which occasionally renders them irreconcilable. When dilemmas emerge, the final choice becomes one between the scientific evidence (based on 'sound science') and the political decision (based on popular-communicative intentions) (Miller and Conko 2000). However, this understanding that there is a clear-cut division between politics and science is hyperbole. Most authors would be careful, especially regarding the assumption of scientific evidence and sound science (Landfried 1999; ESRC 1999; Miller 1999). Sociologists and historians of science are aware that 'scientific logic' has changed historically at least as much as 'political logic', in a way that both are products of their times (Gieryn 1995). Hence, science and politics co-evolve over time, and are in many ways deeply related to each other (Cozzens and Woodhouse 1995). This relativization, or 'historification' does not mean that science and politics are one and the same, nor that science loses its explanatory power for providing answers to complex technical questions. It just means that the claims of universal validity of science need to be contextualized in time and space, and it means as well the recognition that science has its limits.

The recent food safety scandals in the EU touched on the central nerve of the relationship between science and politics in Western Europe, in a way that shows an important change in the relationship between the two. There are two main elements that point to this transformation. One is that these cases have underlined as never before the asymmetry that exists between the real outputs from scientific analysis, and the high social expectations attached to them. What has happened since the late 1990s is that there has been increasing popular awareness that scientific uncertainty exists, and that it is much greater than the public has been willing to accept. The new social values and attitudes that signal the emergence of the current risk society imply a greater intolerance of uncertainty and risk than earlier decades, putting pressure on scientific activity and its outputs. Furthermore, the 1990s saw the emergence of a certain degree of mistrust of science, as the GMOs case in the EU shows. Despite scientists' reiterated statements that products coming from advanced methods of genetic manipulation do not represent a higher risk than those obtained by traditional methods, European consumers continue to dislike GMOs. What does this mean? It means that consumers still see an additional risk attached to GMOs in what has become an outspoken disbelief of biologists' statements.

The second element relates to the political response to this social dynamics, and its changing relationship with science. As Buonanno et al. put it: 'Scientists recognize the impossibility of zero risk, whereas policymakers face personal risks when they attempt to convey to consumers the scientific truth; i.e. even the best conceived and implemented regulatory policy cannot ensure zero risk' (Buonanno et al. 2001: 2). Consumer concerns about food safety have become one of the priorities of European politicians in a way that has transformed some of the basic assumptions of their relationship until now. Not by chance – the GMOs, BSE and Dioxine scandals were not a mere media stunt. These cases gave a very strong impression to consumers that the allegiance of the political and scientific elites was not based on the good of people's health, but on economic interests. In other words, the mistrust placed in science spilled over to the political elite, and the burgeoning societal uneasiness over these matters was related to the ineffective political management of the situation. This helps explain why the European Commission, in charge of risk assessment and risk management, reacted rapidly with various strategic plans, white papers and communications on food safety. It also helps explain why the EU is willing to introduce the precautionary principle when dealing with these matters. Does this mean that the relationship between science and politics is changing? Very probably.

European politicians might no longer rely exclusively on 'scientific evidence available', they might as well rely on 'scientific uncertainty' (lack of information, scientists' disagreements, and so on) as a legal basis for banning specific products or processes. Politicians are coming to grips with the limits of science, and societies' preoccupation with it.

Against this backdrop, the recent debates at EU level about 'science and governance' have started addressing the thorny question of how to reconsider the role of science in politics. As Kyriakou and Rojo state: '"Science and governance" is about the process of devising and controlling the mechanisms to allow science and decision-making in society to work together in ways that are effective, credible, accountable and transparent' (Kyriakou and Rojo 2001: 2). The obvious loss of credibility at EU level impels this debate to help produce a new, more flexible, model where these four adjectives are crucial building blocks. The political question now is, how to do it?

The interesting question at this point is the final shape that the new governance of science at EU level will assume, and to what extent there is continuity and novelty in it. In this regard, Leiss has made a plea for a transition from an old to a new paradigm, as the only way of bridging the widening gap between science and society during the last decade (Leiss 2000) for which accountability is essential.

> Like everything else in the civil service bureaucracy, the scientific advice was given in secret and was thus not open to challenge by the public, which was especially useful for covering up the existence of huge uncertainties and the lack of essential data to support a preferred policy choice. (p. 50)

The new paradigm requires that the government concentrates on being accountable, as the only valid means to regain lost social confidence and credibility in the face of a still growing number of scientific uncertainties. Current endeavours to rebuild the risk assessment and risk management procedures in the EU hold witness to these attempts. The question to be posed is, then, how far does the proposed model represent a true solution to the widening gap between science and society, or how far is it just a continuation of previous practices? The next section addresses this in relation to scientific advice in food safety issues at EU level.

Rethinking the Role of Scientific Advice

Regulatory politics in the area of risk assessment and risk management can be seen as the mediator between science and society, but this mediator is not neutral. As we saw earlier, the credibility crisis that arose out of the food safety cases was not just related to science and the social expectations of it, but was also a credibility crisis for the mode in which the EU had regulated and managed these issues until that time. The system that has been operating until recently was created in 1974, based on three committees: The Standing Committee on Food (StCF) (comitology committee representing member states), the Advisory Committee for Foodstuffs (ACF; representing various economic and social interests), and the Scientific Committee for Food (SCF; a scientific advisory committee). These committees created a complex web of political interaction in the regulation of foodstuffs in the EU. The Commission, the StCF and ACF are in charge of risk management, whereas the SCF is in charge of risk assessment. Ever since its creation, this system had operated on pragmatic considerations, perceived to be satisfactory to most stakeholders and the general public until the upsurge of the crisis (Vos 2000: 231–2).

The crisis of the late 1990s pointed out three problems with this system, rapidly undermining its popular credibility. First, there was a lack of optimal coordination of European policies in the areas of agriculture, the internal market and human health, resulting in undesired effects on food safety. Secondly, member states had been using their position in the comitology system to pursue economic rather than food safety goals. And thirdly, the system was so complex that it lacked transparency and allowed manipulation and disinformation.

These critical points, raised by the Committee of Inquiry of the European Parliament in 1996,[16] impelled a reorganization of the decision-making procedures relating to food safety. The institutional transformation that followed, starting in the last years of the Santer Commission with some adjustments to the organization of committees,[17] is still unfinished business. When Prodi took over the Presidency of the Commission after the resignation of Santer and his Commissioners, he put the issue of a new independent agency for food safety at the top of the political agenda. The idea of such an agency is not new in European politics, but its time had arrived, in the desire to increase the accountability and transparency of scientific advice in risk assessment and management procedures of EU food safety. In late 1999, a report from independent experts came up with some interesting recommendations. Professors James, Kemper and Pascal suggested an independent agency, very similar to the US model, where the Food and Drugs Administration has a significant role in both risk assessment and risk management (Randall 2001). However, their suggestions did not win much political support. When a few weeks later the Commission published its own proposal,[18] it suggested a European Food Safety Authority only focused on risk assessment and on an alert system. Contrary to the experts' suggestions, risk management would continue to be held in the hands of the Commission. The explicit argument was that the transfer of risk management responsibilities, which would imply regulatory powers, to an independent agency could lead to a dilution of democratic accountability. The European Parliament and the Council of Ministers supported the Commission on this matter in what was a political deal on this particular issue (Buonanno et al. 2001: 11–13). Likewise, UNICE, a relevant business association at EU level, expressed its preference for a purely advisory agency, with strong national representation mechanisms.

However, some experts doubt that such a solution would respond fully to the credibility crisis initiated in the late 1990s. Ellen Vos stresses the practical difficulties of separating scientific advice and political administration.

> One has to take into account that in many situations of scientific uncertainty and/or controversy, scientific analysis and management are strongly intertwined and that 'objective scientific facts' simply do not exist. It is for example very likely that scientific evidence relating to a highly sensitive issue such as a request for an EU authorization of a specific novel food will include some socio-economic elements. (Vos 2000: 248)

Giandomenico Majone goes further, lamenting the fact that the institutional transformation has evolved piecemeal and has so far not been able to introduce radically new solutions, like for example giving the European Food Safety Authority independent regulatory powers. This would be the only means of assuring transparency, and accountability, and of being able to restore consumer confidence (Majone 2000).

With or without regulatory powers, industry and consumer organizations seem to support the idea of a European Food Safety Authority, although for different reasons. Large companies in the biotech sector have openly expressed their backing for an independent advisory agency at EU level,[19] as they are 'exasperated by the complex and protracted system for clearing their products' (Buonanno et al. 2001: 10) and want to restore consumer confidence in GMOs, among other issues (Shepherd 2000). Likewise, consumer associations want more transparency in scientific advice at EU level, and a more political focus on human health protection.[20]

According to recent regulations (articles 1 and 2), the tasks of the EFSA are strictly advisory, including:[21]

1. Providing scientific advice and scientific and technical support for EU policy in food and feed safety.
2. Providing independent information and communication on risks.
3. Collecting and analysing data to allow the characterization and monitoring of risks.
4. Providing scientific advice in other fields, such as human nutrition, animal health and welfare, plant health, and GMOs.
5. Cooperating with competent bodies of member states.
6. Cooperating with the Commission and EU member states to promote

coherence between risk assessment, risk management and risk communication.

In view of the essentially advisory nature that the EFSA will assume, it is important to bear in mind, as we saw in the previous section, that advisory functions do have a political dimension. In spite of the large diversity in the way scientific advice has been organized in advanced industrialized countries, and the variation as to the formal status of this advice within the policy-making process (Glynn et al. 2000), scientific advice invariably has an important political component. Along with the argument exposed earlier that science and politics are difficult to separate completely, a key issue emerging for the coming EFSA is how to win back the lost credibility of the previous committee system, and how to bring about the necessary legitimacy, transparency and accountability. In her study of the US's two central scientific bodies in policy-making (the Environmental Protection Agency EPA, and the Food and Drug Administration, FDA), Sheila Jasanoff concluded that: 'Regulatory practices at EPA and FDA support the thesis that negotiation – among scientists as well as between scientists and the lay public – is one of the keys to the success of the advisory process' (Jasanoff 1990: 234). Negotiation, but within different procedures and ethos: science as the negotiation between divergent scientific viewpoints; and politics as the negotiation between divergent social and ideological values. Jasanoff suggests also that there should be a clear boundary between them, not just because they have such a different nature, but mainly because popular legitimacy and the overall credibility of the system rely on this clear separation of spheres.

Drawing from the US experience, the final success of the EFSA model will depend on the way in which these negotiating spaces are institutionalized in practice, and how the spheres of science and politics will be separated from each other. The first of these two factors will make the EFSA a truly deliberative and negotiating space in times of uncertainty; and the second will render the overall system of scientific advice much more transparent, open and accountable. This latter step being the most significant one, given the seriousness of the critiques that the previous committee model of scientific advice at EU level managed to raise (Vos 1999).

CONCLUSIONS

The risk aversion attitude that characterized European societies at the turn of the century has been the background to the high politicization of consumer protection matters at EU and international levels, and of the overall reorganization of the governance of science that is currently taking place in the

EU. Arguably, there is currently as much 'scientific uncertainty' as 'political uncertainty' in the EU. This chapter examined how the Europeanization of this issue followed a rather dramatic path, in the shadow of the food scandals (BSE, dioxine, etc.) and the uneasiness about GMOs. It has been argued that the decision to give EU solutions, rather than purely national solutions, has been based on the combined effect of single market logic and strong societal pressures. A renationalization of these matters would have strongly reversed the single market construction, whereas it was clear to most politicians that the distrust about food safety was a truly EU-wide phenomenon, unlikely to be restored by single state policies. But will the EU solutions envisaged so far be able to achieve the goal of regaining consumers' trust? The regulatory wave relating to GMOs is a good step. However, the co-existence of vertical and horizontal laws draws a rather complex picture (regulatory patchwork), unlikely to enhance transparency and clarity. Nevertheless, the political endeavours to introduce compulsory labelling might have the positive effect of empowering consumers by providing them with the means of choice. The precautionary principle, another cornerstone of the new EU policy, is a powerful legal instrument that has great potential to reassure sceptical European consumers. However, this principle has two problems, namely, that its real impact is still unclear when implemented systematically, and that it is completely unknown among lay people, thus drastically reducing its ability to reassure consumers. Last, the effectiveness of the new EU line of action will depend on the way in which the coming European Food Safety Authority will make use of its advisory capacity, and regain consumers' trust by open and transparent scientific advice. This will depend mostly on the communicative and organizational competences of this institution in its daily praxis, rather than on the institutional engineering of its functions that is currently being negotiated. All this is to say that in the new EU approach to these matters, there are elements of continuity and elements of partial novelty. However, their effectiveness does not necessarily depend on their path-breaking nature as such, but mostly on how well they can render more transparent the difficult process of assessing and managing risk.

The new EU lines of action in this domain have coincided with spectacular developments at international level, most notably the creation of a biotechnological and food safety regime. Despite the inconclusiveness of this regime, defined as it is by the bipolar parameters of the WTO and the Cartagena Protocol, it still represents a step in the right direction as it institutionalizes the common global goals of protection and free trade. What is the role of the EU in this arena? As the chapter made clear, the EU has some difficulties in gaining global acceptance of its high standards of protection when it comes to international trade. Nevertheless, there was a piecemeal approximation to the precautionary 'approach' in most of the binding and non-binding international agreements we examined. Since the actual implementation of this principle is still an open question, it is important to bear in mind its potential consequences for less-developed countries. Forcing exporters to comply with the EU's high safety standards imposes an additional economic burden (i.e. exporters need to acquire an EU-accepted chemical, or change some components in their products), which might render the EU market less accessible in real terms. These arguments over the implicit costs of the precautionary principle have not been widely discussed in the EU, in what seems to be unanimous support for the Commission's diplomatic charm offensive at global level. In contrast with other innovation-related areas, such as intellectual property rights, the EU has so far successfully spoken with one voice in global fora, and in the tense relationship with the US, its major trade partner. Because this is an issue where EU member states agree widely, the negotiating position of the EU in the coming WTO round will probably not suffer from intra-EU friction, but most likely from US–EU disagreement.

Is there a new model of governing science emerging in the EU, and how would the interplay between private and public institutions change in this regard? Current EU efforts to calm the public rows on food safety are the most salient example that there are significant changes in the modes of governing science in the EU. The new mode aims at partly restructuring the relationship that has hitherto existed between science and politics, by separating their respective spheres of action, while searching for more dialogue-seeking procedures within each of them. The US experience analysed by Jasanoff might be interesting in this respect (Jasanoff 1990). However, the guiding principles of the new mode of governance should be transparency, transparency and more transparency. And this cannot simply be achieved by rules defining the public accessibility of administrative documents. It will be only achieved by mechanisms ensuring public information, systematic communication, and two-way dialogue with stakeholders that have divergent interests and hold divergent scientific opinions. Accountability, legitimacy and democracy will be dependent on that enforcement of transparency. In this new mode of governance, the relationship between the private and public spheres will also be slightly changed. The policy of compulsory labelling is an essential element for the empowerment of consumers. European consumers want to choose freely, and want to be well-informed in their choice. In the new mode of governance, risk-taking and risk-aversion attitudes will be moved from the political-productive level back to the individual. Individualizing these decisions is a good way to strike the difficult balance between consumer protection and free trade goals, both at EU and international levels. But above all, it generates new spaces for individual power and responsibility in our complex, contemporary, self-reflexive, late modern societies.

Summing up, there are several interlinked lessons to be learnt from the point of view of innovation policy. The first one is that the controversies that have surrounded food safety matters in the EU underpin the theoretical discussions from the late 1980s that the innovation process is essentially a social process. Rapid scientific advances might suffer from societal backlash, and have an impact on the acceptance of specific technologies. A second lesson is that the GMO rows are not just short-sighted hysteria of ill-informed European consumers, but a more fundamental transformation of societal values and principles that has a tremendous impact on the societal expectations regarding science and politics. A third lesson is that communication, dialogue and participatory endowments are needed to make fully accountable not just risk assessment and management, but also the overall innovation policy as such. A fourth lesson is that the new mode of governing science in the EU has to be rooted in a new understanding of individual responsibility and risk-taking, and based on unequivocal information devices (such as compulsory labelling) and two-way communicative formulae.

NOTES

1. This double nature of risk, which is objective and subjective at the same time, places Beck in a difficult epistemological position between modernity and post-modernity. We will not discuss this in detail. Instead, I will concentrate on two aspects: the increasingly global nature of risks, and the way in which risk is associated with social trust and social values in science.
2. See Manning for an excellent and succinct presentation of the recent advances of biotechnology (Manning 2000).
3. Commission's Green Paper on the General Principles of Food Law in the EU (Com (97) 176 final, 30 April 1997) and the Commission's Communication on Consumer Health and Food Safety (Com (97) 183 final, 30 April 1997).
4. White Paper on Food Safety, Com (1999) 719 final, of 12 January 2000.
5. In February 1999 the EP proposed 78 modifications to the text, but only nine were accepted by the Council of Ministers. In the second hearing the EP suggested 29 amendments but the Council did not want to accept any of them. The final decision took account of a few of those.
6. Regulation EC no. 178/2002 laying down the general principles and requirements of food law, establishing the European Food Safety Authority and laying down procedures in matters of food safety, OJ L 31 of 1 February 2002.
7. Other important but non-binding agreements in the field of biotechnology and GMOs are the Convention on Biological Diversity (CBD), the Codex Alimentarius Commission (Codex) of the FAO–WHO, the OECD's Safety Considerations for Biotechnology, and the FAO's Draft Code of Conduct on Biotechnology.
8. Although the US refused to sign the CBD in 1992, it engaged actively in the negotiations of the new international regulation.
9. The United States, Argentina, Australia, Canada, Chile and Uruguay.
10. AIA: Advance Informed Agreement.
11. This article establishes that in cases where scientific evidence is insufficient, a member may provisionally adopt SPS measures on the basis of the available information.
12. The Clinton Administration introduced pre-market evaluation procedures in April 2000.
13. Report of the Panel 'EC Measures Concerning Meat and Meat Products (Hormones) – Complaint by the US' (WT/DS26/R/USA, 18 August 1997. And Report of the Appellate

Body in 'EC Measures Concerning Meat and Meat Products (Hormones)' WT/DS&/AB/R, of 16 January 1998.
14. The segregation of GMOs from non-GMOs in some countries such as the US or Canada might be almost impossible as they are treated equally. Similarly, labelling processed food might be also difficult as the processing might destroy the DNA fingerprint of the GMO ingredient.
15. European Commission:http://trade-info.cec.eu.int/europa/2001newround/pro.htm, page 2.
16. Temporary Committee of Inquiry into BSE, set up by the European Parliament in July 1996, which came with the report on the Commission's handling of the BSE crisis since 1988 OJ C 261/132, 1996; followed by a Resolution from the EP on the same matter: OJ C 261/75, 1996.
17. This adjustment was the re-allocation of all scientific committees dealing with human health to come under the umbrella of one single Directorate General of the Commission.
18. White Paper on Food Safety Com (1999) 719.
19. Like for example Vice-Chairman of Aventis, Jean-René Fourtou. The industry has recently created an information association: the European Food Information Council, EUFIC.
20. Most notably, BEUC (Le Bureau Européen des Unions de Consommateurs), The European Chamber of Consumer Associations.
21. Regulation (EC)No 178/2002 of the European Parliament and of the Council of 28 January 2002 laying down the general principles and requirements of food law, establishing the European Food Safety Authority and laying down procedures in matters of food safety.

REFERENCES

Beck, U. (1992), *Risk Society - Towards a New Modernity*. London, Sage.
Beck, U. (1999), *World Risk Society*. Cambridge, Polity Press.
Brom, F. (2000), 'Food, consumer concerns, and trust: Food ethics for a globalizing market'. *Journal of Agricultural & Environmental Ethics* **12**(2): 127–39.
Buonanno, L., S. Zablotney and R. Keefer (2001), 'Politics versus science in the making of a new regulatory regime for food in Europe'. *European Integration Online Papers* (EIoP) **5**(12).
Commission, European (2000), *Communication from the Commission on the Precautionary Principle*. Brussels, European Commission COM (2000) 1, Brussels, 2 February.
Commission, European (2001), *Questions and Answers on the Regulation of GMOs in the EU*. Brussels, European Commission.
CORDIS (2001), *Cordis Focus* (183).
Cozzens, S.E. and E.J. Woodhouse (1995), 'Science, government, and the politics of knowledge'. In *Handbook of Science and Technology Studies*, S. Jasanoff, G.E. Markle, J.C. Petersen and T. Pinch. London/Thousand Oaks, Sage.
Davison, A., I. Barns and Renato Schibeci (1997), 'Problematic publics: A critical review of surveys of public attitudes to biotechnology'. *Science, Technology and Human Values* **22**(3): 317–48.
The Economist (1999), 'Frankenstein foods'. *The Economist*, 18 February.
Eike, M.C. (2000), 'GM food: Controversy and uncertainty'. Unpublished paper.
ESRC (1999), 'The politics of GM food: Risk, science and public trust'. *Special Briefing* Economic and Social Research Council.
Eurobarometer (2001), 'Europeans, science and technology'. Eurobarometer 55.2, December 2001. Brussels, European Commission.
Falkner, R. (2000a), 'International trade conflicts over agricultural biotechnology'. In *The International Politics of Biotechnology*, A. Russel and J. Vogler. Manchester,

Manchester University Press.

Falkner, R. (2000b), 'Regulating biotech trade: The Cartagena Protocol on biosafety'. *International Affairs* **76**(2): 299-313.

Foucault, M. (2000), *Power - Essential Works of Foucault 1954-1984, no. 3*. New York, The New Press.

Frewer, L.J., C. Howard and Richard Shepherd (1997), 'Public concerns in the United Kingdom about general and specific applications of genetic engineering: Risk, benefit, and ethics'. *Science, Technology and Human Values* **22**(1): 98-124.

Gieryn, T.F. (1995), 'Boundaries of science'. In *Handbook of Science and Technology Studies*, S. Jasanoff, G.E. Markle, J.C. Petersen and T. Pinch. London, Sage.

Glynn, S., P. Laget, R. Barré, G. Andersson, M. Bourene, R. Vidle, A. Braun and D. Ibarreta (2000), 'Science and governance: Describing and typifying scientific structures'. Paper submitted to the conference on 'Science and Governance in Europe', October 2000.

Gonçalves, M.E. (2000), 'The Importance of being European: The science and politics of BSE in Portugal'. *Science Technology and Human Values* **25**(4): 417-48.

Harhoff, D., P. Régibeau and K. Rocket (2001), 'Some simple economics of GM food'. *Economic Policy* **33**(October): 263-300.

Héritier, A. (1996), 'The accommodation of diversity in European policy-making and its outcomes: Regulatory policy as a patchwork'. *Journal of European Public Policy* **3**(2): 149-67.

Jasanoff, S. (1990), *The Fifth Branch. Science Advisers as Policymakers*. Cambridge, Harvard University Press.

Jensen, P. (2000), 'Public trust in scientific information'. Paper submitted to the conference on Science and Governance in Europe, October 2000.

Kyriakou, D. and J. Rojo (2001), 'Editorial'. *The IPTS Report* **55** (3) (Special Issue: Science and Governance in a Knowledge Society).

Laget, P. and M. Cantley (2001), 'European responses to biotechnology: Research, regulation and dialogue'. *Issues in Science and Technology - Online* Summer 2001.

Landfried, C. (1999), 'The European regulation of biotechnology by polycratic governance'. In *EU Committees: Social Regulation, Law and Politics*, C. Joerges and E. Vos. Oxford, Hart Publishing.

Leiss, W. (2000), 'Between expertise and bureaucracy: Risk management trapped at the science-policy interface'. *Risky Business*, B. Doern and T. Reed. Toronto, University of Toronto Press.

Levidow, L.C., S. Carr, David Wield and Rene von Schomberg (1997), 'European biotechnology regulation: Framing the risk assessment of a herbicide-tolerant crop'. *Science, Technology and Human Values* **22**(4): 472-90.

Majone, G. (2000), 'The credibility crisis of community regulation'. *Journal of Common Market Studies* **38**(2): 273-302.

Manning, F.C.R. (2000), 'Biotechnology: A scientific perspective'. In *The International Politics of Biotechnology*, A. Russell and J. Vogler. Manchester, Manchester University Press.

Miller, D. (1999), 'Risk, science and policy: definitional struggles, information management, the media and BSE'. *Social Science and Medicine* **49**(9): 1239-56.

Miller, H.I. and G. Conko (2000), 'The science of biotechnology meets the politics of global regulation'. *Issues in Science and Technology - Online* Fall 2000.

Noiville, C. (2000), 'Principe de precaution et organisation mondiale du commerce. Le cas du commerce alimentaire'. *Journal du Droit International* **127**(2): 263-98.

Pardo-Quintillán, S. (1999), 'Free trade, public health protection and consumer information in the European and WTO context: hormone-treated beef and genetically modified organisms'. *Journal of World Trade* **33**(6): 147–98.

Phillips, P.W.B. and W.A. Kerr (2000), 'Alternative paradigms – the WTO versus the biosafety protocol for trade in genetically modified organisms'. *Journal of World Trade* **34**(4): 63–75.

Randall, E. (2001). 'Policy and plans: Formulating a food safety and public health strategy for the Union'. http://www.policylibrary.com/Essays/ RandallEFARisk/EFArisk2.htm.

Runge, C.F. and L.-A. Jackson (2000), 'Labelling, trade and genetically modified organisms – a proposed solution'. *Journal of World Trade* **34**(1): 111–22.

Shepherd, I. (2000), 'Science and governance in the European Union – a contribution to the debate'. Paper submitted to the conference on Science and Governance in Europe, October 2000.

Skogstad, G. (2001), 'The WTO and food safety regulatory policy innovation in the European Union'. *Journal of Common Market Studies* **38**(3): 485–505.

Strange, S. (1988), *States and Markets*. London, Pinter.

Teknologirådet (2001), 'GMO-debat i krydsild'. *Fra Rådet til Tinget. Nyhedsbrev* **157**(May).

Vos, E. (1999), 'EU committees: The evolution of unforeseen institutional actors in European product regulation'. In *EU Committees: Social Regulation, Law and Politics*. C. Joerges and E. Vos. Oxford, Hart Publishing.

Vos, E. (2000), 'EU food safety regulation in the aftermath of the BSE Crisis'. *Journal of Consumer Policy* **23**(3): 227–55.

Williams, R. and D. Edge (1996), 'The social shaping of technology'. *Research Policy* **25**: 865–99.

7.   Conclusion

CHARACTERIZING THE GOVERNANCE OF THE INNOVATION POLICY AT EU LEVEL

The astonishingly rapid succession of initiatives and public actions in the innovation arena, and the widening of the policy agenda, reveal important novelties in the way innovation policy is being governed at EU level. It is not easy to put order into this panoply of social, economic and political dynamics that shape the governance structures. Nevertheless, it is important that we can see the wood for the trees and gain an overview of these dynamics.

Taking Table 7.1 as a starting point, we can reach some conclusions about the governance patterns emerging at each of these dimensions; namely, Europeanization, international/global level, the redefinition of public–private realms and the question of disparities and diversity in the EU.

As we saw in the corresponding chapters, each of these areas has a sort of 'internal logic' within which political action and initiatives are articulated. At the same time, however, they form a single collective dimension as they are essential building blocks of the new innovation policy approach. This follows the understanding that innovation is much more than the linear result of RTD efforts, but encompasses a large number of other issues that define the specific regulatory, social, financial and political context where innovations take place. Hence, despite the specific developments of these different areas, some common features can be identified indicating how the general context of the EU has been evolving in the last couple of decades.

Europeanization

In all of these areas, Europeanization has been taking place at breath-taking speed since the mid-1990s. It looks as if the 'logic of the single market' that was so strong in the 1980s was also present in the 1990s and early 2000s. However, the difference with the 1980s was the understanding that market forces alone would not be able to enhance the competitive position of the EU economy as a whole in the context of increasing globalization. The emphasis on knowledge production, its appropriation (IPRs) and exploitation (standards and ICTs) at EU level became an important element of the new strategy towards European competitiveness. The social aspect of all this came later on

Table 7.1 Characterizing the governance of EU innovation policy since the mid-1990s

	Europeanization	International/global level	Public–private	Disparities and diversity
Research and knowledge production	Trends towards a multi-level system of knowledge production	Increasingly blurred borders in the European architecture, and growing EU participation in public global cooperation	Efforts for more private funding, and new role for JRC/public research centres/universities	Emerging triangle with North, South and East
Intellectual property rights	A single IPR regime for the EU and EEA	No unitary EU position at WTO negotiations, and no legal direct effect of TRIPS, but important implications	A relative strong and broad IPR regime	Large differences in patenting propensity across states and industrial sectors
Information society	Rapid process from deregulation to an e-Europe strategy in the digital economy	EU clear position in the current reorganization of global governance	New rules protecting privacy and universal services	Regional divide tackled through EU regional policy. Social divide: public action at national level
Standardization	New approach consolidated, with success and failure cases	Spectacular growth of private consortia, and new EU agreements on mutual recognition	Problems of participation/openness and efficiency	
Risk and social sustainability of innovation	Europeanization of 'risk society' and panoply of EU actions to find solutions	EU defending its high levels of protection in world fora	Current reorganization of scientific advice committees and governance of science	

and somewhat unexpectedly, within the prospects of the information society and the rows about risk and food safety. Here the EU has also launched some initiatives, though of a more 'reactive' character.

Indeed, the most astonishing aspect of this trend towards Europeanization has been its rapidity. The element of time has had paramount importance, because it indicates that this accelerated integration process might be based on a relatively homogeneous understanding of the EU's political action towards innovation and competitiveness. This is something that deserves careful attention. The convergence of political visions is not a random phenomenon – it is rather the fruit of intense political interaction and deliberation among political elites about what the common future will bring and about what lines of political action are most appropriate. This is far from being an easy political process in a game with 15 players. My suggestion here is that this process is not the result of contingency, rather it is the combination of the persuasive work that the Commission has undertaken all the way through, within the cognitive framework of the 'knowledge-based economy' and the prospects of the imminent enlargement eastwards. Despite its undeniable moral decline due to the dismissal of the Santer College in 1999, one could argue that in terms of policy outputs on innovation-related areas, the bulk of the Commission's proposals on these matters have still managed to receive positive support from EU member states. This 'purposeful opportunism' and the effect of the timing of Commission ideas, would never have fallen on good soil if the member states had not shared the very basic political ambition and identity-based vision of a common competitive and innovative EU. This is what, at the end of the day, has made Europeanization an astonishingly rapid political process.

What kind of division of tasks between the EU and its member states is emerging? In one of the chapters we argued that a multi-level system of knowledge production is emerging in the EU. This is not just the case for the framework programme, but most evidently for the ERA initiative that aims at integrating the member countries' different national research systems into one single European space, followed by a strengthening of the 6FP. All this means that the EU and member state levels of research and knowledge production will become increasingly intertwined, but without abandoning the additionality principle of EU involvement. Similar trends can be identified in the recent setting up of the EU–wide intellectual property rights regime. Although the ECJ has for long ruled on the misuse of these rights, it was only at the end of the 1990s that a single EU regulatory regime has gradually been put in place. This means that the EU is now granting these rights in the exercise of constitutional-type powers. Interesting in this regard will be the Community patent, and particularly the organization of the judicial system around it, where the division of powers between national and EU courts will follow the hierarchical system of EU law and judicial order.

After the rapid expansion of EU involvement in these innovation-related areas, the issue coming to the fore now is how to consolidate the public administration of these new EU powers and initiatives. In the case of distributive politics, as in research, consolidation means that a lot of effort has to be placed in the actual implementation of the new measures. In this sense, all stakeholders have to be ready in the coming years to draw some lessons from the novelties in ERA and the 6FP. This is also the case for (de)regulatory politics, such as IPRs, the information society and standardization, where, apart from the lessons on new initiatives, the Commission has to engage stakeholders and member states more actively in addressing more drastically the *already existing impasses* (e.g. the efficiency problems of harmonized standards), *existing rigidities* (e.g. implementing universal services in the information society), and *existing expectation mismatches* between EU rhetoric and actual scope of political competences (e.g. in social aspects of the information society), which require reconsideration and/or better coordination between member states and the EU. Indeed, as mentioned earlier, the consolidation of division of tasks in the question of food safety might turn out to be more challenging, because new principles and new institutional structures are currently re-shaping the governance of science in the EU, and because consumers continue to be extremely sensitive to these matters.

International/Global Level

This rapid Europeanization has been undertaken in the absence of a clear role for the EU on the international scene. It has been as if the political energy used in the goals of generating a single EU space, and in the definition of the adequate transfer of powers to Brussels, has somehow 'forgotten' the international dimension of most of these issues. Paradoxically, when member states have felt relatively at ease with further EU action, they have had second thoughts about letting the EU acquire a more visible and unitary position in negotiations at international level. Examples of this attitude are the relatively low EU profile in the governance structure of the internet, the TRIPS agreement negotiation, or public RTD cooperation schemes. The tendency seems to have been 'first Europeanize, then we will see what role there is for the EU at a global level'. Yet this does not need to be the only logical sequence of political events. The growing internationalization/globalization that these matters have acquired in recent years has had the effect of pushing EU member states to 'Europeanize'. For example, the GATS agreement negotiations – the WTO negotiations about a global liberalization of national ICT markets – were used by the Commission to push reluctant member states to accept the EU liberalization package of telecom markets in 1998. This means that the global/international context for innovation related areas does have an impact in the Europeanization process. It also means that the recursive interaction between Europeanization and internationalization puts a question mark over the linear political logic of 'first one, then the other'. With this I want to argue that a single EU position in international fora, like for example governance of the internet or the regulation of intellectual property rights under TRIPS, in the absence of absolutely completed Europeanization should be possible, and even desirable. Possibly because this recursive interaction between both levels, global and the EU, is already a reality. These are desirable because in recent decades most of the innovation-related issues analysed here (standardization, IPRs, services, food safety matters, or even RTD public funding) are becoming central issues in global negotiations. This does not just refer to 'new trade issues' under the WTO regime and its formal legal arrangements. It also refers to the much wider question of how innovation policies can be articulated in a context where the relevant decisions and structures in this regard are being moved up to the international/global level of politics. To develop a common EU vision about these should not be a difficult task. Ultimately, intra-EU diplomatic coordination and cooperation in these new trade/competitiveness issues depend on the individual member states' willingness to give the EU a single voice in the world, at the time when important pillars of the global economic polity are being designed.

Public and Private Realms

A third trend that manifests itself is that there has been a deep restructuring of the relationship between public and private realms. This has acquired such a dimension that, I argue, it consistently defines an emerging new constitutional order at supra-national level. The economic constitutionality of the EU legal system does not just refer to the EU market-making ethos as such, but essentially to the fact that the EU confers individual rights. All this results in the shaping of a new trans-national space for economic transactions, built on a new level and mode of political and juridical authority (Weiler 1999; Maduro 2000). The activities that fall under innovation policy have actively contributed to the generation of this EU economic constitution in recent years, mainly by profoundly re-shaping the public and private realms and by conferring individual rights. Take for example the case of intellectual property rights regulation at EU level. They are crucial elements in the innovation process by means of knowledge appropriation and exploitation. Their contribution to the economic constitution is that they define the limits and contents of individual property rights and also define the circumstances in which knowledge might be commoditized. Something similar can be said about the protection of privacy in the area of the information society. By defining these individual rights, the

EU is shaping a new political and economic constitutional order, which is different from that existing at national level.

One further question deserves attention here – the argument that this restructuring of public and private realms has, for the most part, been discussed and decided by experts with little public participation. Take again the example of intellectual property rights regulation. This is perhaps the most dramatic reconceptualization of the boundaries between the private and public domains. Admittedly, there have been great rows about biotechnological and software patents, both dealing with the limits of patentability.[1] However, besides these controversies, other, equally crucial, issues have emerged somewhat more quietly. Examples are 'compulsory licensing' and 'fair use' legal caveats in patents and copyright regulations. The 'battles' for further compulsory licensing and fair use have not received much attention from the general public. The EU rules protecting privacy in the information society are another good example of a highly technical matter that did not hit the media headlines, but that has direct implications for the definition of the private realm in the new IT context. This poses the question of representation, democracy and, eventually, the popular legitimacy of the EU as a political and economic project with constitutionalizing effects. We will return to this issue in the next section.

Disparities and Diversity

This analytical dimension was only applicable in the three chapters dealing with knowledge production, intellectual property rights and the information society. Obviously, EU action on territorial disparities has been articulated within the conventional limits of EU regional policy, like for example the regional innovation strategy (RIS) or the actions designed to foster the information society in less developed regions. In other words, the regional policy of the EU has partly integrated the innovation agenda. Indeed, the selected data presented in these chapters show that the picture emerging from the dynamics of the last years and from coming EU enlargement towards the East is of great diversity in innovation indicators and performance. This is likely to persist in the years to come, and the point is whether this diversity will eventually affect the general trends that the innovation policy at EU level has developed over the past few years.

PRACTICAL CONSEQUENCES: THE CHALLENGES AND OPPORTUNITIES

Having examined briefly the dynamics and trends of EU innovation policy, we now discuss some of its practical consequences. It is important to keep in mind that this book is not an evaluation of how effective or how optimal EU endeavours have been in this field. Instead, it analyses the dynamics and political logic of recent years, pointing to the structural transformations in terms of governance. Therefore, when dealing with the opportunities and challenges ahead, I will not focus on the 'substance', but rather on the form of public action as such. In other words, I do not intend to suggest new courses of action or new policy instruments to improve innovativeness or competitiveness. Such a task is much better accomplished by specifically delimited economic studies that look for 'policy implications' for policy-makers. The purpose here is much more modest. The dynamics of EU innovation policy examined earlier bring to the fore some questions about the future governance of this overall policy area. As we saw in the first section, two issues that constantly arise in academic studies on new modes of governance of public administration are management and democratic accountability. We now turn to these.

Management and the Limits of EU Action

With the spectacular spread of EU action in the field of innovation, the question of steering and management is becoming a central one. This is so for the sake of coherence and consistency in the myriad of policy instruments now operating under the innovation realm. Several aspects deserve attention: improving horizontal coordination, shaping a new role for the EU in the 'soft' coordination instruments, and reconsidering communicative devices and strategies.

Starting with the first, the EU should make an effort to establish better horizontal linkages between the areas placed under the umbrella of 'innovation policy'. All these areas coincide in their overall goal of generating a positive environment for innovativeness and, obviously, they differ as to the means for achieving it. However, the way in which the specific policy instruments complement and support one another has so far only been implicitly assumed. This is to say that the EU has to spell out in a clearer way the lines of horizontal coordination between all these actions. This is, for example, the case with the i2i initiative (that lends money), the overall framework programme (that 'gives' money to RTD), and the significant efforts to promote private financing of RTD; one needs to ask what is the overall intention of the EU in terms of financing RTD in the future? And how complementary are they? Another example is the case between the efforts to foster innovation in SMEs and the little attention that these have so far received in the regulation of IPRs (especially the coming software patent), and the systematic low participation of SMEs in the framework programme (likely to continue in the enlarged networks of 6FP). Another example is the unclear effects that the emerging strong regime of IPRs might have on the patterns and dynamics of standards agreements in Europe, particularly in the heavily standard-based ICT sector. These are important examples, and the point to make is that the horizontal connections of problems and instruments need to be spelled out, thus enhancing the coherence and consistency of EU public action.

A second issue is the shaping of a new role for the EU in the 'soft' coordination instruments. With the advent of the 'open method of coordination', the EU is stepping into what was previously strictly the domain of the state. With the idea of benchmarking best practices of national innovation policies, the EU is gaining a new profile, namely, that of scrutinizing national public action and its effects. Arguably, this might have important repercussions. First of all, it might render the 'core business' of the EU public action much more diffused and blurred. Before benchmarking, EU involvement in this area followed the specific goal of generating a positive context for innovation at supra-national level. EU action was then defined in strict complementarity to national efforts, and in the direct pursuit of a single market/economic space. With the idea of analysing 'best practices' at national level, the EU is also now involved (although indirectly) with those areas at national level that have not been transferred to the EU level. In other words, the EU is now concerned with what goes on at national level. Another important repercussion is the effects that the open method of coordination might have on national practices. Learning from others has always been a normal practice of modern national/regional public administration and institutional development, also for innovation policy. The intensive work of the OECD over decades is bearing fruit, and convergence is already visible among several European states even before EU involvement in benchmarking (Biegelbauer and Borrás 2003). The question might then be, why is it necessary to nurture this convergence if the EU is already building a positive context for innovation at trans-national level?

Last but not least, the EU needs to reconsider its communicative strategies. Consumers and citizens are these days constantly exposed to a myriad of data, studies, action plans, green papers, and so forth, in what seems to be an overwhelming flow of information about 'what is going on' that becomes impossible to communicate in everyday terms. To be fair, the Commission has defined the formal areas of EU involvement in innovation in a few programmatic texts, most notably the 1995 Green Paper on innovation (and its corresponding action plan), and in the recent 2000 Commission's Communication. Both serve as 'road maps' of EU action for innovation. However, these two documents are buried under a pile of dozens of others, undermining the ability of the Union to present to its citizens the simple image of 'what the problems are' and 'what the EU is doing about this'. Besides, the EU's website is hardly any help due to the excess of information and documentation. This calls for the provision of a better articulated flow of information, particularly from the Commission side, if one of the objectives of the Union is to strengthen qualified participation in decision-making.

Democratic Accountability: The Achilles' Heel

The areas which fall under innovation policy have traditionally been rather technocratic, detached from the 'high politics' of right–left ideological frays. The interest of the general public in matters like standardization, scientific research, or intellectual property rights has, with some exceptions, been quite minimal. However, the dramatic events in the area of food safety in the late 1990s, and the increasingly ethical dimensions of biotechnology have brought science, technology, and innovation at large back on to the political stage. As we saw in the chapter about risk and the social sustainability of innovation, the rows at EU level foreshadow the reflexive nature of the risk society, where progress is no longer an ultimate social goal per se. Rather, social well-being in a much broader understanding has become the new goal. Despite its initial 'business as usual' attitude, the Commission has understood that the popular concerns about the risks and ethics attached to the innovation process are here to stay, requiring an important rethinking of political structures in these areas. Hence the EU is re-shaping the conventional procedures for scientific advice at EU level. Similarly, ethical matters have been promoted politically through a high-ranking independent commission of experts within the Commission (European Group on Ethics).

However, these transformations are unlikely to restore lost popular confidence in the innovation process and the politics of science if the decision-making procedures of other areas such as research, standardization and intellectual property rights remain as opaque as before. Complex networks of actors interact in formal and informal fora shaping political decisions on the nature and forms of EU involvement in these areas. In other words, innovation policy is still in the hands of experts, civil servants, corporate interests, civic interests and the scientific community, in a constellation of actors where the public at large rarely take part.

Democratic participation is the most severe challenge for EU politics in the coming years, given the decreasing legitimacy that the European project has had since the Maastricht Treaty. With widespread Euro-scepticism, politicians should be aware that the technocratic view of science decision-making in Brussels serves to reinforce the loss of confidence in science and the EU project as a whole. Hence there is a mutually reinforcing process between the legitimacy loss in the EU political project and the legitimacy loss in science as a collective aspiration for improved living conditions. Reversing this situation is not an easy task. At the discursive level, the Commission has acknowledged this double challenge, and it has addressed the new social conditions for governance of science at EU level (mainly in its White Paper on governance, and in the action plan on science and society[2]). However, a more radical approach might be necessary, in order to change the deserved image of technocratic decision-making for scientific matters that the EU has gained over past decades. Introducing more resolute decisions in this regard might be necessary if the EU is to succeed in changing popular wariness. In this sense finding clear ways to enhance popular participation and the openness of bureaucratic procedures in all issues concerning innovation, technology and science would be a step forward. Yet, this implies that democracy has to be redefined from the conventional understanding of strictly representative mechanisms to a more participatory and closer form of democracy that empowers citizens into self-governing procedures (Hirst 2000; Rhodes 2000). At EU level, this might mean that we have to recognize the fact that the 'political' and the 'technical' are not two separate spheres of social action, but one and the same. As Barry puts it: 'Technical controversies are forms of political controversy, although it is open to question whether, in particular instances, such disputes take place in a public political arena' (Barry 2001: 9). Hence, democratizing the governance of science requires empowering citizens and making these technical controversies open political choices, where citizens and consumers are able to grasp and understand the uses, effects and consequences of scientific objects and technical devices. Naturally, this is easier said than done, especially at EU level given the particularities of its political construction (institutional architecture, supra-national nature) and its large 'distance' to individuals (lack of a single political space for public opinion-formation, diverse mass media, diverse political cultures, diverse representative channels). Indeed, popular participation and wider channels for informed political and technical choices are even more necessary than in the national political order so as to bridge the gap between the governed and government. Since legitimacy can no longer be taken for granted, the EU has to earn this legitimacy by public action that no longer is just effective, but is essentially and primarily democratic. In the field of innovation and the politics of science, *politicizing the 'technical', rather than 'technifying' the political, might be a starting point in this regard.*

TWO THEORETICAL CONSEQUENCES

In addition to these 'practical' consequences of the governance of the EU's innovation policy, there are two wider theoretical aspects to consider. The first is the question of whether this approach to innovation, and the subsequent dense EU intervention in a wide range of policy areas, can lead to the suggestion that there is a European system of innovation in the making. The second theoretical question is whether the EU as such is emerging as a 'competition state', and what this means for the 'ethos' of the Union.

Systems of Innovation Theory and the EU

In the early 1990s, industrial economists developed the notion of a 'national system of innovation' (Nelson 1993; Lundvall 1992), which quickly turned out to be widely used. This notion bridged the worlds of academics and policy-makers by providing an intuitively strong frame from which to tackle the naturally pervasiveness of science, technology and innovation in the national societal and economic context. However, implicit in the cognitive premises of the 'system of innovation' idea was the general assumption of its 'national' character, where the diversity of national institutions (in social, economic, cultural, etc. terms) could explain differences in performance by the unrepeat-able form of each system's nature. Consequently, the territorial dimension was not just a mere attribute of the system, but a non-alienable aspect of it.

As we have seen in this book, the gradual, but steady, adoption of the innovation policy paradigm has given rise to an important revamping and expansion of EU policy instruments. This large bundle of EU policy instruments has to be analysed not just individually, but collectively, and in this sense the question of whether there is a European system of innovation in the making looks particularly relevant.

The economic literature on innovation systems still provides different understandings of what a system of innovation is. Nevertheless, common to them all is that they are anchored in evolutionary and institutional economics that dismisses the neo-classical understanding of technical change (Edquist 1997). Nelson and Lundvall have emphasized the institutional basis of the system, and see it as the network of formal–informal, public–private institutions that has shaped and is shaping economic and innovation activity. Other authors emphasize the question of social interaction and point out that a system of innovation is formed by the density of interactions in a given territory. This approach is mostly argued for by economic geographers (Storper 1997; Belussi 1999). When looking collectively at this bundle of policy actions at EU level, and trying to define whether we can talk of a European system of innovation, the emphasis on institutions or on interaction is not banal.

The 'system of innovation' concept needs further theoretical development in order to accommodate the supra-national dimension of EU innovation policy. Nevertheless, a tentative approach would be to stress the building process of a European system of innovation based on some crucial economic institutions (IPRs, or knowledge production), and to emphasize that this institutional construct defines the technological zones where social and political interactions take place (Barry 2001). In other words, that the European system of innovation is an institutional ensemble that is being 'filled up' by social interactions.

The EU as a Competition State

The second theoretical question raised by the findings of this book is the nature and 'ethos' of the economic constitution of the EU. That is, the place of innovation within the overall political and economic goals of the EU, and its ultimate social accomplishment. Here neo-marxist state theorists and political economists have a lot to say. Philip Cerny has discussed the changing architecture of politics, pointing out that there has been a transition from the Keynesian welfare state to a new conception of state, the 'competition state', where the collective goal of improving the competitive position in world markets subsumes the Keynesian principles on which state action has been based since the post-war period (Cerny 1990, 1997). Jessop has called this the transition from the Keynesian welfare nation state (KWNS) to the Shumpeterian workfare post-national regime (SWPR), and he sees this transition partly as the result of the fact that knowledge is being fictitiously commodified (Jessop 2000).

The EU has epitomized this SWPR, especially since the early 1990s, when the competitiveness matter became a central issue after the successful Single European Market Project. This has led some to point to the state-formation nature of the EU as a 'competition state' (Bohle 2001) from the contestation of different grand ideological projects (Johansen 1998). Some go further and, following neo-marxist tradition, point to the material basis for the transition, seeing it as the direct fruit of specific private capitalist interests expressed through powerful business associations in the EU arena (Apeldoorn 2000; Bohle 2001).

Without entering into detailed discussion of these critical views, which I do not share, it is correct to interpret that the legitimacy crises resulting from the food safety issues shocked the political basis of the EU action towards competitiveness. Social distrust was essentially a distrust of the technical and scientific basis for policy decisions, and of the overall political structures for decision-making. Indeed, the distrust of Europeans also pointed out that competitiveness and technical progress are no longer a social goal in themselves. The contemporary technological society is reflexive and looks beyond the economic comfort of progress, and asks itself what price this is worth, what are the risks associated with the use, abuse and non-use of technology, and what is the nature of scientific knowledge as opposed to non-scientific knowledge. All this indicates that there is a need to enhance the political openness and visibility of the current self-reflexive process. Without going as far as to denounce the 'contradictions' of the competition state, or to invalidate the goals of improving competitiveness (as neo-marxist critics seem to do), the voice of societal uneasiness with the political and the technical needs to be heard in a far more constructive way. This might also require the reconsideration that competitiveness and innovation, although very important, are no longer social goals in themselves.

NOTES

1. Ethical groups were mobilized against what they saw as threatening privatization of life forms, and IT groups were mobilized on what they saw as threatening IT creativity and free development.
2. European Commission (2001) White Paper on Governance, COM (2001) 428 final; and European Commission (2002): Science and society action plan, http://www.cordis.lu/science-society.

REFERENCES

Apeldoorn, B. v. (2000), 'Transnational class agency and European governance: The case of the European roundtable of industrialists'. *New Political Economy* **4**(2): 157–81.

Barry, A. (2001), *Political Machines. Governing a Technological Society.* London, The Athlone Press.

Belussi, F. (1999), 'Policies for the development of knowledge-intensive local production systems'. *Cambridge Journal of Economics* **23**: 729–47.

Biegelbauer, P. and S. Borrás (eds) (2003), *Innovation Policies in Europe and the US: The New Agenda.* Aldershot, Ashgate.

Bohle, D. (2001), 'European integration and eastern enlargement: Dimensions for a new European disorder'. Unpublished paper.

Cerny, P. (1990), *The Changing Architecture of Politics. Structure, Agency and the Future of the State.* London, Sage.

Cerny, P. (1997), 'Paradoxes of the competition state: The dynamics of political globalization'. *Government and Opposition* **32**(2): 251–74.

Edquist, C. (1997), 'Introduction'. In *Systems of Innovation. Technologies, Institutions and Organisations*, C. Edquist. London, Pinter.

Hirst, P. (2000), 'Democracy and governance'. In *Debating Governance*, J. Pierre. Oxford, Oxford University Press.

Jessop, B. (2000), 'The state and the contradictions of the knowledge-driven economy'. In *Knowledge, Space, Economy*, J.R. Bryson, P.W. Daniels, N.D. Henry and J. Pollard. London, Routledge.

Johansen, H. (1998), 'Exploring the colour of the beast: Hegemony and political projects in the European Union'. In *Explaining European Integration*, A. Wivel. Copenhagen, Copenhagen Political Studies Press.

Lundvall, B.-Å. (ed.) (1992), *National Systems of Innovation: Towards a Theory of Innovation and Interactive Learning*. London, Pinter.

Maduro, M.P. (2000), 'Europe and the constitution: What if this is as good as it takes?' Unpublished paper.

Nelson, R.R. (ed.) (1993), *National Innovation Systems. A Comparative Analysis*. Oxford, Oxford University Press.

Rhodes, R.A.W. (2000), 'Governance and public administration'. In *Debating Governance*, J. Pierre. Oxford, Oxford University Press.

Sharp, M. (1997), 'Towards a federal system of science in Europe'. In *Science in Tomorrow's Europe*, R. Barré, M. Gibbons, J.S. Maddox, B. Martin and P. Papon. Paris, Economica International, 201–18.

Storper, M. (1997), *The Regional World. Territorial Development in a Global Economy*. New York/London, The Guilford Press.

Weiler, J. (1999), *The Constitution of Europe*. Cambridge, Cambridge University Press.

Index